ATTITUDES AND
ATTITUDE CHANGE

Attitudes and Attitude Change

Gerd Bohner
Universität Bielefeld
and
Michaela Wänke
Universität Erfurt

PSYCHOLOGY PRESS
ALERE FLAMMAM
Taylor & Francis Group

First published 2002 by Psychology Press Ltd
27 Church Road, Hove, East Sussex, BN3 2FA, UK

Simultaneously published in the USA and Canada
by Taylor & Francis Inc
29 West 35th Street, New York, NY 10001

Psychology Press is part of the Taylor & Francis Group

© 2002 Psychology Press

British Library Cataloguing in Publication Data
A catalogue record for this book is available from the British Library

Library of Congress Cataloging-in-Publication Data
Bohner, Gerd, 1959–
    Attitudes and attitude change / Gerd Bohner and Michaela Wänke.
        p.   cm. – (Social psychology)
    Includes bibliographical references and index.
    ISBN 0-86377-778-3 – ISBN 0-86377-779-1 (Pbk)
    1. Attitude (Psychology). 2. Attitude change. I. Wänke, Michaela.
    II. Title.   III. Social psychology (Philadelphia, Pa.)
    BF327 .B64 2002
    153.8'5–dc21

                                                    2001048425

    ISBN 0-86377-778-3 (I Ibk)
    ISBN 0-86377-779-1 (Pbk)
    ISSN 1368-4574

Cover design by Joyce Chester
Cover illustration by Bipinchandra J. Mistry
Typeset in Palatino by Mayhew Typesetting, Rhayader, Powys
Printed and bound in the UK by TJ International Ltd, Padstow, Cornwall

Contents

Acknowledgements

Our collaboration in writing this book extended over several years. During this time each of us moved between universities more than once. Parts of the book were written and revised at the Universities of Heidelberg, Mannheim, Erfurt, Würzburg, New South Wales and Kent. Although our moves inevitably slowed down the production of the book, both the series editor, Miles Hewstone, and the people at Psychology Press were very patient with us and provided a lot of help and encouragement. It was a pleasure to work with them.

Mark Conner, Greg Maio and Norbert Schwarz read and commented on the manuscript of this book. We are grateful for their time and their many insightful comments, which have led to substantial improvements of the text.

We would further like to thank several colleagues and students who helped with specific tasks. Hieke Gerger, Nargis Islam and Hanna Kley provided technical assistance and proof-read the manuscript; Kerry Dineen and Frank Siebler helped with the stimulus selection and programming of the English-Irish IAT presented in Figure 2.6; Sabina Aharpour, Michelle Levy, Kerry Rees and Tendayi Viki posed as models for photo illustrations (Figures 2.4, 2.5 and 5.5).

During part of the time working on the book, one of us (MW) was supported by a Heisenberg fellowship from the Deutsche Forschungsgemeinschaft, enjoying the hospitality of the Social Psychology Departments at the Universities of Heidelberg and of New South Wales.

We would like to thank the psychology departments—and especially the social psychology groups—at both these universities and at the University of Kent, where GB spent most of the time working on the book, for providing good facilities, excellent staff support and a stimulating research environment.

Series preface

Social Psychology: A Modular Course, edited by Miles Hewstone, aims to provide undergraduates with stimulating, readable, affordable, and brief texts by leading experts committed to presenting a fair and accurate view of the work in each field, sharing their enthusiasm with students, and presenting their work in an approachable way. Together with three other modular series, these texts will cover all the major topics studied at undergraduate level in psychology. The companion series are: *Clinical Psychology*, edited by Chris R. Brewin; *Developmental Psychology*, edited by Peter Bryant; and *Cognitive Psychology*, edited by Gerry Altmann and Susan E. Gathercole. The series will appeal to those who want to go deeper into the subject than the traditional textbook will allow, and base their examination answers, research, projects, assignments, or practical decisions on a clearer and more rounded appreciation of the research evidence.

Basic issues in attitude research I

What is an attitude, and why is it important? 1

Throughout history, people have fought for freedom of belief, thought and speech. The storming of the Bastille and, 200 years later, the brave protests at Tiananmen Square, testify to how dear individuals hold their attitudes. Attitudes are a central part of human individuality.

Figure 1.1. History provides many examples of people ready to risk their lives standing up for their convictions. During the Tiananmen Square protests of 1989, this Beijing citizen stood motionless in the path of approaching tanks. The tanks did not stop but turned around the man, who was not injured. Copyright © Popperfoto/Reuters.

Many examples can be found for people ready to die for their convictions. On the dark side, even today people kill, persecute and inflict suffering because of misguided attitudes such as nationalism, racism or religious fanaticism. People love and hate, like and dislike, favour and oppose. They agree, disagree, argue, persuade and sometimes even convince each other. Every day, each of us is exposed to countless attempts at changing or reinforcing our attitudes through personal communication, the mass media or the Internet. Every day, social scientists and market researchers conduct studies and polls. They report that the percentage of Britons who favoured their country's membership in the European Union rose from 29% in 1982 to a majority of 52% in 1990 (Commission of the European Community, 1982, 1990), that more than 70% of people are usually satisfied with their work (Furnham, 1997), or that young singles living in urban areas value health aspects and gourmet appeal in convenience food. Such findings in turn provide input to political, organisational or marketing decisions. Moreover, when individual attitudes turn into public opinion, then these attitudes determine the social, political and cultural climate in a society, which in turn affects the individual lives of the people in that society. Forty years ago, in an era of more conservative sexual attitudes, unmarried student couples would have had very different experiences had they moved in together. Until quite recently, homosexual couples were virtually nonexistent on TV, because producers shied away from such controversial issues. If you are not convinced yet that attitudes might be an important concept, we have more and hopefully more convincing arguments below.

In any case, you may come up with many questions. For example, you may wonder how one can know the views of the British regarding their nation's EU membership. How is it that people have different attitudes, and how do these attitudes change over time? Can one really influence attitudes, and if so, how? What are attitudes good for? Will a person who opposes animal testing also act upon her attitude and boycott products involving animal testing? Social psychology has a lot to say about such issues—in fact much more than we can cover in this book. In our attempt to answer some of these questions we will first provide you with a more formal definition of what attitudes are.

What is an attitude?

Above we already gave some examples of attitudes. Others would be sexism, liberalism, opposition to animal testing, love for chocolate, or the belief that the Rolling Stones are the greatest rock band ever. As different as these are they are all examples of an attitude, because they represent an evaluative response toward an object. We define an attitude as a summary evaluation of an object of thought. An **attitude object** can be anything a person discriminates or holds in mind. Attitude objects may be concrete (e.g. pizza) or abstract (e.g. freedom of speech), may be inanimate things (e.g. sports cars), persons (e.g. Slobodan Milosevic, oneself) or groups (e.g. conservative politicians, foreigners).

Attitudes may encompass affective, behavioural and cognitive responses (see chapter 3 below). For example, an environmentalist may strongly believe that air pollution destroys the ozone layer, which increases the risk of cancer (cognitive); she may get angry or sad about the extinction of endangered species (affective); and she may use public transportation rather than a car and participate in recycling (behavioural). It should be noted that contrary to earlier theorising (e.g. Katz & Stotland, 1959) these three response classes are not necessarily separable from each other and do not necessarily represent three independent factors. Our example may already have illustrated that it is intuitively, as well as empirically, difficult to separate the different classes from each other. Moreover, attitudes may consist entirely of cognitive or of affective components and it is not necessary that all three classes are represented. For that reason we adopted a one-dimensional definition of attitude as a summary evaluation.

Our definition is congruent with the perspectives taken by most attitude researchers (e.g. Eagly & Chaiken, 1993; Petty, Wegener, & Fabrigar, 1997). What is debated regarding attitude conceptualisations is whether evaluations have to be stable over a longer time period and have to be stored in long-term memory to qualify as an attitude. Some definitions characterise attitudes as enduring concepts which are stored in memory and can be retrieved accordingly (e.g. Allport, 1935; Petty, Priester, & Wegener, 1994, for a classic and a contemporary reference). This perspective was termed the **"file-drawer model"*** because it perceives attitudes as mental files which individuals consult for the evaluation of the object in question (Wilson, Lisle, & Kraft, 1990). In contrast, other researchers have proposed the idea of attitudes as temporary constructions, which individuals construct at the time an evaluative judgment is needed (e.g. Tesser, 1978; Tourangeau & Rasinski, 1988; for reviews see Schwarz & Bohner, 2001; Wilson &

---

* Throughout this book, key terms appear in bold. These terms are defined in a Glossary towards the end of the book.

Hodges, 1992). According to the **attitudes-as-constructions perspective**, people do not retrieve any previously stored attitude from their memory. Rather they generate an evaluative judgment based on the information that comes to mind in the situation.

Both perspectives can draw upon supporting evidence. On the one hand, some attitudes, for example political attitudes (e.g. Marwell, Aiken, & Demerath, 1987) have been shown to be relatively stable over time. On the other hand, numerous studies have shown that people report different attitudes depending on the context, for example when they experience different mood states (e.g. Schwarz & Clore, 1983), when the situation brings different contents to mind (e.g. Tourangeau & Rasinski, 1988), or towards different interviewers (e.g. Schuman & Converse, 1971). We will extend this discussion in chapter 5.

Why do people have attitudes?

Over the years social psychologists have suggested different classes of psychological needs or goals which may be served by holding attitudes. Because almost any conceptualisation of attitude functions has introduced a different taxonomy, and unfortunately often used the same terms for different concepts or different terms for the same concepts, students often find the whole matter rather confusing. However, social psychologists have not thought about attitude functions in order to propose elaborate classifications, nor did they assume to capture each and every possible function in their systems. The assumption that guided initial thoughts and research was that in order to change a particular attitude one needs to know which function it serves. Consequently, researchers who were concerned with prejudice focused on functions possibly underlying prejudice. Katz (1960), for example, suggested an "ego-defensive" function whose name reveals its foundations in psychoanalytical theory. Other researchers looked at functions relevant in consumer behaviour and distinguished, for example, between product attitudes based on image concerns, which serve the function of presenting oneself favourably, and those based on product quality concerns, which serve the function of evaluating the utilitarian aspects of the product (Shavitt, 1990; Snyder & DeBono, 1987). For example, you may favour a restaurant because you find its food tasty (utilitarian) or because you want to cast the impression (social identity) of being one of the (cool, fashionable etc.) people who frequent this restaurant (Shavitt, Swan, Lowrey, & Wänke, 1994).

Although each theoretical analysis needs to be understood within the specific context in which it evolved, most taxonomies overlap to some extent. We suggest here two main **attitude functions** that can be seen as the essence of different theoretical approaches:

(1) serving knowledge organisation and guiding approach and avoidance;
(2) serving higher psychological needs.

Knowledge organisation and regulating approach and avoidance

Dividing the world into good and bad at the most basic level seems to be a fundamental process (although this tendency may differ in extent between individuals; see Jarvis & Petty, 1996). Not only do people judge objects mainly according to this dimension (Osgood, Suci, & Tannenbaum, 1957), recent work further shows that they are doing so incredibly fast. Regardless of whether research participants were presented with familiar or novel stimuli, words or pictures, typical response latencies for deciding whether the stimulus was good or bad were below one second. Results such as this suggest that determining the favourability of objects may be an automatic process[1] at least for some objects (e.g. Bargh, Chaiken, Raymond, & Hymes, 1996; Fazio, Sanbonmatsu, Powell, & Kardes, 1986).

Identifying good and bad or categorising the environment into friendly and hostile seems to be the most obvious and essential function, and not surprisingly it is part of all analyses of attitude functions. Katz (1960), who developed one of the earlier classifications termed this function the "**knowledge function**". Attitudes provide a simple structure for organising and handling an otherwise complex and ambiguous environment. In this sense, an attitude represents a cognitive **schema** (see Bless, Fiedler, & Strack, in press, for a review of the schema concept in social cognition; see also chapter 9).

Knowledge may be desirable in itself, but moreover knowledge fulfils a **utilitarian function**. Knowing whether something is good or bad is quite useful when it comes to approach or avoidance. Individuals approach people they find attractive and eat food they find tasty. Many researchers proposed a function that serves achieving rewards and avoiding punishments; based on Katz' taxonomy, this function is often referred to as "utilitarian". Note, however, that in contrast to Katz' approach most other conceptualisations, whether contemporary or classic, do not separate between a function of helping to understand and organise the environment and a function of maximising benefits and minimising costs. Rather, in most analyses, what is called "utilitarian" or "instrumental" in modern classifications (e.g. Abelson & Prentice, 1989; Shavitt, 1989), or "object-appraisal" in the first study on attitude functions (Smith, Bruner, & White, 1956), embraces both aspects. A general example of attitudes serving such a utilitarian function are attitudes based on self-interest, for example when nonsmokers favour stricter smoking regulations (Green & Gerken, 1989).

Higher psychological needs

Of course, most experiences may generally be classified as pleasant or unpleasant, thus representing rewards and punishments, and accordingly most attitudes would serve the utilitarian function. Herek (1986) has proposed a useful distinction between pleasantness or unpleasantness resulting from the attitude object, corresponding to a utilitarian function, and pleasantness or unpleasantness arising from expressing an attitude, corresponding to an expressive or **symbolic function**. Some attitudes may be central to a person's self-concept, and by expressing or activating this attitude a person affirms his or her central values. With this in mind, Prentice and Carlsmith (2000) have likened attitudes to other valued possessions of a person (see also Abelson, 1986).

Attitudes may also serve the maintenance of social relationships, for example holding attitudes that are viewed favourably by one's peers. These value-expressive (Katz, 1960) and social-adjustive (Smith et al., 1956) functions may be subsumed under the label of **social identity functions** (Shavitt, 1989). Examples for other symbolic functions are the maintenance of self-esteem (Shavitt 1989), the reduction of fear or inner conflict and the coping with threats to the self (Katz, 1960), or coping with one's mortality (Greenberg, Solomon, & Pyszczynski, 1997). The latter function has been investigated in an interesting research programme whose central claim is that knowing about one's mortality, which is unique to humans among all species, has the potential of creating fear or terror in humans. According to **terror management theory**, one strategy to cope with this fear is to focus less on one's individual mortality but more on the larger picture of being part of a group and culture which will remain. Indeed, many studies have suggested that mortality salience engenders defence of one's cultural worldview (for a review see Greenberg et al., 1997) and increased prejudice against members of other groups. For example, when Christian research participants had spent some time thinking about what will happen to them after they physically die and what emotions thoughts of their own death would elicit, they evaluated a Christian more positively and a Jew more negatively as compared to those participants for whom their own mortality had not been made salient (Greenberg, Pyszcynski, Solomon, Rosenblatt, Veeder, Kirkland, & Lyon, 1990). It is believed that the upgrading of ingroup members and the downgrading of outgroup members serve the function of managing the terror induced by being reminded of one's mortality.

Research applying attitude functions

Implicit in the guiding hypothesis that persuasive attempts need to match the underlying attitude functions (*functional matching hypothesis*) is that identical attitudes may serve different functions for different people. For example, a woman may oppose gender discrimination in job promotions because it decreases her chances of a successful career (utilitarian), or because such practices violate her sense of social justice and equal opportunities (value-expressive), or in order to align herself with her feminist peers (social adjustive). People may be prejudiced against a social group because by degrading others, amongst many other things, they may elevate their own self-esteem (e.g. Tajfel, 1981), they may conform to the norm of their social group, or they may justify existing power differentials within a society. This example also demonstrates that the same attitude may serve different functions for different people. And the same attitude may serve different functions for the same person at different times. Moreover, the same person may hold different attitudes pertaining to different functions at different times. But most likely, all of the functions in our example may play a role, implying that attitudes may be multifunctional. Still any attempt to improve the plight of the prejudice victims and extinguish prejudice would have to take into account what function being prejudiced fulfils for those who hold the negative views.

Measuring attitude functions, however, has proved to be cumbersome, which may have contributed to the fact that attitude functions were long neglected in social psychological research, until their revival in the 1980s. One research programme that tested the matching hypothesis—the assumption that persuasive attempts need to apply to the underlying function of the attitude—used the individual difference measure of **self-monitoring** (for a review see DeBono, 2000); we have described one of these studies in Box 1.1. Many other studies have also found support for the hypothesis that a persuasive appeal will be most effective in changing an attitude if the message is designed to address the underlying functions of the attitude (e.g. DeBono & Harnish, 1988; DeBono & Packer, 1991; Shavitt, 1990; Shavitt et al., 1994; for a review see Maio & Olson, 2000b).

Although still concerned with individual differences in attitude functions, recent research also looks at whether particular functions are related to particular classes of attitude objects. Political attitudes seem to correspond more to symbolic functions than to self-interest (for a review see Sears & Funk, 1990). Attitudes toward some consumer goods, for example air conditioners, may serve more of a utilitarian function, whereas attitudes toward other products, for instance wedding rings, may serve more of a value-expressive need (Shavitt, 1989). Advertisers often target a product's most salient function. For example, deodorant adverts are typically image-related, although one can find utilitarian adverts as well (see Figure 1.3).

Most attitudes do not serve just a single function but may well be multi-functional. For example, the negative reactions of some people towards persons who are HIV positive may be simultaneously based on instrumental aspects, such as avoiding transmission of the virus, and value-expressive aspects, such as objection to homosexuality (Reeder & Pryor, 2000; interestingly, this seemed to be the case even when the HIV patients were not homosexuals). Most importantly, however, contemporary research acknowledges that an attitude may serve different functions for the same person at different times. You may keep this aspect tucked in the back of your head as we will come back to it in chapter 10.

Why study attitudes?

No introduction to the psychology of attitudes will fail to quote that "attitudes are probably the most distinctive and indispensable

High self-monitors are mainly concerned with fitting well into a social situation, whereas low self-monitors are concerned with their behaviour reflecting their own values. Snyder and DeBono (1985) assumed that for high self-monitors attitudes fulfil a social-adjustive function but not so for low self-monitors. These researchers therefore hypothesised different reactions of these two groups to advertising strategies. They presented both groups with adverts for different products that focused either on the image conveyed by the product or on product quality. For example, a print advert displayed a bottle of whisky resting on a set of house blueprints. In the image version the copy in the whisky advert read "you're not just moving in, you're moving up". In the quality version the copy read "When it comes to great taste everyone draws the same conclusion." Snyder and DeBono found that high self-monitors were more responsive to adverts that appealed to the images supported by product use than to adverts that focused on the inherent quality of the product. The reverse relationship was found for low self-monitors (see Figure 1.2).

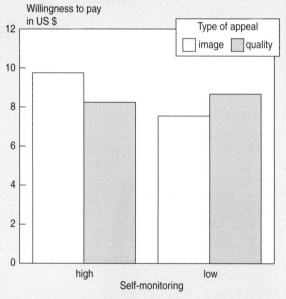

Figure 1.2.   Self-monitoring and attitude functions: Amount of US dollars that recipients of an advert were willing to pay for the advertised whisky as a function of the advertising strategy and recipients' level of self-monitoring (data from Snyder & DeBono, 1985).

concept in contemporary social psychology" (Allport, 1935, p. 798). Despite some fluctuations in popularity, attitude research has continuously featured prominently in social psychology throughout the decades. Few texts however explain why attitudes are so important (for an exception see Greenwald, 1989). Why indeed?

Loves skin.
Hates sweat.

New Dove Deodorant.
Made to pass any woman's test.

Figure 1.3. These two adverts represent different advertising strategies, which seem to appeal to different functions underlying the recipient's attitude towards deodorants. The Natrel advert appeals to a self-expressive function, whereas the Dove advert uses a utilitarian approach.

Students typically reply that *attitudes influence behaviour*. Although the relationship between attitudes and behaviour is complex (see chapter 10) and not always straightforward, it is most certainly the case that a person's attitude toward a particular attitude object may influence his or her behaviour toward this object. If you like pizza you will be more likely to order it than a person who is disgusted by the mere thought of pizza. If you oppose animal testing you are more likely to sign a petition against animal testing than a person who favours animal testing. Moreover, your attitude toward one attitude object may influence your behaviour (and attitudes) toward other attitude objects. For example, you may boycott consumer products involving animal tests or you may support political candidates who have a history of voting for animal rights. In addition, one person's attitude may influence other persons' behaviour. For instance, if you want to impress your peers who are all environmentalists you are likely to use your bike more often than your car. In that sense, your peers' attitude influenced your behaviour (for a thorough discussion see chapter 10).

But apart from the attitude–behaviour relationship there are other reasons why the concept of attitudes has been central to social psychology for the last 60 years. Imagine yourself during your first week at university. You don't know anybody but bravely strike up a conversation with a fellow class-mate. Think of the topics you would address. We bet that after having established name, hometown and other descriptives your conversation will turn to such topics as what kind of music (movies, books etc.) you like or what you think of university so far. In other words, you will try to find out something about your new acquaintance's attitudes while trying to express yours. As a consequence you will develop an attitude toward that person which may lead you to continue, intensify or discontinue your relationship. We argue that attitudes are central to social psychology because they are central to our social lives. People approach and like others whose attitudes are similar to their own (e.g. Byrne, 1971) but they avoid and dislike people who hold different attitudes (e.g. Rosenbaum, 1986). We categorise people according to their attitudes (e.g. as "conservatives" or "feminists"; see Hymes, 1986) and infer other attitudes they may hold. For example, conservative people are likely to oppose a woman's right of abortion whereas feminists are likely to endorse it. In turn, by expressing our own attitudes we re-affirm our own identity. And, as we explained above, attitudes may serve other important psychological functions.

Finally, attitudes do not only influence behaviour and other attitudes, they also determine how we *process information* regarding the attitude object (for a review see Pratkanis, 1989). As we will discuss in more detail in chapters 8 and 9, individuals often search for and select information that confirms their beliefs and attitudes rather than information that may disconfirm them. Moreover, when exposed to information that cannot be avoided, people tend to interpret it in line with their attitudes. In a classic study, Hastorf and Cantril (1954) asked students from two rival universities, Princeton and Dartmouth, to view a film of the Princeton v. Dartmouth football match and to report the fouls of each team. Although they watched the same film, Princeton students reported more fouls of the Dartmouth team than the Dartmouth students. We will review such processes in chapter 9.

In summary, the construct of attitudes seems to be an important mediating link between the social information we perceive in our environment and how we respond to it. Attitudes may determine to a large extent how we react to social stimuli including ourselves, how we feel, think and act relative to them. Consequently, a large part of social psychology deals with attitudes in one form or another, for example, attitudes toward other people (liking, attraction), toward specific groups of people (prejudice), toward oneself (self-esteem) or toward abstract principles (values, opinions). As our examples illustrated, the importance of attitudes becomes apparent at various levels of analysis which are all subject of social psychological and social research:

- At the *individual level*, attitudes influence perception, thinking, other attitudes and behaviour. Accordingly, attitudes contribute heavily to a person's psychological make-up.
- At the *interpersonal level*, information about attitudes is routinely requested and communicated. If we know others' attitudes, the world becomes a more predictable place. Our own thought and behaviour may be shaped by this knowledge, and we may try to control others' behaviour by changing their attitudes.
- At the *societal level*, attitudes toward one's own groups and other groups are at the core of intergroup cooperation and conflict. A negative outgroup attitude or prejudice (e.g. held by heterosexuals toward lesbians and gays) can cause discriminatory behaviour (e.g. refusing to employ members of these groups) or even direct violence.

In sum, attitudes are a central concept in many topics social psychologists study. And, perhaps more importantly, by shaping the social world for individuals, groups and societies at large, attitudes are most relevant for everybody's daily life. So read on.

Overview of the book

This volume is supposed to give you an overview of classic and contemporary issues in attitude research, but we will refer you to further reading at the end of each chapter if you want a more detailed and exhaustive perspective. We divided the topics into four parts: What is an attitude, where does it come from, what are its consequences?, and a postscript. In part I (Basic issues in attitude research) we address such basic issues as the nature of attitudes. You have already seen that valence is the most central property of an attitude: One may like or dislike something. Moreover, one may like or dislike things to different degrees. If we think of attitudes as different degrees of evaluation it becomes obvious that one of the basic topics in attitude research is the measurement of attitudes. Chapter 2 will show you how attitudes can be measured. But there is more to attitudes than their degree of favourability; in chapter 3, we will give a more detailed account of the structure of attitudes.

Part II (Where do attitudes come from?) will deal with the origins of attitudes and how attitudes can be influenced. Would you have thought that attitudes may have a genetic component? It appears that some attitudes are genetically influenced, an issue which we will address in chapter 4. In that chapter, we will not only review evidence for nature as a source of attitudes, but also for nurture, and we will review how attitudes may be acquired via basic principles of learning, mere exposure to an attitude object, or through the observation of role models. A contemporary perspective views attitudes not as enduring concepts which are stored in memory but as mental constructions that are formed "on the spot" when needed in a particular situation. Accordingly, many situational variables influence the formation of attitudes, and we will discuss some of these in chapter 5. We will outline how context provides the building blocks of evaluative judgments, determines their valence, and finally influences how these building blocks are put together. More about these processes will be said in chapters 6 and 7 on persuasion. We will review several classic approaches to persuasion in chapter 6, then focus on the currently most influential dual process models in chapter 7. The latter distinguish processes of attitude change on a continuum ranging from relatively superficial and effortless mechanisms to rather deep and exhaustive thinking. Concluding Part II, in chapter 8 we will look at yet another source of attitudes, namely people's behaviour. We will present different theoretical perspectives on the question when people will hold attitudes that are in line with their overt behaviour, and when they will not.

In Part III (Consequences of attitudes) we will address influences of attitudes on how people interact with their environment: How they process information about the social world (chapter 9) and, last not least, how they behave (chapter 10). You will see, amongst other issues, that what information about an object people attend to, how they interpret it and how they further process it is quite substantially influenced by their attitudes towards that object. Finally, researchers and practitioners alike have been interested to what extent people's attitudes guide their overt behaviour. Can we change what people do by changing how they think and feel about an issue? The relationship between attitudes and behaviour is quite complex, and we will discuss some of its boundary conditions.

Part IV (Postscript) presents some concluding remarks. In chapter 11, we will take a brief look back at what we have learned and present some thoughts on what might lie ahead in the dynamic endeavour of attitude research.

Chapter summary

(1) An attitude represents a summary evaluation of an attitude object. Components of this summary evaluation may be affective, behavioural and cognitive, and may encompass any type of information which holds evaluative implication.

(2) Some researchers have conceptualised attitudes as relatively stable and enduring concepts, which are retrieved from memory upon encounter with the attitude object. Alternatively, others conceive of attitudes as being constructed in the respective situation and influenced by information that comes to mind in this particular situation.

(3) Common to all attitudes is the function of organising and categorising a complex environment. Attitudes may be utilitarian inasfar as people hold positive attitudes toward objects that promise benefits or rewards and negative attitudes toward objects that are associated with costs or punishment. Attitudes

may serve higher psychological needs such as the expression of values, social adjustment, the reduction of threat to the self or the reduction of inner conflict.

(4) The same attitude may serve different functions for different people. The same attitude may serve different functions for the same person at different times. And, of course, the same person may hold different attitudes pertaining to different functions at different times. Most attitudes serve multiple functions.

(5) Attitudes are central in social psychology because they influence behaviour (own and others') (see chapter 10), they influence information processing (see chapter 9), they influence social encounters and they form part of a person's self-concept.

(6) Different forms of attitudes are the topic of main research areas in the social sciences and in social psychology: e.g. prejudice and stereotyping, values, self-esteem.

Exercises

(1) Make a list of as many attitudes of yours you can think of. Can you find some order? Are some related, are some part of a hierarchy etc.? Are some more important to you than others? This will lead you to chapter 3.

(2) Try to think of how you got those attitudes. This is a preparation for chapter 4.

(3) Think of some examples of how you are affected by other people's (e.g. your parents', friends') attitudes.

(4) Think of different attitudes of yours and try to analyse their main function.

(5) Thumb through a magazine and try to explain which attitudinal function(s) various adverts address. Which ones seem most appealing to you and why?

Note

(1) Social psychologists use the term "automatic" for cognitive processes that occur without intention, are efficient in the sense that they do not take up much cognitive capacity, often occur outside of awareness and are difficult to control for the individual (e.g. Bargh, 1994). We will discuss such automatic responses in chapters 5 and 9.

Further reading

Definition of the attitude concept:

Eagly, A. H., & Chaiken, S. (1993). *The psychology of attitudes*. Fort Worth, TX: Harcourt Brace Jovanovich. (chapter 1)

Why study attitudes?

Greenwald, A. (1989). Why are attitudes important? In A. R. Pratkanis, S. J. Breckler, & A. G. Greenwald (Eds.), *Attitude structure and function* (pp. 429–440). Hillsdale, NJ: Lawrence Erlbaum Associates Inc.

Attitude functions:

Maio, G. R., & Olson, J. M. (Eds.). (2000). *Why we evaluate*. Mahwah, NJ: Lawrence Erlbaum Associates Inc.

Shavitt, S. (1989). Operationalizing functional theories of attitude. In A. R. Pratkanis, S. J. Breckler, & A. G. Greenwald (Eds.), *Attitude structure and function* (pp. 311–337). Hillsdale, NJ: Lawrence Erlbaum Associates Inc.

Snyder, M., & DeBono, K. G. (1989). Understanding the functions of attitudes: Lessons from personality and social behavior. In A. R. Pratkanis, S. J. Breckler, & A. G. Greenwald (Eds.), *Attitude structure and function* (pp. 339–359). Hillsdale, NJ: Lawrence Erlbaum Associates Inc.

The measurement of attitudes 2

Attitudes are not directly observable, so if one wants to know a person's attitude one has to find some other way of assessing it. Probably the easiest way is to simply ask the person. Not surprisingly, such direct measures are most commonly used in both academic and applied research. You may have experienced this yourself when answering a questionnaire on consumer satisfaction or evaluating your university courses. As easy as this may seem, there are many issues involved in this kind of measurement, and different instruments have been developed.

As an alternative to direct questions, attitudes may be inferred from other cues. In that case, the person may not even know that her attitude is being assessed. In fact, some indirect measures have been designed to reveal attitudes that the person is not even aware of, so-called implicit attitudes. Independent of whether attitudes are measured directly or indirectly, a good instrument should be reliable and valid. By **reliability** we mean that it should measure consistently whatever it measures, and by **validity** we mean that it should measure the attitude it is designed to measure, rather than something else. Before we turn to particular direct and indirect measures let us start with a closer look at the general logic underlying the concept of measurement.

The concept of measurement

When we speak of measurement, we mean the assignment of numbers to objects according to rules (Stevens, 1946) in such a way that properties of the numbers reflect certain relations of the objects to each other. There are several levels of measurement, which are

TABLE 2.1

Levels of measurement

Scale level	Examples	Relations represented	Permissible scale transformations[a]
Nominal	gender; religion	$= \neq$	any that leave equality and inequality of scores intact
Ordinal	degree class in college; Richter scale of seismic activity	$= \neq$ $< >$	any that leave order of scores intact
Interval	Celsius and Fahrenheit scales of temperature; IQ measures	as Ordinal, plus: ratio between differences among scores	any positive linear transformation: $y' = by + a$
Ratio	response time; frequency of target behaviour	as Interval, plus: ratio between scores	any positive multiplicative transformation: $y' = by$

Note: [a] y' = new scale value; y = old scale value; b = any positive real number; a = any real number.

characterised by different amounts of information about the relation between objects that are reflected in the numbers assigned (see Table 2.1). At the lowest level are *nominal scales*; their numbers reflect only equality versus difference with respect to the property being measured. Examples would be measuring research participants' gender by assigning the number 0 to males and the number 1 to females, or measuring religion by assigning the numbers 1, 2, 3, 4 and 5, respectively, to Christians, Hindus, Jews, Muslims and "others". All that these nominal scales tell us is that two objects sharing the same number are equal, and that two objects not sharing the same number are unequal, with respect to their gender or religion. Any other relations between the numbers are obviously meaningless; e.g. Hindus are not characterised by "twice as much religion" or "one scale unit more religion" than Christians.

Of course we would not be content with knowing if two individuals' attitudes are the same or different. We also want to know how people compare along a continuum of evaluation: whose attitude is more favourable, whose is less favourable? This is achieved by an *ordinal scale*, where the numbers assigned also reflect the ordering of objects with respect to the property being measured. If Wolfgang likes pizza more than Hans does, who in turn likes pizza more than Christiane does, the largest number would be assigned to Wolfgang's attitude, the next largest to Hans', and the smallest to Christiane's. Thus, the numbers 3, 2 and 1 would do, but so would 6, 4 and 2 (or 17, 5.3 and 4); with an ordinal scale, any scale transformation that preserves the rank order of objects measured is permissible. However, the numbers would not tell us how much Wolfgang, Hans and Christiane differ in their liking for pizza.

The representation of the amount of difference would be achieved by the next level of measurement: an *interval scale*. Here, in addition to the properties of an ordinal scale, the relative differences between scores represent the relative differences between the objects measured with respect to the measured property. If we know that the difference between Wolfgang and Hans regarding their liking of pizza is twice as large as the difference between Hans and Christiane, this could be expressed in an interval scale by assigning values 3, 1 and 0, respectively, to their three attitudes. Equivalent sets of numbers would be 2, 0 and −1 or 4, 3 and 2.5. Thus, any positive linear transformation of an interval scale is permissible as it leaves intact not only the rank order of scores, but also the ratios between differences of pairs of scores (see Table 2.1).

The highest level of measurement is a *ratio scale*. It has all the properties of an interval scale and in addition allows for the representation of ratios between the scores themselves. To achieve this, a ratio scale must have a meaningful and fixed zero point. Permissible transformations that leave all properties represented in a ratio scale intact are positive multiplications (see Table 2.1). Examples for ratio scales in the domain of attitude measurement are difference scores of response latencies, which are used to assess implicit attitudes (see the later section in this chapter). But although it makes perfect sense to say that person A's responses were twice as fast as person B's, translating this into a statement about attitudes (i.e. "A's attitude is twice as positive as B's attitude") may be doubtful.

Indeed, attitude researchers are usually content with scales that approximate the interval level of measurement, i.e. scales that have reasonably equal intervals between adjacent scale points but typically lack a meaningful zero point. These allow for the computation of arithmetic means and correlations and most of the statistical operations psychologists use in analysing data (for a more extensive discussion, see Himmelfarb, 1993).

In the next two sections we will take a closer look at the methods by which attitudes are assigned such scale values and then discuss the criteria that a high-quality scale should meet.

Direct measurement

As mentioned above the simplest way to find out about someone's attitude is to ask directly. Most likely, one will get an answer. But how good—or in technical terms, how valid—is that answer: To what extent does it reflect the person's attitude? Although we will discuss the general concept of validity in measurement only later, the validity of direct measures can be best understood within a theoretical framework of the cognitive and communicative processes involved in answering attitude questions. Researchers who were interested in improving survey techniques and data quality have investigated extensively what happens between the question and answer (for a review, see Sudman, Bradburn, & Schwarz, 1996). These processes apply whenever respondents are confronted with attitude questions, whether measurement consists of only one question or of multiple items.

The question-answering processes

What happens when people are asked for their attitude, for example, when a person is asked for an evaluative reaction to strawberries, Tony Blair, or educational contributions? Most people will know what strawberries are, and most Britons will know Tony Blair, but even so one may wonder whether one should react to his politics or to him as a person. And what exactly is an educational contribution? These examples demonstrate that as a first step respondents have to interpret the question and decide what they are asked to report. In the case of strawberries this may not require much thought but a concept will spring to mind automatically from one's world knowledge. Respondents may further make sense of the meaning of a question by using the context in which it is embedded, even if they have no knowledge whatsoever about the attitude object. Strack, Schwarz, and Wänke (1991) asked German students to indicate their attitude toward a (fictitious) "educational contribution" in two different contexts: In one condition, the preceding question referred to the average tuition fees that U.S. students have to pay; in another condition, the preceding question concerned financial support that the Swedish government pays every student. Strack and his colleagues found that participants' attitudes toward the ominous "educational contribution" were more favourable in the "Swedish" than in the "U.S." context. Apparently, respondents were more likely to interpret the educational contribution as something students receive (rather than as a fee they have to pay) when the question about financial support for students, rather than the question about tuition fees, preceded it. Such contextual cues may guide interpretation automatically or because respondents deliberately look for them.

Once respondents have identified the attitude object they will retrieve their attitude towards it provided they had previously formed one and stored it in memory.[1] Or, if they had not "filed" an evaluation or cannot find it in their mental "file drawer", they will need to build one on the spot. To do so, they will use the information that comes to mind in the specific situation. Extensive research has shown how such situational information can influence judgments (see chapter 5), which presents a particular problem for surveys because the specific context created by the measurement may influence the measurement. Possible influences come from the response alternatives or scales provided, the interviewer (if present) or the purpose of the survey, its introduction and literally all other survey elements. The most prominent and best researched influences are those of question order (see Box 2.1).

From the retrieved information respondents will "compute" a judgment (see chapter 5 for details), but the answering process does not end here. Respondents may be unwilling to report these privately computed attitudes and may wish to adjust them, for example to conform to the social norms they infer in the situation, or because of other motives (DeMaio, 1984). Finally, respondents report their judgment, which usually involves accommodating it to certain response alternatives or translating it into a scale value. We present examples of such standardised response formats later in this section. A flowchart of the question-answering process is provided in Figure 2.1 (see also Sudman et al., 1996).

To summarise, the attitudes reported in direct assessments are subject to a number of influences, some of which originate from the measurement process itself. The latter phenomenon has been termed **reactivity** (Weick, 1985). However, a crucial distinction needs to be made. Some effects of measurement reflect motivational distortions of the attitude report, and below we will address how to deal with this particular aspect of reactivity. The other type of effect, which we

BOX 2.1   Question order effects in attitude surveys

Research on **question order effects** dates back to the 1930s when Janet Sayre systematically investigated attitudes towards radio advertising (1939) and found that responses to an attitude question differed systematically depending on what question had preceded it. Since then survey researchers have documented a wide range of question order effects (for reviews see Schuman & Presser, 1981; Schwarz & Sudman, 1992; Tourangeau & Rasinski, 1988). Of course, question order is merely a technical variable and its effects may be due to different psychological processes, namely how respondents make sense of the question, which information they retrieve for this response, how they interpret the response alternatives or scale values, or what they think is appropriate to report in the situation (for a review, see Wänke & Schwarz, 1997). The following example illustrates how previous questions may affect the information retrieval for constructing the attitude under scrutiny.

In a telephone survey, Tourangeau, Rasinski, Bradburn, and D'Andrade (1989) asked 1056 Chicago residents about their opinions on increased welfare spending. For about half of the respondents, this question was preceded by four items related to the liberal side of the target issue, which is concerned with government responsibility for the poor, for example: "Do you agree or disagree: Some people in America really need help from the government." For the other half of the respondents, the target question was preceded by four questions linked to the conservative side of the issue, which could be labelled "economic individualism", for example: "Do you agree or disagree: In America, any person who is willing to work hard has a good chance of succeeding."

The context items were selected because they all showed a high ratio of agreement in the population. They were supposed to affect how respondents thought about welfare by rendering specific related beliefs about welfare more accessible (e.g. "there are many people in need" versus "people in need are just too lazy to work"). Later the target question was asked: "Do you favour or oppose increased spending for welfare programs?" Tourangeau and his colleagues found that the context had a profound influence on responses. In the liberal context, a majority of respondents (61.7%) favoured increased welfare spending, whereas in the conservative context, this was true only of 46.2%.

discussed in this section, are not errors but reflect processes inherent to the construction of the attitude in question (see also chapter 5). In interpreting empirical findings, it is therefore always a good idea to take contextual factors into consideration and to look closely at the methods that were used to measure an attitude (Schwarz & Bohner, 2001; Schwarz & Sudman, 1992; Wänke, 1997).

Instruments for direct attitude measurement

The simplest way to assess a person's attitude is to ask a single question about her general evaluation of the attitude object, and to

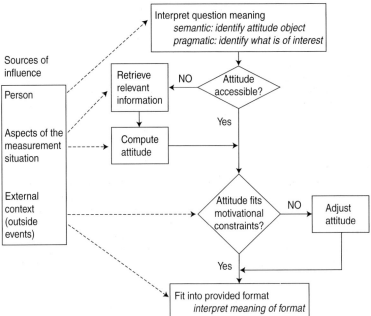

Figure 2.1. Flowchart representation of the question-answering process.

have her mark a response alternative along a numeric response scale. Although multi-item scales are often superior in reliability (e.g. Himmelfarb, 1993; see next section), **single-item measures** are in fact most common in survey research (see above) and are also employed in experimental studies. For instance, Bargh, Chaiken, Govender, and Pratto (1992) used single items to assess attitudes toward each of a large number of objects. Respondents were instructed to give their personal evaluation of each object listed, for example:

Strawberries

extremely bad   –5   –4   –3   –2   –1   0   +1   +2   +3   +4   +5   extremely good

An obvious advantage of single-item measures is that they are highly economical. They also have been found to be reasonably reliable and valid (e.g. Jaccard, Weber, & Lundmark, 1975; see next section). Sometimes they are clearly preferable to more complex measures, for instance when an attitude's **accessibility** is of crucial interest. (Accessibility means the ease with which information can be retrieved from memory, which is mainly a function of the frequency and recency of its prior use; see chapter 5.)[2] This may be exemplified by another phase of the Bargh et al. (1992) research. Here, evaluations were assessed with one-item measures that featured only two response alternatives. Participants were asked to press either a button labelled "good" or one labelled "bad" as quickly as possible each time an attitude object was displayed on the computer screen (see also Fazio et al., 1986). The response latency, i.e. how long it takes an individual to indicate that strawberries are "good" (or "bad"), is thought to reflect the accessibility of the attitude studied. Obviously, response latency is a meaningful indicator of accessibility only with a single, global response rather than a multitude of items, because answering the first item in a series would itself increase the accessibility of the attitude object, affecting response latencies on items presented later. Thus, in many research contexts, single items have proved adequate for the assessment of attitudes.

The major disadvantage of single-item measures is that their reliability may be low (or at least difficult to assess). Any item score not only reflects the attitude under consideration, but also chance variations in measurement, known as random error. In *multi-item scales*, greater reliability can be achieved because the final score is computed as the sum or mean of all items, which compensates for random error in any single item. Furthermore, in the construction phase of a multi-item scale inappropriate items that do not meet certain measurement criteria are eliminated (see next section for detail). Moreover, with complex attitude objects such as the death penalty or European unification, a single item may not be sufficiently differentiated to cover all the various facets of an attitude. Therefore, it is often preferable to assess attitudes with multi-item scales.

The most widely used multi-item attitude scales are the **semantic differential** (Osgood et al., 1957) and the **Likert scale** (Likert, 1932). Another, less frequently employed variant is the **Thurstone scale** (Thurstone, 1928). We briefly describe the central properties of these scales (for a more comprehensive treatment, see Himmelfarb, 1993); some item examples for each scale type are given in Table 2.2.

The semantic differential is perhaps the most commonly used type of multi-item attitude measure. It consists of a list of bipolar adjective scales, usually divided into seven response categories. Respondents rate an attitude object by marking one of the seven categories for each of the bipolar adjective pairs. These ratings are later scored −3 to +3, with positive numbers attached to the positive adjective in each pair. A total attitude score is computed for each respondent by summing or averaging scores across the bipolar scales (see Table 2.2). The

TABLE 2.2

Attitude scales: Item examples for common self-report measures

(a) *Semantic differential* on attitudes toward Germans. (Numbers for scoring are given in parentheses; these are not normally presented to respondents.)

Germans

| lazy | -3 -2 -1 0 +1 +2 +3 industrious |

| friendly | +3 +2 +1 0 -1 -2 -3 unfriendly |

| bad | -3 -2 -1 0 +1 +2 +3 good |

(b) *Likert scale* items assessing sexist attitudes toward women (from the Neosexism Scale; Tougas, Brown, Beaton, & Joly, 1995). Each item is presented with a scale from 1 to 7, with 1 indicating total disagreement and 7 indicating total agreement; items with an asterisk are later reverse-scored.

Discrimination against women in the labor force is no longer a problem in Canada.
I consider the present employment system to be unfair to women.*
It is difficult to work for a female boss.
In order not to appear sexist, many men are inclined to overcompensate women.
In a fair employment system, men and women would be considered equal.*

(c) *Thurstone scale* items assessing attitudes toward euthanasia (Tordella & Neutens, 1979). (The items' scale values, here ranging from 1 to 5, are given in parentheses; these are not presented to respondents.)

A person with a terminal illness has the right to decide to die.	(4.15)
Inducing death for merciful reasons is wrong.	(1.65)
A person should not be kept alive by machines.	(2.44)
Euthanasia gives a person a chance to die with dignity.	(4.29)
The taking of human life is wrong no matter what the circumstances.	(1.36)

original work of Osgood et al. (1957) with the semantic differential was aimed at studying the meaning of concepts. In a large number of studies using long lists of adjective pairs and a multitude of concepts, these researchers found that mainly three underlying dimensions or factors accounted for the interrelations of the scales; these were labelled *evaluation* (e.g. "good–bad"), *potency* (e.g. "strong–weak"), and *activity* (e.g. "fast–slow"). The evaluation factor usually explained the largest proportion of variability.[3] Semantic differentials designed to measure attitude (rather than meaning in general) are made up exclusively of items that load on the evaluation dimension (as those items shown in Table 2.2).

Another highly popular scaling technique was developed earlier by Likert (1932). In his method of summated ratings (better known simply as the *Likert scale*), respondents indicate the extent of their agreement, usually on a five-point or seven-point scale, with each of several statements pertaining to an attitude object. These have been pre-selected from a larger pool of statements so that agreement with each item unambiguously implies either a favourable or an unfavourable attitude. Usually, the statements can be characterised as beliefs about the attitude object, but it is also possible to use statements about affective reactions or behaviours toward the attitude object (e.g. Kothandapani, 1971). As with the semantic differential, an attitude score on a Likert scale is defined as the sum or mean across all items, after reverse-scoring those items on which agreement implies an unfavourable attitude (e.g. items marked with an asterisk in Table 2.2).

Both semantic differentials and Likert scales provide a comparison of respondents and are thus examples of person scaling. Due to the fact that each of their items is constructed to represent an unambiguous evaluation of the attitude object, semantic differential and Likert scales usually achieve high internal consistency, which means that item scores are highly intercorrelated (see next section). However, these scales do not strictly fulfil the criterion of equal-interval scaling, which is a prerequisite for a variety of statistical analyses. The assumption that pairs of scores differing by the same amount (say, 5 and 6 compared to 3 and 4) represent equal differences in subjective evaluation is true only to the extent that respondents interpret each pair of adjacent numbers on the response scale as equidistant and weight each item equally in deriving their overall attitude.

Scaling techniques that are more sensitive to the aim of creating an equal-interval scale were first proposed by Thurstone (1928). His **method of equal-appearing intervals** (Thurstone & Chave, 1929) includes a first step of stimulus scaling: Judges are asked to sort a large number of belief statements, which vary considerably in their direction and extremity, into a specified number of categories defined as equally spaced according to their subjective favourability (e.g. from "1 = least favourable", to "5 = most favourable"). Then each item is given a scale value that corresponds to the median of category numbers it was assigned to. For the second step of person scaling, a subset of items is selected from the initial item pool; most importantly, these items should have elicited high agreement among the judges regarding their favourability, and should represent the whole range of the favourability continuum. This subset is presented to respondents, who are asked to mark those items with which they agree. A respondent's attitude score is then defined as the median of the scale values of all items that she agreed with. Table 2.2 shows items from a Thurstone scale measuring attitudes toward euthanasia (Tordella & Neutens, 1979), along with their scale values.

Each type of multi-item attitude scale has its specific advantages and disadvantages. Semantic differentials provide the benefit that identical item sets can be used with different attitude objects, allowing for comparisons between objects (e.g. attitudes toward public transportation may directly be compared to attitudes toward individual traffic). By contrast, Likert and Thurstone scales need to be constructed specifically for each attitude object and generally require more extensive pilot work. Thurstone scales offer the unique advantage of using the assumption of equal-appearing intervals as a construction principle, which is not true of Likert and semantic differential scales.

Motivated response distortions and how to deal with them

The organisation of an attitude questionnaire, the context of a study, or subtle cues in the experimenter's behaviour may indicate to participants that certain hypotheses are being tested. Participants may then choose to respond to these *demand characteristics* (Orne, 1962) in a fashion that either confirms or disconfirms these hypotheses. They may also engage in **impression management** (Tedeschi, 1981; see chapter 8), trying to present themselves favourably or giving a response that seems to meet with social approval (Crowne & Marlowe, 1964) rather than responding truthfully. To reduce such motivated biases, researchers have proposed strategies that range from temporarily misinforming participants about the purpose of a study to asking for their cooperation by emphasising the importance of truthful responses (Aronson, Ellsworth, Carlsmith, & Gonzales, 1990; Rosenthal & Rosnow, 1991).

One strategy of controlling for distortions is to administer other self-report scales that measure tendencies of self-enhancement, such as Crowne and Marlowe's (1964) social desirability scale or Paulhus' (1998) Balanced Inventory of Desirable Responding. These scales contain negative statements that are likely to be true for virtually everyone (e.g. "I have some pretty awful habits") and positive statements that are true of hardly anyone (e.g. "I never take things that don't belong to me"); endorsement of the positive statements and rejection of the negative statements are thus interpreted as self-enhancement. By correlating an attitude measure with one of these control scales, the extent of response bias can be estimated and controlled for.

An interesting attempt at changing respondents' motivation from self-enhancement to a concern for truthful responding is the **bogus pipeline technique**, which was introduced by Jones and Sigall (1971). In this procedure, the respondent is hooked up to impressive-looking psychophysiological machinery, which purportedly gives the experimenter access to the respondent's true attitudes. A typical bogus pipeline experiment includes some warm-up trials in which the respondent is instructed to give false responses to some questions whose correct answers the experimenter knew beforehand; thus the alleged power of the apparatus to tell true from false responses can be convincingly "demonstrated". In the main trials, then, the respondent's motivation to distort responses is assumed to be reduced. We will review some studies in which this method was used in chapter 8. Although it has been criticised for various reasons, including its cumbersome procedure and the amount of deception involved (e.g. Ostrom, 1973), a recent meta-analysis shows that bogus pipeline conditions do tend to reduce motivated response distortions compared to standard self-report conditions (Roese & Jamieson, 1993). Nonetheless, Roese and Jamieson warn against the use of bogus pipeline procedures for assessing attitudes that are presumably weak or inaccessible, because the procedure might lead respondents to form stronger attitudes on the spot, thereby introducing a different kind of reactivity bias.

To avoid the problem of motivational distortions, researchers sometimes rely on indirect measures. Before we turn to the many facets of these methods, however, we will address some basic criteria of the quality of any measurement, be it direct or indirect.

How do we know if the measurement is good?

A score on an attitude scale is thought to reflect an attitude, a construct that is not directly observable. However, like any measured variable, an attitude score is influenced not only by the construct of interest, but also by other factors (see Himmelfarb, 1993). On one hand, there are influences known as **random error**, which can be thought of as chance fluctuations in measurement. Sources of random error include participants' misreading or misinterpretation of questions, measurement at different times of day, coding errors in the process of inputting data into a computer file and many others. Importantly, random error increases the variability of scores but not their central tendency. In other words, it tends to cancel itself out; whereas some respondents' attitude scores are increased due to random error, others' scores are decreased, and the increases and decreases nullify each other in the long run.

On the other hand, the attitude score may be influenced by other constructs that are not part of the attitude construct to be measured. As this type of influence may systematically increase or decrease the attitude score, it is called **systematic error**. For example, if respondents assume that the experimenter expects positive evaluations from them and then answer attitude items accordingly to please the experimenter, their attitude scores partly reflect the respondents' motivation to comply rather than their attitude.

Two criteria for good measurement are related to the degrees to which the two sources of error are avoided. The *reliability* of an attitude measure is high to the extent that attitude measurement is free from random error; in other words, a reliable scale measures consistently whatever it measures. *Construct validity* is said to be high when measurement is free from both random and systematic error; in other words, a construct valid procedure measures consistently the attitude it is designed to measure (and not something else). The association of random and systematic error with an attitude measure's reliability and construct validity is illustrated in Figure 2.2.

Reliability

One way of assessing a scale's reliability is by computing its *test–retest reliability*, which is the extent to which attitude scores assessed at two different points in time correlate with each other. If one assumes that the attitude under study is relatively stable, a reliable scale should yield stable results and thus high test–retest correlations. Unfortunately, the retesting procedure itself may affect the attitude under study; for example, people may start thinking about the

Figure 2.2. The constructs affecting the score on an attitude measure and their association with reliability and validity: The larger the proportion representing the target attitude, the higher the construct validity. Panels A and B represent attitude measures that are equal in construct validity. Although measure B exhibits lower random error and thus greater reliability, its construct validity is not higher than that of measure A due its higher proportion of systematic error. This shows that greater reliability is not a sufficient condition for greater validity.

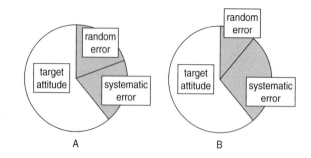

A   B

topic and revise their attitudes between measurements. Furthermore, researchers disagree about whether attitudes should be expected to be stable over time at all (see chapters 1 and 5). Thus, low test–retest correlations may reflect a change in the attitude rather than a problem of the measurement scale.

For these reasons, more popular indices of reliability are based on a scale's *internal consistency*. Internal consistency is the degree to which the items of a scale correlate with each other and thus reflect the attitude construct of interest rather than random error. It can be assessed by correlating the score on one half of a scale's items with the score on the other half; the resulting coefficient is known as the *split-half reliability*. As any scale can be split into halves in different ways, split-half reliability varies somewhat with the particular split being made. This problem is avoided by the most widely used index of internal consistency, **Cronbach's alpha**. It can be thought of as the mean of all possible split-half coefficients (Cronbach, 1951). All else being equal, the alpha coefficient increases with an increasing number of items. This increased reliability of longer scales simply reflects that all items contribute to measuring the attitude construct, thus sharing systematic variance, whereas random error components are uncorrelated and tend to be cancelled out. Thus, reliability can be enhanced by using a sufficiently large number of items to measure an attitude.

You should note that coefficients of internal consistency such as Cronbach's alpha are meaningful indicators of reliability only for scales where each item can be regarded as equally representing the target attitude. This is the case for Likert and semantic differential scales. With Thurstone scales, however, whose items represent different points along the attitude continuum, reliability needs to be estimated differently, e.g. from correlations between parallel forms of a scale or from test–retest correlations (see Himmelfarb, 1993).

Validity

Obviously, an instrument that fluctuates in precision is not very useful. Imagine your watch being fast on some days and slow on others. You would have difficulty being on time. Now imagine you own a highly reliable precision watch but because you have set it incorrectly it still does not show the correct time. Although its measurement is highly reliable, it is not valid. Thus, reliability is a prerequisite of validity but not vice versa (see Figure 2.2). So once high reliability is established, a researcher should be concerned with optimising construct validity. Again, there are various ways of assessing and improving this criterion. Two facets of construct validity are *convergent* and *discriminant validity*. These are high to the extent that attitude scores are closely related to scores from other scales designed to measure the same attitude, and are unrelated to measures designed to assess different constructs. For example, a Likert scale measuring attitudes toward smoking would be expected to correlate highly with a semantic differential scale on smoking (thus exhibiting convergent validity) but would be expected to be uncorrelated with a measure of social desirability (thus exhibiting discriminant validity).

Often validity is assessed with respect to an external criterion thought to be theoretically related to the construct of interest. For example, if a theory posits that attitudes guide behaviour, then measures of attitude should be good predictors of behavioural measures (see chapter 10), which would reflect their *predictive* or *criterion validity*. Generally, the types of multi-item scale we discussed have comparable levels of reliability and validity, and accordingly tend to be highly correlated with each other when applied to the same attitude object (e.g. Jaccard et al., 1975; Kothandapani, 1971).

Indirect measurement

Knowing that their attitudes are being probed respondents may change them for motivational reasons as explained above or may report attitudes construed in the specific situation that they may not be representative to other situations. To avoid sources of invalidity that are associated with the reactive nature of most measures commonly used, various indirect attitude measures have been devised. Some of these are still reactive in the sense that participants respond to a researcher's questions; however, participants are unaware at the time of measurement that their **attitudes** are being studied. One variant of this approach are *"disguised attitude measures"*; another are *projective measurement techniques*. Finally, researchers have designed an assortment of truly **nonreactive measures**.

Disguised attitude measures

Some measures exploit the fact that attitudes can systematically distort information processing (see chapter 9) and use these distortions as indicators of attitude. In Hammond's (1948) **error-choice method**, for example, respondents receive forced-choice questions that ostensibly measure knowledge. However, neither of the provided response alternatives is factually correct; instead, they deviate from the correct answer in opposite directions. An error-choice item assessing Europeans' attitudes toward saving energy might read:

> "Between 1980 and 1995, consumption of electric energy in European Union countries has . . . (*tick one*):
>
> ___ (a) increased by 25%
> ___ (b) increased by 75%."

Objectively, the increase in consumption during the specified period was about 50%.[4] People with positive attitudes toward saving energy are expected to overestimate the urgency of saving and thus to choose the higher alternative, whereas respondents with negative attitudes would be more likely to choose the lower alternative. Note, however, that attitudes toward conservation of energy are just one of a number of factors that might plausibly influence consumption estimates, so that the construct validity of this type of measure may not be particularly high.

A disguised attitude measure based on logical reasoning errors has been proposed by Thistlethwaite (1950). This method capitalises on the finding that people are more likely to judge logically incorrect syllogistic conclusions to be correct if the content of these statements is consistent with their attitudes. For example, White students at colleges in the Southern and Northern United States were presented with the following set of statements (p. 444):

(a) Given: If production is important, then peaceful industrial relations are desirable. If production is important, then it is a mistake to have Negroes [sic] for foremen and leaders over Whites.

(b) Therefore: If peaceful industrial relations are desirable, then it is a mistake to have Negroes [sic] for foremen and leaders over Whites.

Southern students, who presumably held negative stereotypes of Blacks, were more likely than Northern students to indicate incorrectly that (b) logically followed from (a). Yet again, we have to bear in mind that factors other than attitude are reflected in respondents' judgments as well.

Another type of disguised attitude measures are called **projective techniques**. These usually involve the presentation of unstructured or ambiguous material and the assessment of how individuals interpret these stimuli. Examples are association tasks, where respondents are given a word and freely list whatever associations come to mind, or picture interpretation tasks, where respondents are asked to interpret ambiguous drawings or photos. The rationale behind this approach is that respondents will inadvertently reveal their hidden feelings and opinions in their responses. Although their validity is doubtful, projective techniques have been popular in applied areas such as consumer research (for a review, see Fram & Cibotti, 1991). One classic instance of projective attitude assessment is the *shopping list* procedure. In the original study (Haire, 1950), two shopping lists were prepared that were identical but for one item: They contained either "Maxwell House drip ground coffee" or "Nescafe instant coffee". Each list was given to 50 housewives, who were asked to describe what they thought of the woman who had put together that list. Nearly half of the respondents described the Nescafe buyer as lazy and disorganised, whereas only a small minority reported similar thoughts about the woman who bought standard coffee. Haire concluded that these responses revealed negative attitudes toward instant coffee, a novelty at that time.

Nonreactive measures

We speak of *nonreactive measures* if research participants are completely unaware that a measurement is taking place. Thus, nonreactive measures do not involve respondents' cooperation at all. An impressive collection of such "unobtrusive" techniques of data gathering was presented by Webb, Campbell, Schwartz, Sechrest, and Grove (1981) in a book that is both scholarly and entertaining. Their compilation includes techniques of *behavioural observation* in natural settings, the study of *physical traces* of behaviour and *archival records*.

Many behaviours are related to attitudes and open to unobtrusive *observation*, for example: being present at a meeting, throwing away a flier, growing a beard, or posting a "lost letter" (e.g. Milgram, Mann, & Harter, 1965; see Box 2.2). Various aspects of behaviour can be observed, such as frequency, speed, duration, or intensity (Aronson et al., 1990). Unfortunately, however, a person's behaviour is influenced by many variables other than attitude (see chapter 10), which means that purely behaviour-based measures provide an imperfect assessment of attitude.

As an example for a *physical trace* measure, the wear on floor tiles in front of museum exhibits can indicate the exhibits' popularity (Webb et al., 1981, p. 7). *Archival records* can also yield indicators of attitude: To examine potential preferences for male offspring in families of high socio-economic status, Winston (1932) obtained from official birth records the sex and birth order of each child. He hypothesised that, in families estimated to be complete, a preference for sons over daughters would be reflected in a larger boy-to-girl ratio among the children born last, compared to the boy-to-girl ratio among all children of these families. Winston's hypothesis was strongly supported.

Thus, disguised and nonreactive attitude measures can provide important insights in sensitive areas. They are rarely used, however, because they tend to be remote from the attitude under study and therefore low in construct validity. Also, they often yield only aggregated instead of individual data, and a study's sample is difficult to specify: How much did any specific individual contribute to the wear on the museum floor? What do we know about the individuals who posted (or opened, or ignored) the lost letters? Finally, ethical problems arise because unobtrusiveness may clash with the principle of obtaining research participants' informed consent (see chapter 5 of Webb et al., 1981).

Physiological measures are a special case of observational data. Although they cannot be recorded unobtrusively, we discuss them here as they are largely outside of participants' voluntary control. Among the physiological measures that have been used as indicators of attitude are the *galvanic skin response, pupillary dilatation versus*

This nonreactive behavioural measure of attitude involves leaving addressed letters in public places, as if they had been lost, and then recording the return rate and condition of the returned letters. The attitude object studied is reflected in the address printed on the letter; by varying the address, attitudes toward different objects may be compared. Other variations may involve the location where the letter is dropped (e.g. different neighbourhoods) and the condition of the letter (e.g. sealed vs unsealed). The general assumption behind the lost-letter technique is that among those individuals who find a letter, those with positive attitudes toward the addressee are more likely to post it unopened than those with negative attitudes. Thus, a behavioural outcome (was the letter posted or not?) is used, often in combination with physical traces (does the condition of the letter indicate that it has been opened?) to infer attitudes.

In a classic demonstration of this technique, Milgram and his colleagues (1965) dispersed 400 sealed, stamped and addressed envelopes in various public places (shops, pavements etc.) in a U.S. town. One hundred letters were assigned to each of the following addresses: "Friends of the Communist Party", "Friends of the Nazi Party", "Medical Research Associates" and "Mr Walter Carnap". The researchers expected that the prevailing negative attitudes toward extremist political organisations would lead to a reduced return rate for the letters addressed to either the Communist or the Nazi organisation. Their results supported this hypothesis, as can be seen in Figure 2.3: Return rates were equally low at 25% for each extremist organisation but much higher for the "Medical Research Associates" (72%) as well as the personal address (71%).

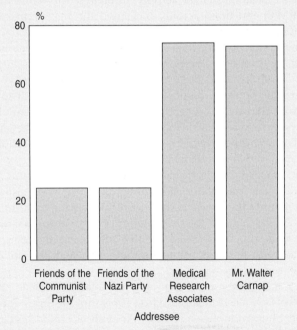

Figure 2.3. Return rates of "lost letters" as a function of the addressee (data from Milgram et al., 1965).

The **lost-letter technique** was used to study attitudes toward a variety of issues, including political candidates, public transportation, capital punishment and racial attitudes (for a review, see Webb et al., 1981, pp. 276–281). A modern adaptation involving "lost e-mail" was proposed by Stern and Faber (1997).

Although the lost-letter approach has a number of advantages—the observed behaviour is a common, everyday action; the procedure is truly nonreactive; responses can conveniently be collected from a mailbox—its major problem is its questionable construct validity. As with many other unobtrusive procedures, the behaviour of posting versus not posting a found letter may be affected by factors other than attitude. A plausible rival explanation for the Milgram et al. (1965) results would be differences in curiosity evoked by the different addresses. Perhaps people were more nosy about the content of letters to the Nazi party than to Mr Carnap, and thus more likely to open the former than the latter. To test this explanation, Sechrest, Grove, and Cosgrove (1980; as cited in Webb et al., 1981) "lost" letters bearing one of the following addresses: "Education Research Project", "Marijuana Research Project" and "Sex Research Project". In line with the curiosity hypothesis, most letters were returned to the education research project, fewer to the marijuana researchers, and the lowest number to the sex research project.

constriction, facial muscular activity measured through *electromyography* (EMG) and brain activity measured through *electroencephalography* (EEG).

However, skin conductance and pupillary measures mainly reflect the intensity of affective responses and the attentiveness to stimuli, respectively, rather than the evaluative direction (favourable versus unfavourable) of these responses; they are therefore ill-suited as measures of attitude (Himmelfarb, 1993). The measurement of subtle changes in individuals' facial expressions via EMG fared better in this regard. For example, Schwartz, Ahern, and Brown (1979) found that participants showed greater EMG activity in their zygomatic (smiling) muscles when exposed to positive stimuli, but greater activity in their corrugator (frowning) muscles when exposed to negative stimuli. In a study related to attitude change, Cacioppo and Petty (1979) showed that the presentation of a proattitudinal message, which was assumed to evoke positive affect and thoughts, led to more zygomatic and less corrugator activity than presentation of a counterattitudinal message.

Finally, EEG, the recording of small electric signals of brain activity through electrodes placed on the scalp, has been applied as a method of attitude measurement. As with electrodermal activity, however, this procedure does not allow for a direct assessment of positive or negative responses. Instead, it exploits the observation that unexpected stimuli elicit brain wave activity that differs from the activity elicited by expected stimuli. Therefore, one may infer the evaluation of a target object by embedding its presentation in a series of other objects whose evaluation is known and invariable. The brain activity that the target object elicits will then indicate if its evaluation is consistent or inconsistent with the evaluation of the other objects. A handy introduction to these and related procedures is provided by Cacioppo, Petty, Losch, and Crites (1994).

What kind of attitude measures do researchers typically use?

In practice, direct attitude measures clearly prevail. Greenwald and Banaji (1995) reviewed the methodology used in 47 attitude studies that had been published in four major social psychology journals in 1989. They found that all 47 studies had used direct measures, while only six had used some indirect measure as well. From a methodological viewpoint this preference for direct measures makes sense, because these are generally easier to administrate, more precise and reliable than indirect measures (e.g. Lemon, 1973).

In using direct measures, researchers often try to strike a balance between the high reliability but effortful construction of a fully validated multi-item scale and the high efficiency but doubtful reliability of a single-item response by formulating ad hoc a handful of items designed to assess a specific attitude. Also, researchers can minimise reactivity and context effects by using appropriate instructions, ensuring confidentiality of responses, and experimentally controlling for question order and other contextual factors. However, these considerations presuppose that respondents are able to report their attitudes truthfully and accurately if only they intend to do so. This may not always be the case.

Implicit attitudes: A conceptual case for indirect attitude measurement

Traditionally, alternatives to direct attitude measurement were considered mainly as a *methodological* improvement—a means of increasing validity by decreasing motivated response distortions. If one assumes, however, that social information processing, including attitudinal processing, often operates outside of conscious awareness, indirect attitude measures become necessary for *theoretical* reasons. After all, people can give truthful self-reports of their attitudes only to the extent that they have introspective access to them.

As we have already noted, however, the mere presence of an attitude object may automatically elicit an evaluative response, without any conscious thought or recollection of prior experience being involved (Bargh, 1997; Bargh et al., 1992). Greenwald and Banaji (1995) define **implicit attitudes** as evaluations whose origin is unknown to the individual and that affect implicit responses. The latter responses are either outside of voluntary control or not identified by the individual as an expression of their attitude. For example, when asked to evaluate letters of the alphabet, people tend to prefer those letters that are part of their own name over other letters, without being aware of the name–letter connection (Nuttin, 1985). Nuttin suggested that this pattern of preference reflects implicit positive attitudes toward the self.

But people may even be unaware of their implicit attitudes themselves, as in the case of implicit prejudice, where negative evaluations toward an outgroup may show, e.g. in a person's nonverbal behaviour, yet this person may consciously disavow of any negative feelings toward this group (for discussion, see Wilson, Lindsey, & Schooler, 2000). Greenwald and Banaji (1995) discussed a wide range of evidence for implicit attitude phenomena, and advocated the development of sensitive measures of implicit attitude. Before concluding this chapter, we will discuss two recent examples of implicit attitude measures.

Priming and the bona fide pipeline

Studies on attitude accessibility suggested that **priming** procedures might provide access to implicit attitudes. In this paradigm, the presentation of evaluatively uncontroversial target words (e.g. "horrible") on a computer screen is immediately preceded by the presentation of attitude objects that serve as primes. In earlier studies (e.g. Fazio et al., 1986), the primes were usually words (e.g. "politicians"). Respondents' task is to categorise the target word as quickly as possible by pressing a "good" or a "bad" response key. If the evaluations of prime and target match (as should be the case in our example for people holding a negative attitude toward politicians), responses to the target are faster than if the two evaluations mismatch. It has been suggested that the magnitude of relative facilitation (i.e. reduction in response time to matching versus nonmatching targets) caused by a given attitude–object prime may be used as an indicator of a person's attitude toward that prime (Fazio et al., 1986).

More recently, taking advantage of technological progress, Fazio, Jackson, Dunton, and Williams (1995) began using high-resolution colour pictures of persons as primes. To assess racial attitudes, they briefly presented faces of White and Black persons, followed by positive or negative target adjectives. The participants' task again was to categorise the target adjectives as good or bad as quickly as possible (see Figure 2.4). This procedure is nonreactive, as participants are never asked to consider their attitude toward the primes—the rationale they are given for the primes appearing is that a recognition test will follow.

Alluding to the bogus pipeline method (Jones & Sigall, 1971), Fazio and his colleagues (1995) called their priming procedure a "bona fide pipeline" to people's implicit attitudes. Interestingly, racial attitudes as measured by the bona fide pipeline predicted White participants' nonverbal behaviour toward a Black experimenter (see Figure 2.5). Participants with more negative implicit attitudes toward Blacks were rated as behaving in a less friendly and less interested manner by their Black interaction partner (who was blind to participants' attitude results).

Furthermore, implicit racial attitudes were positively correlated with a direct self-report measure of racial attitude only for those respondents whose motivation to control their prejudice was low. Presumably, students who were motivated to appear nonprejudiced managed to do so on the explicit self-report measure but could not conceal their more automatic responses in the bona fide pipeline procedure.

The implicit association test

Another technique of indirect attitude measurement, the **implicit association test (IAT)**, was introduced by Greenwald, McGhee, and Schwartz (1998). The IAT measures the differential association of two target concepts (e.g. "flower" versus "insect") with positive versus negative evaluations (e.g. "pleasant words" versus "unpleasant words"). As a participant in an IAT, you learn to use two keys, one on

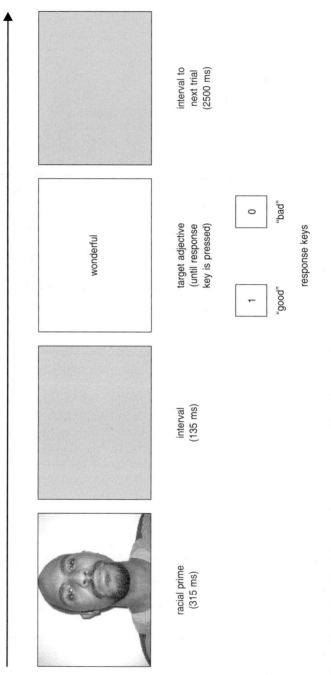

Figure 2.4. The bona fide pipeline procedure of measuring implicit racial attitudes. Stimulus sequence of one trial, as introduced by Fazio et al. (1995).

Figure 2.5. Implicit negative attitudes may transpire in nonverbal behaviour, for example when a White participant interacts with a Black experimenter.

the left and one on the right, to quickly respond to stimuli on the screen. For example, you may first learn to press the left-hand key each time a flower name appears, and the right-hand key each time an insect name appears. Then you learn to respond with the same two keys to pleasant words (left-hand key) and to unpleasant words (right-hand key). Later, both target stimuli and evaluation words are presented in a random sequence, and you are still asked to perform the responses previously learned. This combined task is performed more rapidly when highly associated categories (flower and pleasant) share the same key than when less associated categories (insect and pleasant) do so. This performance difference implicitly measures differences in evaluation of the two target concepts. Figure 2.6 shows an IAT that we designed to measure implicit attitudes toward the English versus the Irish.

Greenwald et al. (1998) found that the IAT was sensitive not only to near-universal explicit differences in evaluation (like "flowers = positive" versus "insects = negative"), but also to between-group

Sequence	1	2	3	4	5
Task description	Initial target-concept discrimination	Associated attribute discrimination	Initial combined task	Reversed target-concept discrimination	Reversed combined task
Task instructions	• Irish English •	• pleasant unpleasant •	• Irish • pleasant English • unpleasant •	Irish • • English	Irish • • pleasant • English unpleasant •
Sample stimuli	✓ Casey Clark ✓ ✓ Duffy Brown ✓ Richardson ✓ ✓ Fitzpatrick ✓ Twoomey	✓ diamond disaster ✓ ✓ heaven ✓ friend cancer ✓ rotten ✓ ✓ joyful	✓ Driscoll ✓ happy Johnson ✓ ✓ joyful ✓ Flanagan abuse ✓ failure ✓	✓ Clifford Kelley ✓ ✓ Foster ✓ Stevens Duffy ✓ ✓ Johnson ✓ Clark	✓ loyal Flanagan ✓ evil ✓ ✓ Clifford Kelley ✓ ✓ Foster ✓ lucky

Figure 2.6. Illustration of the implicit association test (IAT; adapted from Greenwald et al., 1998). Participants perform a series of five discrimination tasks (columns 1 to 5). In this example, an attribute dimension ("pleasant–unpleasant") and a pair of target concepts ("Irish" and "English") are presented in the first two steps. The black circles in the third row indicate that discriminations are assigned to a left–right response. Both discrimination tasks are combined in the third step and later recombined in the fifth step, after response assignments for the target-concept discrimination have been reversed in the fourth step. Correct responses are indicated by ticks to the left or right in the bottom row. To control for order effects, the positions of tasks 4 and 1 as well as tasks 5 and 3 are switched for half the participants. *Note*: Using this IAT, we found that English students showed mean response latencies per item that were 94 ms faster when English names and pleasant words (vs Irish names and pleasant words) shared the same key, a result that significantly differs from zero. Thus, English students exhibited a clear-cut implicit preference for their own nation. This was not paralleled by the results of an explicit measure of preference, on which the same students indicated that they equally liked the English and the Irish ($M = 2.93$ on a semantic differential ranging from 1, preference for the Irish, to 5, preference for the English). Moreover, the correlation between the implicit and explicit measure was nonsignificant, $r = .12$.

differences in implicit evaluation: Japanese Americans showed faster responses when Japanese names shared a key with pleasant words and Korean names shared a key with unpleasant words, whereas the reverse was true for Korean Americans. Most interestingly, the IAT detected evaluative differences that participants consciously denied, with "White and pleasant" responses being faster than "Black and pleasant" responses for White participants who describe themselves as unprejudiced.[5]

As the last example indicates again, explicit and implicit attitudes toward the same object need not be highly correlated; in fact, the correlations reported by Greenwald et al. (1998) are often near zero (see also Note to Figure 2.6). Reviewing work on the relationship between implicit and explicit measures of intergroup attitudes, Dovidio, Kawakami, and Beach (2001) found low to moderate correlations overall. This does not necessarily render implicit measures invalid but may reflect that different aspects of an attitude or indeed different attitudes are being measured. In line with this possibility, Florack, Scarabis, and Bless (2001) found that the IAT score towards a group (Turks) predicted judgments towards an exemplar (a specific Turkish person) independent of explicit attitudes towards the group. However, this was only the case for research participants who invested little processing effort when judging the exemplar.

With regard to reliability, the IAT seems to exhibit low test–retest coefficients but high internal consistency (Greenwald & Nosek, 2001). Studying priming measures of implicit stereotyping, Kawakami and Dovidio (2001) found modest test–retest reliability coefficients of about .5 over a period of up to 15 days. Future research will have to examine the psychometric properties of implicit evaluations more closely, as well as their relationship to explicit, self-reported attitudes (for discussions, see Greenwald & Banaji, 1995; Greenwald, Banaji, Rudman, Farnham, Nosek, & Rosier, 2000; Schwarz & Bohner, 2001). At present, a growing body of research explores the specific conditions under which IAT scores predict other judgments or behaviour (for a review see Plessner & Banse, 2001). It seems uncontroversial, however, that both types of evaluation may coexist in a person's cognitive system (Wilson et al., 2000) and may correspond to each other more closely for less socially sensitive issues (Dovidio et al., 2001).

Chapter summary

(1) Attitudes can be measured directly by asking respondents to report their beliefs or evaluations, or indirectly by studying responses that are thought to be related to attitudes.

(2) Direct attitude measures may consist of a single item accompanied by a numeric response scale, or of a series of such items.

(3) When responding to a direct measurement, the respondent must complete a sequence of steps: interpreting the meaning of the question, retrieving or constructing an evaluation, and translating it into the answer format provided. Prior to reporting, the privately formed judgment may be edited, e.g. to make a favourable impression. The context of the measurement can influence all steps of the question-answering process and thus affect the response.

(4) Scores on an attitude scale are a function of the attitude studied, but also contain random error (chance fluctuations of measure-

ment) and systematic error (influences by constructs other than the attitude being measured). A scale is reliable to the extent that it is free from random error, and valid to the extent that it is free from both random and systematic error.

(5) Three common multi-item scales are the semantic differential, the Likert scale, and the Thurstone scale. They are generally higher in reliability than single-item measures, but their construction involves considerable effort. Researchers therefore often resort to measuring attitudes with one or a few items compiled ad hoc.

(6) To avoid reactivity effects (i.e. a change in the target attitude due to the measurement), indirect measures have been used. These include disguised attitude measures, physiological measures and truly nonreactive measures. Although they are a useful (and often entertaining) methodological tool, indirect attitude measures typically suffer from low construct validity.

(7) A special class of measurement techniques, including priming measures and the implicit association test, is used to assess implicit attitudes. These are evaluations that a person is not aware of or whose source a person cannot introspectively identify.

(8) Implicit and explicit measures often do not correspond well, but researchers are only beginning to explore and understand the psychometric properties of implicit attitude measures.

Exercises

(1) Find examples of nominal, ordinal, interval and ratio scales we use in everyday life. Why would you aim for an attitude measure having at least interval scale level?

(2) Which of the following statements are true?
(a) If reliability increases, then construct validity increases.
(b) If reliability decreases, then construct validity decreases.
(c) A measure can be reliable without being valid.
(d) A measure can be valid without being reliable.

(3) Think of context effects that might affect a person's evaluation of their job. Specifically, what preceding questions might elevate (lower) responses to a question on work satisfaction?

(4) Generate items that could be included in a Likert (Thurstone) scale measuring attitudes toward genetically modified food.

(5) What external criteria would you use to construct-validate the scale you generated in exercise 4?

(6) Consider attitudes toward the following groups, objects and behaviours: asylum seekers; political parties; beef; the European Union; pornography; using condoms; working overtime. Which of these attitudes might show a discrepancy between explicit and implicit measures, and what might be the reason in each case?

(7) Think of stimuli that might be used in an IAT for measuring implicit self-esteem.

Notes

(1) As mentioned in chapter 1, for some attitude objects an affective response may spring to mind immediately. For example, many people experience a kind of "yuck" reaction when seeing a snake (see also chapter 5).

(2) Accessibility is an important characteristic of attitudes. Among other things, it moderates how attitudes guide behaviour (see chapter 10).

(3) This finding attests to the importance of attitudes for making sense of all objects in a person's environment (see chapters 1 and 9).

(4) See information by the United Nations in the World Wide Web (http://www.undp.org/hdro/ienergy.htm).

(5) Further examples of IAT measures designed by Greenwald and his colleagues that can be self-administered are available in the World Wide Web (http://www.yale.edu/implicit/).

Further reading

Technical aspects of measurement, reliability, validity:

Himmelfarb, S. (1993). The measurement of attitudes. In A. H. Eagly & S. Chaiken, *The psychology of attitudes* (pp. 23–87). Fort Worth, TX: Harcourt Brace Jovanovich.

Psychological aspects of the question-answering process:

Sudman, S., Bradburn, M. N., & Schwarz, N. (1996). *Thinking about answers: The application of cognitive processes to survey methodology*. San Francisco: Jossey-Bass.

Nonreactive measures:

Webb, E. J., Campbell, D. T., Schwartz, R. D., Sechrest, L., & Grove, J. B. (1981). *Nonreactive measures in the social sciences* (2nd ed.). Boston, MA: Houghton Mifflin.

Implicit versus explicit attitudes:

Dovidio, J. F., Kawakami, K., & Beach, K. R. (2001). Implicit and explicit attitudes: Examination of the relationship between measures of intergroup bias. In R. Brown & S. Gaertner (Eds.), *Blackwell handbook of social psychology: Vol. 4. Intergroup processes* (pp. 175–197). Oxford, UK: Blackwell.

Beyond valence: structure and strength 3

There is more to attitudes than simply being favourable or unfavourable. You have already seen that attitudes of the same valence may have different underlying functions, but there is yet more to come. In this chapter we will first deal with aspects of **attitude structure**. Research on *intra-attitudinal structure* has investigated how an attitude is represented in memory. This concerns the representation of the attitude itself, for example as a point on an evaluative continuum, as the one-dimensional definition we adopted in chapter 1 would suggest, or as a point in a multidimensional space, as other conceptualisations would suggest. This also involves questions of how the individual components that make up the summary evaluation are organised in memory, how they relate to each other and the overall attitude, and how they are integrated. Research on inter-attitudinal structure deals with the question how attitudes toward different attitude objects are related to each other in a person's mind. A further property of attitudes that recent conceptualisations increasingly emphasise is **attitude strength**. Attitude strength more or less reflects the intensity of one's feelings and beliefs.

The insight that attitudes can be described by more aspects than merely valence will certainly contribute to a better understanding of the construct; for this reason we address them here. However, researchers have looked at these properties mostly in terms of how they relate to the dynamics of attitude change, for example to what extent the stability of an attitude depends on its structure, or whether structural properties moderate the influence of attitudes on behaviour and information processing. As we will take up some of these issues later in part III of the book, you may alternatively postpone reading this chapter until then.

Intra-attitudinal structure

If we rigidly adhere to our definition of attitude as a summary evaluation, then the question of how specific beliefs or feelings about an attitude object may be organised do not, strictly speaking, pertain to the structure of the attitude. Instead, the issue of attitude structure should be restricted to the representation of the summary evaluation itself, for example as a point on an evaluative continuum. However, several theorists have included the specific memory contents which serve as input to attitudes—such as beliefs and feelings about the attitude object—in their conceptualisations of attitude structure. For example, Pratkanis (1989), in his socio-cognitive model of attitude structure, describes the representation of a fully developed attitude as consisting of three parts: (a) an attitude-object category (e.g. skinheads), (b) an evaluative summary (e.g. unfavourable), and (c) a supporting knowledge structure (e.g. "skinheads are stupid, violent, fascist . . ." etc.). This model is inferred from the observation that attitudes produce particular effects on cognitive processes (which we will discuss in detail in chapter 9). Other models of attitude structure derive from the three-component view we briefly mentioned in chapter 1 (e.g. Maio & Olson, 2000a); yet others describe attitude structure as an aggregate of belief-by-evaluation products (e.g. Fishbein & Ajzen, 1975). In keeping with these traditions, we will discuss intra-attitudinal structure by addressing the properties of the representation of the attitude itself, such as polarity and dimensionality, and then turning to the organisation and integration of the underlying components.

Polarity of attitudes

If we define attitudes as representing a point on an evaluative continuum you may ask about the range of the continuum. Like a fan heater, which you can turn from neutral—just blowing air—to warm and hot, attitudes could range from neutral to favourable.

How much do you like jazz, ice cream or movies by Woody Allen? Chances are that these are examples of unipolar attitudes. You probably think about these attitude objects mainly in terms of how much pleasure you can derive from them and you are likely to think of the extent of pleasure along a *unipolar* continuum, ranging from no pleasure at all to a lot of pleasure. However, some attitude objects may elicit more polarised attitudes. For example, some people are very much in favour of legalising abortion, whereas others are not just less in favour but rather are violently opposed. To keep with our metaphor, bipolar attitude representations are analogous to a climate control where you can switch from hot air over warm to cool and cold air lowering the existing room temperature.

Does it matter whether the one-dimensional continuum as which we defined attitudes is unipolar and ranges from neutral to pro (or anti) or bipolar and ranges from anti to pro? Whether a particular attitude is bipolar or unipolar affects how the attitude and its components are organised in memory, how people react to new information and how attitudes may change. Pratkanis (1989) argued that in the case of bipolar attitudes, proponents of *either* side of the bipolar continuum often know very well the arguments on *both* sides, although they agree only with one side and disagree with the other. In other words, supporters and opponents possess similar knowledge structures. Figure 3.1 illustrates a possible bipolar representation.

In the case of unipolar issues, people with positive or negative attitudes usually possess a lot of knowledge congruent with their attitude and not much that is incongruent (like the Manchester United fan who knows by heart all the national and international titles that the club has ever won since its foundation), whereas people with less extreme or neutral attitudes generally know little about the attitude object. Figure 3.2 shows the attitudinal knowledge structure of an Ally McBeal fan as an example.

Whether an attitude is represented as unipolar or bipolar may vary between individuals, but Pratkanis (1989) suggested that the type of representation also depends on the attitude object. He assumed that bipolar representations are most common for issues which are controversially discussed in one's social environment, so that information of both sides is available, whereas unipolar structures are usually found for less disputed topics like music and sports.

The polarity of an attitude is also important for deciding how to measure it. For example, if satisfaction is represented in a bipolar way and ranges from dissatisfaction to satisfaction, then the scale needs to capture the appropriate extremes. A scale ranging from low or no satisfaction (rather than dissatisfaction) to high satisfaction would not adequately represent all possible degrees. Box 3.1 gives an example how unipolar and bipolar scales used to measure the same attitude can lead to rather different conclusions.

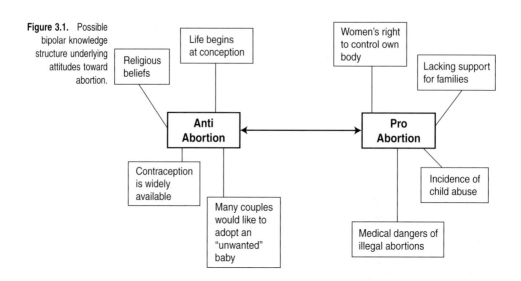

Figure 3.1. Possible bipolar knowledge structure underlying attitudes toward abortion.

- Religious beliefs
- Life begins at conception
- Women's right to control own body
- Lacking support for families

Anti Abortion ←→ **Pro Abortion**

- Contraception is widely available
- Many couples would like to adopt an "unwanted" baby
- Medical dangers of illegal abortions
- Incidence of child abuse

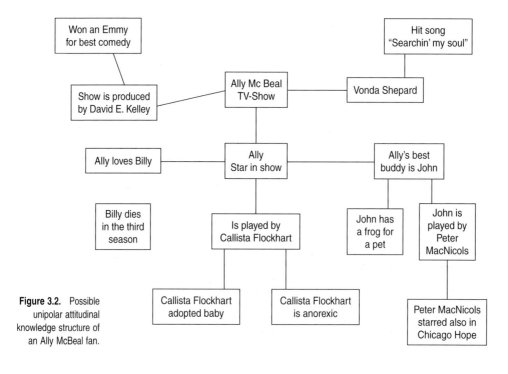

Figure 3.2. Possible unipolar attitudinal knowledge structure of an Ally McBeal fan.

- Won an Emmy for best comedy
- Show is produced by David E. Kelley
- Ally Mc Beal TV-Show
- Vonda Shepard
- Hit song "Searchin' my soul"
- Ally loves Billy
- Ally Star in show
- Ally's best buddy is John
- Billy dies in the third season
- Is played by Callista Flockhart
- John has a frog for a pet
- John is played by Peter MacNicols
- Callista Flockhart adopted baby
- Callista Flockhart is anorexic
- Peter MacNicols starred also in Chicago Hope

BOX 3.1 The polarity of response scales may affect the interpretation of attitude objects

Schwarz and Hippler (1995) asked respondents for their opinion about several politicians. One group of respondents reported their opinion on scale A, the other on scale B.

Scale A

I dont think highly   0 1 2 3 4 5 6 7 8 9 10   I think highly of
of this politician   this politician

Scale B

I dont think highly   −5 −4 −3 −2 −1 0 +1 +2 +3 +4 +5   I think highly of
of this politician   this politician

Note that both scales have identically labelled poles, and both represent 11-point rating scales. If they were fully equivalent, then for example a score of "3" on scale A would correspond to a score of "−2" on scale B, and we would not expect the two groups of respondents to differ in their reported opinion (see chapter 2 on permissible scale transformations). The results of Schwarz and Hippler's study, however, suggest otherwise. As Figure 3.3 shows, respondents seemed to report a more positive opinion of each politician when scale B was used. Only about 29% of these respondents reported a score below the scale mid-point, reflecting an unfavourable opinion, as opposed to about 40% who did so when scale A was used.

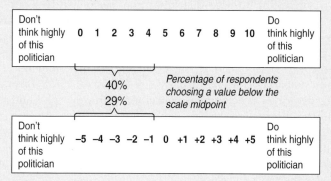

Figure 3.3. The polarity of response scales affects attitudinal responses (data from Schwarz & Hippler, 1995).

The authors explain their finding as follows. A unipolar scale suggests that the measured attitude is unipolar, i.e. that it ranges from no support to high support. A bipolar scale, however, suggests that the measured attitude is bipolar, i.e. that it ranges from high opposition through a neutral midpoint to high support. Accordingly, when faced with scale A, participants with a rather neutral attitude presumably chose a response option at the low end, thus making their responses indistinguishable from the responses of those participants that were clearly opposed. When faced with scale B, however, participants with neutral attitudes presumably selected a response option near the midpoint of the scale, whereas participants with opposing attitudes would still have chosen a response option near the low end of the scale.

Dimensions and components

In chapter 1 we defined attitudes as one-dimensional. This means that they can be described by one single score, or as suggested above as a point on an evaluative continuum, rather than a point in a two- or more-dimensional space. This does not mean to imply, however, that the summary evaluation may not consist of evaluative responses on different dimensions. Most obviously one's responses may pertain to different content areas. For example, a vegetarian may be "turned off" by meat because she does not want to kill animals and thinks the way animals are raised is cruel. Her evaluative beliefs all pertain to something we may term moral obligations toward animals. Another vegetarian may additionally believe that eating meat causes gout and that high cholesterol intake associated with meat consumption causes heart disease. Her negative attitude toward eating meat would thus be based on two dimensions: morals and health. A similar two-dimensional structure was revealed in a study on Britons' attitudes toward genetically manipulated food, where risk-related aspects formed one dimension and moral issues the other (Sparks, 1999).

It is interesting to note that what may seem like two opposing poles on a continuum often actually constitutes two different—and to some extent independent—dimensions. Political ideologies are a most prominent example. While one may think of liberalism as the opposite of conservatism it has been argued that both may well embody disparate concerns (Conover & Feldman, 1981). Liberalism may be described as being more concerned with civil rights and social equality, conservatism more with order, security and economic growth. You will probably find that the programmes of left-wing, socialist parties are not a mirror image of those of right-wing, conservative parties, but rather that both political camps differ in the emphasis they put on issues.

Carrying these ideas one step further would imply that positive and negative responses are not necessarily reciprocal or antagonistic as a bipolar model would suggest. In the above analogy of the climate control, cold and heat are reciprocal insofar as more heat means less cold and vice versa. This perspective has most recently been criticised by Cacioppo, Gardner, and Berntson (1997) in their bivariate model. They posit that "reciprocal effects between positive and negative evaluative processes do exist but so do nonreciprocal effects" (p. 6). Note that this of course denies a one-dimensional representation of attitudes and calls for a two-dimensional representation of positive and negative reactions.

What is the advantage of such a two-dimensional model? Importantly, the conceptualisation of positivity and negativity as independent underlying dimensions allows for finer distinctions between attitudinal positions. By rough categorisations four groups result from the combinations of the scores on both dimensions. Positive and negative attitudes, respectively, are described by high scores on one dimension and low scores on the other. Low scores on both dimensions reflect indifferent attitudes. Finally, some people may score high on both dimensions and endorse positive as well as negative responses. One may say that they have ambivalent attitudes. Note that a bipolar (rather than bi-dimensional) conceptualisation would lump the latter two groups together. However, research has shown differences between such positions. For example, people who were classified as indifferent to donating blood according to their responses to positive and negative items were less willing to actually donate blood than those who were classified as ambivalent (Gardner & Cacioppo, 1996; as cited in Cacioppo et al., 1997). **Ambivalence**, of course, is not a new concept. It has intrigued researchers for decades and we will come back to it later.

So far we have categorised the components which make up the overall attitude according to content (moral, health, social equality etc.) and favourability. Yet one may also classify them according to their nature as affective, cognitive or behavioural (**tripartite model**), as briefly mentioned in chapter 1. It has been argued that these response classes constitute separable dimensions, a view which would call for a three-dimensional conceptualisation. However, research has only partly supported this idea (for a review see Breckler, 1984). For example, our vegetarian may believe that all creatures are equal and thus humans do not have the right to kill another species. These cognitive beliefs are likely to be more strongly correlated to her affective feelings of sadness and guilt when she thinks of slaughtering animals than to her other cognitive beliefs about what constitutes a healthy diet. In fact, Eagly and Chaiken (1993) have pointed out that the different response classes may exist in a synergistic relationship. A person who for whatever reasons finds meat disgusting (for example because she once experienced food poisoning from eating spoilt meat) and lives a vegetarian life-style may be more prone to be exposed to and pay attention to consistent information and develop cognitive beliefs that eating meat is unhealthy.

It may come as no surprise that some attitudes may be more affectively determined (for example liking your mother) whereas others may be more cognitive (supporting an increase in tuition fees).

This may also imply that for some attitudes, or for some people, affective components may be better predictors of overall attitudes while for others cognitive components work better (e.g. Haddock & Zanna, 1998). From this also follows that the response classes are not necessarily consistent with each other nor with the overall summary. However, before we discuss consistency and return to the issue of ambivalence, let us address another question of intra-attitudinal structure, namely how attitudes are composed of more elementary components, in particular cognitions about the attitude object.

Aggregating components

Several theorists have proposed mathematical models that describe attitudes as aggregated *beliefs* (e.g. Anderson, 1971, 1981; Fishbein, 1967a,b). Fishbein's approach, which he later integrated into the theory of reasoned action (Fishbein & Ajzen, 1975; see chapter 10), emphasises the **expectancy-value principle** that is a central feature of various motivation theories (see Feather, 1982). An attitude toward an object is described as the sum of "expectancy × value"-products:

$$A_o = \sum_{i=1}^{n} b_i \, e_i$$

In this equation, A_o represents the attitude toward object O, b_i the belief or subjective probability that the object possesses a certain attribute I, and e_i the subjective evaluation of that attribute. Only *salient* attributes are included in the equation, i.e. those that a person regards as relevant and attends to. The model can be illustrated by computing someone's attitude toward regular exercise. Meet Mark who believes that regular exercise most probably ($b_1 = +3$) leads to weight reduction, which he would welcome ($e_1 = +2$). Further, Mark thinks that exercise possibly ($b_2 = +2$) prevents heart disease ($e_2 = +3$), and may perhaps ($b_3 = +1$) help him meet people ($e_3 = +3$), both of which he strongly desires. On the other hand, exercising may perhaps ($b_4 = +1$) be painful ($e_4 - -3$) and possibly ($b_5 = +2$) boring ($e_5 = -1$).[1] Overall, Mark's attitude toward exercising would be rather positive as the sum of these products is positive (see last entry in "cumulative sum" column of Table 3.1).

Attitude scores derived from summing belief-evaluation products usually correlate highly with attitude measures that are based on self-reported summary evaluations (e.g. Fishbein & Coombs, 1974; Jaccard

TABLE 3.1

Adding and averaging models of belief integration

Beliefs about the attitude object "regular exercise"	Subjective probability	Evaluation	Product	Attitude (cumulative sum)	Attitude (cumulative average)
Leads to weight reduction	+3	+2	+6	+6	+6
Prevents heart disease	+2	+3	+6	+12	+6
Helps meet people	+1	+3	+3	+15	+5
Is painful	+1	−3	−3	+12	+3
Is boring	+2	−1	−2	+10	+2

& Davidson, 1972). However, as you will certainly recall, correlation does not imply causation. Although the model was intended to propose that beliefs determine attitudes, a person's beliefs may also be derived from the overall attitude at the time these beliefs are expressed (see Eagly, Mladinic, & Otto, 1994). For practical aspects the question of causality may not matter much. Either way beliefs may be used as predictors of attitudes and thus contribute to the prediction of behaviour, which is the theoretical focus of Fishbein's approach. We will discuss this application and the problem of causal relations between attitudes and behaviour further in chapter 10.

With regard to the cognitive processes involved, one may ask whether people always have to retrieve attributes and integrate them—or could they simply "know" their attitudes? This corresponds to the debate between the "attitudes-as-constructions" view and the file-drawer model introduced in chapter 1. We will take up this issue in chapter 5. Suffice it to say here that the expectancy-value model was not much concerned with this debate. It focused on how cognitive beliefs determined overall attitudes but is not incompatible with the notion that summary evaluations are stored separately from the supporting beliefs and may be retrieved directly.

The expectancy-value model is a special case of a more general mathematical approach to the aggregation of elementary units of information into aggregate judgments: **information integration theory** (e.g. Anderson, 1971, 1981, 1991). Whereas the Fishbein model applies only to *attitudes*, which it describes as a *sum* of evaluations weighted by subjective probabilities, Anderson's approach can be applied to *any judgment* and allows for a *variety of algebraic functions* by which items of information are integrated. The most prominent algebraic functions are the *adding* and *averaging* models. Applied to attitudes, both the adding and the averaging model contain the assumption that individuals interpret information with regard to its meaning concerning the attitude object (evaluation), determine its relevance (weighting) and integrate this information with their previous attitude provided they can retrieve one from memory. The final step of integration is done either by adding elements (as in the Fishbein approach) or by averaging elements.

The latter type of integration is illustrated in the rightmost column of Table 3.1. Moving down the last two columns, you can directly compare the adding and averaging models by considering how the overall attitude score would change as additional beliefs are entered successively. For example, according to a summation model, any new positive belief makes the overall attitude more positive, and any new negative belief makes it less positive. By contrast, according to an averaging model, only new beliefs that are more positive (negative) than the existing attitude will make it more positive (negative). Also, in a summation model new beliefs have the same impact no matter how many other beliefs already form the basis of an attitude, whereas in an averaging model the relative impact of new information decreases with a larger existing belief structure. Research has examined which algebraic function best describes attitudes. Although this of course depends on other conditions as well, the averaging approach seems to be of wider applicability.[2]

In contrast to the Fishbein model, information integration theory is not meant as a process model. The fact that attitudes can be described or predicted by the algebraic functions does not imply that this is what people actually do. Both models agree in that they conceptualise attitudes in purely cognitive terms and do not consider the role of affect. Moreover, beliefs are rather narrowly understood as propositions. A somewhat wider and more modern frame might conceptualise attitudes as a function of any information with evaluative implications that comes to mind, including mental images, past experiences, affective responses and other types of information. With this understanding of information in mind, information integration theory can offer a useful, albeit rather general, model.

Consistency

Although integration models take into account various elements of an attitude, the degree to which these elements are consistent or inconsistent with each other is not reflected in the final aggregate judgment. In our above example, Mark arrives at a favourable attitude toward exercise but a closer look at his beliefs reveals that he holds both positively and negatively evaluated beliefs toward this object. As mentioned above his attitude may be described as ambivalent. Ambivalence can be measured by assessing the positive and negative aspects of an attitude object separately, each on a unipolar dimension; the larger and the more similar the absolute values on these two dimensions, the greater the ambivalence (e.g. Kaplan, 1972).

Probably everyone has experienced some degree of ambivalence toward an attitude object. People often hold ambivalent attitudes toward health-related behaviours, for example drinking, smoking etc. On the one hand jogging is good for you, on the other hand it is such a drag; smoking causes cancer, but you enjoy it; or you really like your boyfriend but do not want to commit to a long-term relationship. The examples are endless and demonstrate that in order to change many undesirable attitudes it may not be enough to instil negative beliefs or feelings toward the issue. A more effective strategy would need to eliminate the positive beliefs as well. Of course, not only beliefs may be inconsistent with each other; feelings may be mutually inconsistent as well, or one's beliefs may be inconsistent with one's feelings. The proverbial being torn between one's head and one's heart is an example for such an affective–cognitive inconsistency. Likewise behavioural components may be inconsistent either with each other or with feelings or beliefs.

When elements or classes of elements are inconsistent with each other, then also the overall attitude is consistent with some elements but inconsistent with others. In the above example, Mark's beliefs that exercise is painful and boring is inconsistent with his overall rather favourable attitude. As this example illustrates, an overall evaluation may be more or less consistent with its cognitive basis (*evaluative–cognitive consistency*), its affective basis (*evaluative–affective consistency*), or its behavioural basis (*evaluative–behavioural consistency*; see Eagly & Chaiken, 1998). Early studies on evaluative–cognitive consistency were conducted by Rosenberg (1960).[3] He believed that low correlations between a person's beliefs and their overall attitude implied a "vacuous attitude" or "nonattitude" (Converse, 1970), which would lead respondents to answer belief and attitude questions in an unreliable, erratic way (Rosenberg, 1968). Clearly this conclusion is based on a purely cognitive perspective of attitudes. Anyone who has sentimentally clung to a keepsake no matter how ugly and useless would doubt this assumption. Indeed, recent work showed that attitudes low in evaluative–cognitive consistency may well be high in evaluative–affective consistency (Chaiken, Pomerantz, & Giner-Sorolla, 1995). In other words, people who hold such attitudes may rely more on their feelings than on their beliefs.

Researchers were mainly interested in the consequences of inconsistency and ambivalence. They suggest that inconsistencies go with less stable attitudes (e.g. Bargh et al., 1992; Erber, Hodges, & Wilson, 1995), a fact that is easily explained if we assume that not all potentially relevant information is accessible at any one point in time. For example, when Mark is asked how he feels about exercise he may not think of all the beliefs listed above. Instead, he may only think of how exercising keeps him attractive and healthy and thus he comes to view exercising highly favourably. At another time, it may also occur to him that exercising is rather boring and painful and consequently he reports a much less favourable attitude.

If attitudes are more consistent and nonambivalent, the evaluative implications of beliefs that come to mind at any given time are bound to be more similar, and greater stability should result. Indeed, Chaiken and her colleagues (1995) showed that attitudes high in either evaluative–cognitive consistency or evaluative–affective consistency were quite stable over time. Only attitudes low in both types of consistency showed low stability, i.e. the somewhat erratic response pattern that Rosenberg (1968) had described.

A different question is whether inconsistencies themselves are particularly stable. Some research findings suggest that ambivalence or inconsistency of beliefs may motivate an individual to think more about an attitude object (e.g. Jonas, Diehl, & Brömer, 1997), which may eventually lead to less ambivalent and more consistent beliefs (see chapter 8). The dynamics of inconsistency reduction have also been addressed extensively in research on *inter-attitudinal consistency*, where researchers are concerned with how attitudes toward different objects are related to each other.

Inter-attitudinal structure

How are attitudes toward different objects linked to each other in a person's mind? This question has been addressed mainly in two ways. One approach emphasised the hierarchical nature of thematically consistent cognitive structures, or **ideologies**, in which attitudes are embedded. According to this approach, an attitude toward a novel political or social issue may be derived from more central and general values an individual holds in that area (e.g. Converse, 1964; Kinder & Sears, 1985). For example, a person who holds social equality as a core value is likely to derive favourable attitudes toward anti-discrimination laws and negative attitudes toward policies that promote social stratification. In yet a different manner attitudes may be formed in terms of their consistency with the individual's cognitive system. Assume for example that in your local newspaper you read about a proposal to regulate building construction in the area. You realise that you do not have enough information to really conclude whether this is a good and sensible suggestion with which you agree or not. It turns out that the proposal is endorsed by the Conservative Party but opposed by Labour. How would that influence your opinion of the proposal? Chances are that you may go according to your general political views, unless you care enough to really get informed about the issue (see chapters 6 and 7). People may side in a conflict according to the rule "my enemy's enemy is my friend".

This leads us to the other approach to inter-attitudinal structure: Heider's (1946, 1958) **balance theory**. An early example of a *cognitive consistency theory*, balance theory shares core assumptions with other formulations in that family of approaches (for a review, see Abelson et al., 1968; see also chapter 8 on dissonance theory). It assumes that people strive for consistency or equilibrium among their cognitions and describes the conditions of such equilibrium; it states that a lack of equilibrium is felt as an unpleasant state which motivates the person to restore equilibrium; and it describes the processes by which consistency can be restored. Of particular interest in both Heider's analyses and subsequent research was how attitudes toward issues and attitudes toward people are related in a perceiver's mind (Heider, 1946). As an example imagine Jenny who loves her new partner Tom and dreams of joint holidays in the mountains. The stability of each of these two cognitions (loving Tom; wanting to spend time together in the mountains) is influenced by a third cognition: Jenny's perception of Tom's attitude toward mountain holidays. In Heider's terminology, these three cognitions form a *triad* involving the perceiver (*p*; e.g. Jenny), another person (*o*; e.g. Tom), and some nonperson object (*x*; e.g. mountain holidays). These elements may be linked to each other in two ways. Attitudinal bonds were called sentiment relations (e.g. "Jenny loves Tom"), and bonds that are determined by something other than evaluation, such as proximity, similarity, or ownership, were called unit relations (e.g.

Figure 3.4. Balanced and imbalanced cognitive triads. (See text for details.)

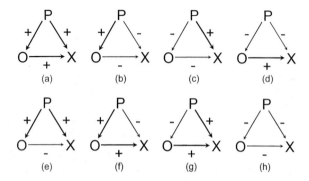

"Jenny and Tom are dating"). Both sentiment and unit relations can be positive or negative. According to Heider (1946), a balanced state among the elements in a three-element structure "exists if all three relations are positive in all respects, or if two are negative and one positive" (p. 110)—in other words, balance exists when the product of all three signs in the triad is positive. Balanced and imbalanced triads are depicted in Figure 3.4.

If Jenny perceives that Tom dislikes the mountains (a negative *o–x*-relation), one relation would be negative and two positive (triad e in Figure 3.4). As this triad would be in a state of imbalance, Jenny should feel uncomfortable and be motivated to change her cognitive structure toward balance. She could do so in several ways: Firstly, she could change the sign of the *p–x*-relation by adopting a negative attitude toward mountain holidays; secondly, she could change the sign of the *p–o*-relation by feeling less affection for Tom; finally, she could try to change the sign of the *o–x*-relation, e.g. by persuading Tom that the mountains are more fun than he thought.

People's goal to maintain attitudinal balance may easily be exploited in persuasion attempts, when celebrities support a political cause or endorse a consumer product. Just imagine the person in the Figure 3.5 were Slobodan Milosevic instead of the Princess of Wales, what do you think people's reaction to the campaign against landmines would have been?

Attitude strength

In our above example, what do you think is more likely: that Jenny will change her feelings for Tom or for the mountains? This depends

Figure 3.5. Endorsement of a product or policy by a celebrity, such as Princess Diana's support for a campaign to ban landmines, can influence attitudes via the balance principle. Copyright © Popperfoto/Reuters.

very much on the strength of each attitude. Let us assume that Tom is the love of her life; then she will most likely cool her mountaineering desires a bit. If, on the other hand, Tom is just a nice guy she happens to date and mountains are a real passion of hers, unfortunately for Tom she may not intensify her feelings for him and will go camping in the mountains with someone else.

In fact, various structural and experiential aspects of attitudes have been studied under the heading of *attitude strength*. One can say that everything attitudes are assumed to do (e.g. to guide information processing; to cause behaviour), *strong* attitudes are assumed to do better. They are thought to be more resistant to change, more persistent over time and more consistent with behaviour (e.g. Petty, Haugtvedt, & Smith, 1995). As intuitively plausible as this sounds, there is some confusion in the literature as to what attitude strength means and how it should be conceptualised. Different researchers proposed a variety of conceptual underpinnings of attitude strength

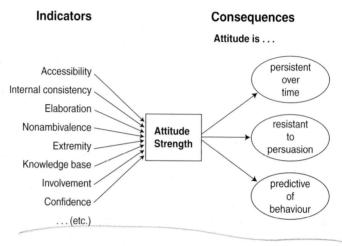

Figure 3.6. Proposed indicators and consequences of attitude strength.

Indicators

Accessibility
Internal consistency
Elaboration
Nonambivalence
Extremity
Knowledge base
Involvement
Confidence
. . . (etc.)

Attitude Strength

Consequences

Attitude is . . .

persistent over time

resistant to persuasion

predictive of behaviour

(see Figure 3.6). For examples, strength has been linked to *non-ambivalence* (Thompson, Zanna, & Griffin, 1995), *intra-attitudinal consistency* (Chaiken et al., 1995), and *extremity* of the attitude (Abelson, 1995); it has been operationalised as the *amount of thinking* about the attitude object (Tesser, Martin, & Mendolia, 1995) or about attitude-relevant information (Petty et al., 1995) that a perceiver engages in; other definitions include the degree of *vested interest* in an issue (Crano, 1995), the *confidence* with which the attitude is held (Gross, Holtz, & Miller, 1995), and the *accessibility* of the attitude (Fazio, 1995), that is the ease with which it comes to mind.

The various indicators of strength may legitimately be treated as independent properties of attitudes. It is plausible that people's attitudes may not only differ in valence (Mark may like exercising but his brother Tim may dislike it) but also in accessibility, ambivalence, extremity, confidence and so on (both Mark and Tim may strongly favour their local football team, but whereas Mark doesn't really think this is an important issue, Tim is a passionate supporter who would never miss a match). So it seems useful to take these characteristics into account when studying attitudinal processing. What may be true for extreme attitudes may not apply for more moderate ones, for example. Indeed, strength indicators are becoming increasingly investigated (see Petty & Krosnick, 1995).

The research strategies that have been applied to studying attitude strength include the measurement or manipulation of one or more strength indicators (e.g. accessibility) and assessing their covariation with (or effect on) one or more of the hypothesised consequences (e.g. persistence; see Wegener, Downing, Krosnick, & Petty, 1995). Two broad classes of attitude strength indicators have been distinguished (Bassili, 1996): *meta-judgmental indices*, which are based on research participants' self-reports concerning the strength variable of interest (e.g. subjective feelings of confidence; ratings of the attitude's importance), and *operative indices*, which are more objectively derived from the process of forming an attitude judgment or from its outcomes (e.g. response time as a measure of attitude accessibility; absolute difference of an attitude score from the scale midpoint as a measure of the attitude's extremity).

You may wonder to what extent the variety of strength measures used in research reflects a unitary underlying construct. Factor-analytic studies have addressed this question empirically by assessing the intercorrelations of a variety of attitude strength measures and looking for underlying dimensions. Although most measures tend to be positively correlated, it was generally concluded that attitude strength is not a unidimensional construct (e.g. Krosnick, Boninger, Chuang, Berent, & Carnot, 1993; Prislin, 1996). In a direct comparison of meta-judgmental and operative measures, Bassili (1996) found that only operative measures explained unique variance in outcome variables such as attitudinal persistence and resistance. One reason for this difference may be that meta-judgmental measures suffer more from reactivity effects (see chapter 2) than operative measures.

In any case, it should be noted that meta-judgmental as well as operative measures are context dependent and so may not reflect a stable property of an attitude. For example, research participants who were made to repeatedly express their attitudes subsequently showed a higher attitude accessibility and also rated their attitudes as more important (Roese & Olson, 1994). This example also demonstrates that the unique impact of one strength-related variable (accessibility or importance) can be reliably assessed only if other strength-related variables are also measured and controlled for (for discussion, see Wegener, Downing, Krosnick, & Petty, 1995), which is most often not the case. These methodological difficulties notwithstanding, we will present further examples for research on attitude strength when discussing persuasion (see chapter 7) and the relationship between attitudes and behaviour (see chapter 10).

Before ending this section, we should note that many attitudes seem to be much weaker than the traditional view of attitudes as stable knowledge structures might suggest. In a highly interesting programme of research, Wilson and his colleagues found that simply asking people to think about the reasons why they hold a certain attitude may be enough to cause striking change (Wilson, Dunn, Kraft, & Lisle, 1989). Asking research participants to think about the reasons for their attitudes led to pronounced attitude change with objects as diverse as posters, jam, psychology courses and others.[4] In the light of such findings, various researchers have proposed that attitudes are best understood as context-dependent, temporary constructions (Schwarz & Bohner, 2001; Wilson & Hodges, 1992; we will elaborate on this point in chapter 5).

Concluding comments

In this chapter, which concludes the part on basic issues, we reviewed some conceptualisations of attitude structure and strength. It should be emphasised again that the significance of attitudinal properties like structure, strength and also function, which was covered in chapter 1, comes primarily from their moderating role regarding attitude change and the impact of attitudes on further processing and behaviour. It is entirely irrelevant whether we classify an attitude as utilitarian or value-expressive, one- or two-dimensional, strong or weak unless this helps us in any way to improve its measurement or our understanding of attitudinal phenomena and dynamics. In this respect, part I laid the ground for the more fascinating issues in attitude research, namely attitudes' origin (see part II) and consequences (see part III).

Chapter summary

(1) Attitudes can have unipolar or bipolar structures. The structure determines how one attends to new information regarding the attitude object and remembers information about it (see chapter 9).

(2) Attitudes may have more than one underlying dimension. Each dimension may encompass elements of different response classes (cognitive, affective) or may consist entirely of one class.

(3) Elements within one dimension or between dimensions are not necessarily evaluatively consistent, nor are different dimensions necessarily consistent with each other. People may experience some degree of ambivalence toward some attitude objects.

(4) The fact that attitudes may be ambivalent led some researchers to postulate a bi-dimensional rather than a uni-dimensional conceptualisation of attitudes in which positivity and negativity represent independent dimensions.

(5) Different attitudes may be organised in a hierarchical fashion so that more specific attitudes may be derived from more general attitudes.

(6) Heider's balance theory, the ancestor of a family of theories of cognitive consistency, addresses the dynamics of inter-attitudinal structure. Balanced states are differentiated from imbalanced states, which are inherently unpleasant and motivate change toward a more balanced structure.

(7) Different properties of attitudes such as extremity, confidence, accessibility, non-ambivalence and others have been proposed as indicators of attitude strength. These aspects are related to an attitudes' stability over time, resistance to change and may moderate attitudes' influences on information processing and behaviour.

Exercises

(1) Give examples for what you think may be unipolar and bipolar attitudes. Why is the underlying polarity important for measurement?

(2) According to the information integration model, which factors may cause attitude differences between different people? What does this imply for attitude change? (Think of different ways how Mark would change his opinion on exercising.)

(3) Find examples for cognitive triads. How could imbalanced ones be turned into balanced ones?

(4) Think of attitudes you hold that are particularly strong, and of others that are less strong. How does attitude strength manifest itself subjectively? Which of these attitudes are likely to change over the next year? Is likelihood of change related to strength?

Notes

(1) These five beliefs may be seen as representing three dimensions: health, social aspects and hedonism.

(2) When comparing averaging and adding approaches it is difficult to make unequivocal predictions. Disregarding subjective probabilities for a moment, if attitude object X features two equally positive beliefs of +3, and attitude object Y features three beliefs of +3, an adding model would predict that Y (sum = +9) is liked better than X (sum = +6), whereas an averaging model would predict that both X and Y are equally liked (average = +3 in each case). However, if one assumes that people might integrate an initial neutral attitude (0) with the features of each object, an averaging model would also predict the attitude toward Y ([0 + 3 + 3 + 3] / 4 = 2.25) to be more positive than that toward X ([0 + 3 + 3] / 3 = 2; for further discussion, see Eagly & Chaiken, 1993; Petty & Cacioppo, 1981).

(3) In line with general usage in the 1950s, where "affect" was often synonymous with "evaluation", Rosenberg himself used the term "affective–cognitive consistency" to denote an inconsistency between beliefs and overall evaluation.

(4) Interestingly, a greater amount of thinking does not necessarily benefit attitudes and attitude-based decisions. In one experiment, students who had been asked to analyse the reasons for their attitudes toward various psychology courses changed their attitudes about these courses and subsequently made poorer behavioural decisions. Specifically, they were less likely to register for high-quality (as opposed to low-quality) courses, whereas students in a control condition who had not been induced to think about reasons were more likely to enrol in the high-quality courses (Wilson & Schooler, 1991).

Further reading

A review of research on attitude structure and function:

Eagly, A. H., & Chaiken, S. (1998). Attitude structure and function. In D. Gilbert, S. T. Fiske, & G. Lindzey (Eds.), *Handbook of social psychology* (4th ed., pp. 269–322). New York: McGraw-Hill.

A reader that presents the many facets of attitude strength and summarises related research findings:

Petty, R. E., & Krosnick, J. A. (Eds.). (1995). *Attitude strength: Antecedents and consequences.* Mahwah, NJ: Lawrence Erlbaum Associates Inc.

A reader that presents views on attitude structure, and its link to attitude function, from different theoretical perspectives:

Pratkanis, A. R., Breckler, S. J., & Greenwald, A. G. (Eds.). (1989). *Attitude structure and function.* Hillsdale, NJ: Lawrence Erlbaum Associates Inc.

Where do attitudes come from? **II**

In part I, we defined attitudes as evaluative responses. In this part, we look at the factors that determine whether the evaluative response is positive or negative. Is there anything inherently good or bad about a given attitude object? Although there are stimuli which elicit a wide consensus in their evaluation—most people find kittens cute and spiders ugly—we would not have written this book if the evaluation of a stimulus were inherent to the stimulus. Rather, evaluation is in the eye of the beholder. Different people differ in their evaluations and attitudes, and the same people differ over time or circumstances.

Imagine Joanna, who is rather religious, opposes abortion, prefers classical music to rock, and reported rather high consumer satisfaction with the local public transport system in a recent survey. Then there is Brian, who feels rather indifferent about church and religion in general, favours abortion, whom classical music gives the creeps, and who in the same consumer survey as Joanna gave rather low satisfaction ratings to the public transport system. Was Joanna born religious or did she acquire this attitude during her lifetime? If Joanna and Brian were to discuss abortion with each other, would they change their views to some degree? Would Joanna begin to like rock music more if she and Brian became friends? How come they both show so different opinions regarding the public transport service? After all it is exactly the same service they both evaluated. These are the kinds of question we will address in the following chapters.

The literature sometimes distinguishes between the areas of attitude formation and attitude change. Yet the processes regarding attitude formation and attitude change are often overlapping and hardly separable. Any process by which individuals form an attitude toward a novel attitude object may equally contribute to changing existing attitudes. And vice versa, processes typically studied in the area of attitude change would also apply to establishing new attitudes. In fact, persuasion research, which is usually characterised as the study of attitude change—often employs persuasive communications on *fictitious* issues, brands or other attitude objects to control for the influence of pre-existing attitudes, which mocks the notion of attitude *change* (see chapters 6 and 7). Thus, we reject this classic division and instead dedicate this section to the different processes that contribute to an individual's holding or reporting a specific attitude at a specific point in time.

In chapter 4 we will review a few basic influences on how attitudes come about. This discussion will be centred around two broad classes of influence: those of nature, i.e. the direct or indirect impact of genes on attitudes, and those of nurture, i.e. external or social influences, learning and exposure to stimuli. In chapter 5 we will discuss in more detail the situational variability of attitudes from a temporary-construal perspective. In chapters 6 and 7 we will dwell extensively on one particular form of social and informational influences: persuasion. Finally, in chapter 8, we will address behavioural influences on attitudes.

Nature and nurture as sources of attitudes 4

When psychologists explore the origins of a particular psychological phenomenon like a behaviour, trait or ability, they typically investigate to what extent the phenomenon is related to genes and to what extent it is acquired via environmental or social influences. Quite often this may involve agitated debates over the contribution of "nature versus nurture",[1] as may be exemplified by the controversy around the origins of individual differences in intelligence. Surprisingly, this kind of debate has not played a prominent role in attitude research at all. Until quite recently, it was taken for granted that attitudes are acquired and socially formed, and we will review several of the processes by which attitudes may be learned in the second part of this chapter. In recent years, however, some researchers propagated the notion that some attitudes may be inherited (for a review see Tesser, 1993), and we will review some of the evidence below.

Genetic influences

According to Tesser and Martin (1996), a biological influence on an evaluative response is plausible if (a) it is difficult to identify an experiential source, (b) there is cross-cultural evidence for uniformity of the response, (c) the response is compatible with evolution theory, and (d) the response covaries with biological factors. An example for attitudinal responses that are difficult to connect with an experiential source is the observation that newborns seem to show preferences for particular facial patterns versus other patterns, as early as one hour after birth. Given the young age at which this preference occurs it can hardly—although not impossibly—be accounted for by experience. However, the absence of evidence is not a strong epistemological cue.

Stronger evidence comes from an evolutionary approach. **Evolutionary psychology** explains human behaviour (including personality, preferences etc.) as mechanisms that evolved through natural selection (e.g. Cosmides, Tooby, & Barkow, 1992). According to this perspective, modern humans inherited the behaviour (or more precisely the genes for the behaviour) that increased early humans' selective fitness and enabled them to reproduce successfully. For example, a preference for sweet and fatty food helped prehistoric humans to survive, and consequently individuals with such a preference will have produced more offspring than individuals who disliked such high calorie food. Given that this preference is linked to a gene, it is likely that the offspring inherited the gene. Over several generations, the gene for a sugar preference will have successfully multiplied while a gene for sugar aversion would have fared less well. In the long run, liking for sugar would have been widespread in the human population. This preference would persist even though it does not provide a selective advantage any more in affluent societies.

Evolutionary psychologists have suggested quite a number of preferences which may reflect such functional adaptations, including which landscape people prefer and find beautiful: In general, humans prefer lush vegetation to deserts, and trees to built features or grassy expanses (for a review see Orians & Heerwagen, 1992). The best investigated area, however, is mating preferences (e.g. Buss & Schmitt, 1993). For both sexes, attraction to features indicative of a high quality mate would indicate an adaptation for choosing a high quality mate. According to this view, what individuals evaluate as attractive is not a culturally shaped standard but the product of biological evolution. Humans consider those features as attractive which indicate fertility. In females those are youthful looks—as women reach their peak fertility in their mid 20s and female fertility is constrained by age—and other indicators of health such as clear skin and lustrous hair. Youthful looks are less important in male attractiveness as male fertility is less constrained by age, but health cues are important. Cross-cultural consensus in what is attractive is interpreted as evidence for this adaptionist perspective on beauty. For example, large eyes, a small nose and full lips are considered both as indicating youth and—if one takes the winners of national beauty contests as evidence—such features are considered as being attractive in women in different cultures (Cunningham, 1986). Singh (1993) reported that whereas many beauty marks are subject to fashion, a low waist-to-hip ratio in women has been considered highly attractive throughout history. It was argued that facial attractiveness and a low waist-to-hip-ratio in a woman is an indicator of fecundity and less medical problems, and thus men's preference for hourglass-shaped figures and attractive faces in women may have secured greater reproductive success. Although current evidence does not unequivocally support that beauty advertises health (for reviews see Kallick, Zebrowitz, Langlois, & Johnson, 1998; Tassinary & Hansen, 1998) we cannot exclude a positive beauty–health relationship for the environment where such preferences originally evolved. However, the universality claim of the hourglass figure attractiveness was shattered when researchers recently reported about a preference for convex figures amongst the Matsigenka, a Peruvian tribe isolated from western culture (Yu & Shepard, 1998). Although there is strong evidence that some criteria of what we find attractive are biologically determined, the evidence is not conclusive and the debate of biology versus culture will continue.

Of course, conception alone does not guarantee reproductive success. Just like other animals, human males and females may have evolved different strategies to secure surviving offspring which in turn has shaped their preferences (or attitudes) in various regards (Buss & Schmitt, 1993; for a general theory of parental investment and sexual selection, see Trivers, 1972). Men have relatively little costs in producing offspring and are rather unlimited in the number of children they can produce. Whether mating results in surviving offspring depends to a large extent on the female's fecundity (see above) and her success in securing resources for her offspring. Men thus have two options: a quantity strategy in which they increase the probability of surviving offspring by having a large number of short-term mates, and a long-term strategy in which they actively contribute to the survival of offspring by supplying resources to them. From this Buss and Schmitt derived predictions about men's preferences for different features in short-term versus long-term mates.

The fact that men, to a greater extent than women, may increase their selective fitness by having many partners explains why men hold more positive attitudes toward casual sex than women, which is perhaps the largest documented sex difference in psychology (see Buss & Schmitt, 1993). In a study by Clark and Hatfield (1989), students were approached on campus by an attractive person of the "opposite" sex. What this confederate said was experimentally varied in three conditions (a to c):

> "I have been noticing you around campus. I find you very attractive."

(a) ". . . Would you go out with me tonight?"
(b) ". . . Would you come over to my apartment tonight?"
(c) ". . . Would you go to bed with me tonight?"

The answer depended very much on whether the person approached was male or female. Whereas about half of the men and half of the women approached in condition (a) accepted the invitation for a date, virtually none of the women, but more than two-thirds of the men, accepted the invitation in conditions (b) and (c). Thus, men were more willing to have sex with a strange woman than to go out with her!

Females, on the other hand, have relatively high costs by carrying a child to term, giving birth and nursing. Moreover, they are relatively limited in the absolute number of offspring they can produce during their lifetime. Consequently, they have a high interest to secure the survival of the relatively few children they can have. Because a mate who provides the necessary resources will improve their offspring's success, in long-term mate choices women should be more interested in a man's potential resources, such as wealth, status, earning ability etc. Indeed, cross-cultural data show that women more than men value the economic resources in prospective long-term mates, whereas males value good housekeeping in a mate more than females do (Buss et al., 1990). Again, however, the evolutionary hypothesis and thus biological explanation for the sex differences in mate selection criteria has been challenged. For example, Eagly and Wood (1999) point out that the tendency for women to weigh a potential spouse's economic capacity higher than men, and men's tendency to weigh housekeeping ability higher than women, decrease with an increasing level of gender equality in a society. This suggest that social or societal influences are at least partially responsible for these differences in mate preferences.

The most convincing case for a genetic influence on attitudes comes from twin studies, which allow to link variance in attitudes to variance in genes. Researchers have found a **heritability factor** of up to .5 on some attitudes, which means that 50% of the variance in this attitude between individuals of a population may be attributed to genetic variance in this population. Although there may be doubt regarding the exact height of the heritability estimates (amongst other problems, these estimates neglect the interaction between environmental and genetic influences), the data support the notion that some differences in attitudes between people may be partly due to genetic differences. Attitudes for which such a relationship have been reported are religiosity (Waller, Kojetin, Bouchard, Lykken, & Tellegen, 1990), job satisfaction (Arvey, Bouchard, Segal, & Abraham, 1989), vocational attitudes and interest (Keller, Bouchard, Arvey, Segal, & Dawes, 1992; Roberts & Johannson, 1974; Scarr & Weinberg, 1978), authoritarianism (Scarr, 1981), liking of jazz, attitudes toward capital punishment (both Martin, Eaves, Heath, Jardine, Feingold, & Eysenck, 1986), white supremacy and patriotism (Eaves, Eysenck, & Martin, 1989) and many others (for a review see Tesser, 1993).

Are we supposed to believe that there is a gene for becoming religious or liking jazz? Maybe, but a more plausible explanation lies in the assumption of mediating variables, which are partly controlled by genes and in turn influence attitudes. People form attitudes that are compatible with their dispositions, such as personalities and abilities. To the extent that these have a genetic component one would also observe a genetic component in the related attitudes. For example, it may be safe to assume that mathematical ability is moderately correlated with liking for maths. People who find maths easy are by and large likely to enjoy a maths class. If we assume that a gift for maths is to some extent genetically influenced, this might imply an indirect genetic influence on liking for maths. Examples for potential mediators (for a detailed discussion see Tesser, 1993) may be genetic differences in sensory structures (e.g. taste, hearing etc.), body chemistry, intelligence, temperament and activity level, and conditionability, which is the ease with which one can be conditioned (see next section).

Because the issue of heritability and genetic influences is highly sensitive and often leads to misunderstandings we would like to explicitly point out a few caveats. First, the heritability factor applies to the variance of a variable in populations but does not apply to individuals and does not express the extent to which a particular variable is produced by a particular gene. One could not say, for example "I owe 50% of my religiosity to my genes". Second, even if genes influence a trait, a behaviour or an attitude, their influence is neither exclusive nor irreversible nor impervious to modification by other factors. To quote Richard Dawkins, one of the most eloquent proponents of modern evolution theory:

> It is a fallacy . . . to suppose that genetically inherited traits are by definition fixed and unmodifiable. Our genes may instruct us to be selfish, but we are not necessarily compelled to obey them all our lives. It may just be more

difficult to learn altruism than it would be if we were genetically programmed to be altruistic. Among animals, man is uniquely dominated by culture, by influences learned and handed down.

(Dawkins, 1989, p. 3)

This leads us directly to those other—and much better researched—factors influencing attitudes.

Attitudes may be acquired

While human beings may bring inherited dispositions with them, which may influence which attitudes they tend to form in later life, external influences undoubtedly play a large part in shaping attitudes. Research has identified several different processes by which associations between an attitude object and an evaluation may be acquired. We begin here with some external influences that are relatively direct and are often presumed to require little mediating thought processes compared to the types of influence we turn to in later chapters when we address explicit persuasion. As you will see, however, whether the processes we discuss in the following paragraphs are really so "thoughtless" is in fact a matter of debate.

Mere exposure

When a new song comes out, do you like it better the very first time you hear it or after a few exposures? There is some evidence that liking increases with exposure. Of course, we may like a new acquaintance better after we get to know her more closely but in fact a prolonged interaction in which we acquire more information about her is not necessary. Saegert, Swap, and Zajonc (1973) manipulated how often students who participated in a "taste perception study" passed each other when they moved between experimental cubicles where they tasted different samples of liquids. Although the participants did not communicate with each other, they later gave higher ratings of liking for those other participants that they had passed more often. Because simple exposure to stimuli is sufficient to increase their perceived favourability, this effect is known as the **mere exposure effect** (Zajonc, 1968). Many studies have documented this

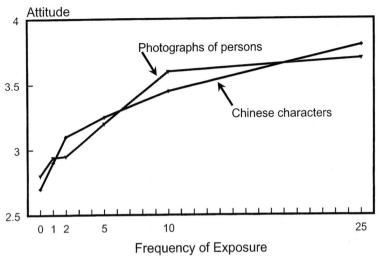

Figure 4.1. The mere exposure effect: The more frequently people are exposed to initially novel objects, the more positive their attitudes towards these objects become. Here the effect is shown for yearbook photographs and Chinese characters.

phenomenon. Bornstein (1989) reviewed 200 studies with quite different stimulus materials (e.g. nonsense words, ideographs, geometric forms, photographs) and concluded from this evidence that overall, increased exposure to a stimulus increases liking for that stimulus. But as you may have guessed the mere exposure effect also has its limitations. The increase in liking is strongest at a *moderate* level of repetition and levels off at higher levels of exposure, as shown in Figure 4.1.

Moreover, Bornstein's (1989) meta-analysis showed that the effect is stronger for more complex stimuli, for shorter exposure times including **subliminal exposure**, for longer delays between exposure and evaluation, and for exposure sequences in which many other stimuli are presented as well. Finally, it is not necessary that participants recognise the stimulus as having been presented earlier—in fact conscious recognition seems to attenuate the effect. The fact that exposure may be subliminal and recognition is not necessary may tell us something about why the effect occurs. At least, it rules out earlier explanations which had been built on the positive affect elicited by the recognition of familiar stimuli.

Based on the finding that explicit recognition does not contribute to the mere exposure effect, Zajonc (1980) argued that "preferences need no inferences", meaning that a stimulus may directly elicit affect without any cognitive mediation. This assumption of a so-called "hot" path from stimuli to affective response elicited an equally hot debate, which to some extent revolved around the question of what defines cognition (e.g. Lazarus, 1984; Zajonc, 1984; for a recent revival see Zajonc, 2000). In any case, it seems somewhat overdrawn to equal absence of awareness with the absence of cognition and this position is untenable in light of more recent findings (for reviews see Banaji, Lemm, & Carpenter, 2001; Bargh, 1997). Some researchers (e.g. Bornstein & D'Agostino, 1994) suggested that individuals may experience a facilitated encoding when perceiving a stimulus at a repeated time, something Jacoby and colleagues termed "perceptual fluency" (Jacoby, Kelley, Brown, & Jasechko, 1989). Individuals may attribute this pleasant experience of facilitated processing to the favourability of the stimulus. In line with this argument, Reber and his colleagues found that any variable that facilitates processing, for example visual contrast in reading, increases liking (Reber, Winkielman, & Schwarz, 1998). However, other results clash with this interpretation (see Klinger & Greenwald, 1994) and as of today there is no single satisfactory account for the mere exposure effect. If you feel disappointed by the lack of a solution to the puzzle you may take some comfort in the fact that the effects themselves are very reliable. As an exercise you may think about how they can be applied.

Conditioning and imitation

When psychologists investigated how people acquire behaviour they identified three main principles: learning by contiguity, learning by reinforcement, and learning by observation. Attitude researchers have applied these processes to the acquisition of attitudes.

Learning by stimulus contiguity

Mere exposure to previously neutral stimuli may suffice to develop a liking for these stimuli, but we may also come to like something because exposure to it was paired with experiencing positive affect elicited by other sources. And we may come to dislike something because it was combined with aversive stimuli. Attitude researchers showed that covert positive or negative evaluations can be created in humans if novel stimuli are paired with stimuli that already elicit positive or negative responses. This is the principle known as **evaluative conditioning**.

The most basic conditioning involves learning the meaning of evaluative connotations, as children do when they acquire concepts

(Staats, 1983; Staats, Staats, & Crawford, 1962). Good or bad, positive or negative are merely words. They assume their meaning by being associated with pleasant or unpleasant affective states, most likely caused by physical experiences such as hunger, pain or their respective offset. Once an evaluative meaning has been established, the word itself may become an unconditioned stimulus when paired with another stimulus.

Razran (1940) repeatedly exposed research participants to various slogans, such as "Workers of the world, unite!", under one of three conditions: (a) eating a free lunch, (b) inhaling unpleasant smells, (c) sitting in a neutral setting. Both before and after exposure, participants' agreement with each slogan was assessed. Although participants were unable to recall which slogan was paired with which environment, they showed increased agreement with slogans that were paired with the free lunch, decreased agreement with slogans paired with disagreeable odours, and did not change their evaluation of slogans paired with the neutral setting. Staats and Staats (1958) used spoken words as unconditioned stimuli and names of nationalities, presented visually, as conditioned stimuli. Half of the participants saw "Dutch" several times followed by a negative word (e.g. "sour") and "Swedish" followed by a positive word (e.g. "beautiful"); for the other half, the pairing of nationality and valence was opposite. Staats and Staats found that post-conditioning attitudes toward the nationalities, assessed with a semantic differential scale, reflected the valence of the adjectives the nationalities had been paired with.

This was just an experiment but one may easily imagine how individuals may develop negative or positive attitudes towards certain groups or people by hearing others refer to them in positive or negative terms. Note, however, that evaluative conditioning is not limited to verbal stimuli. Why do you think advertisements show products in beautiful surroundings or feature gorgeous models? An effect of music in conditioning consumer attitudes was demonstrated by Gorn (1982; see Box 4.1).

Earlier research conceived of evaluative conditioning as a form of classical conditioning: As Pavlov's dog learned to salivate (conditioned response = CR) when hearing a bell (conditioned stimulus = CS) because previously the bell had always signalled receiving food (unconditioned stimulus = US), attitudes may also develop as conditioned responses to an attitude object (CS) as a result of having been paired with another affect-eliciting stimulus (US). The contemporary view of classical conditioning in humans, however, which assumes that the individual acquires an expectancy that the unconditioned

BOX 4.1   A study on the influence of music on consumer attitudes

Participants in a study by Gorn (1982) were told that an advertising agency wanted to select music for a pen commercial. They were shown an advert featuring a pen, which was either beige or light-blue. The music played was either from "Grease", an up-beat musical, or a piece of classical East Indian music. According to pilot studies, "Grease" generally produced a positive emotional response whereas the East Indian music evoked mainly a negative response. Thus, four conditions were run, with each of the two colours being paired with either liked or disliked music. After viewing the advert and rating the music, participants were told that they could select a pen as a gift for their participation. Two colours were available: light-blue and beige. If music had an influence, one would expect that participants would prefer the colour that was paired with "Grease" or the colour that was *not* paired with the East Indian music. The results (see Figure 4.2) showed that when "Grease" was played, the advertised colour, independent of whether it was blue or beige, was chosen by 79% of the advert-recipients, whereas only 21% chose the nonadvertised colour. This alone could merely reflect that people chose what they had seen before in advertising. Indeed, mere exposure would also predict a preference for the advertised pen. However, when the disliked Indian music was played, the advantage for the advertised colour was gone. More precisely, only 30% preferred the advertised colour and 70% chose the nonadvertised colour.

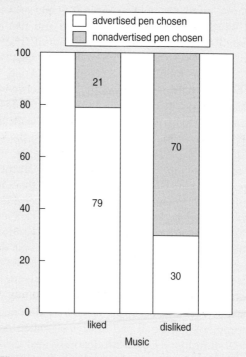

Figure 4.2. Effects of music on consumer attitudes: Percentages of participants who chose the advertised and nonadvertised pen, respectively, depending on the favourability of the music presented with the advert (data from Gorn, 1982).

stimulus will follow the conditioned stimulus (e.g. Dawson & Schell, 1987), is not quite compatible with many findings regarding evaluative conditioning.

First, evaluative conditioning occurs independent of the awareness of stimulus pairings (Baeyens, Eelen, & van den Bergh, 1990). Using the Staats and Staats (1958) paradigm, Berkowitz and Knurek (1969) created negative and positive attitudes, respectively, towards the names "Ed" and "George". Later, in an ostensibly unrelated experiment, each of their participants discussed with two confederates who introduced themselves as Ed and George. After the discussion, both participants' ratings of the confederates and confederates' ratings of the participants' behaviour showed an effect of the previous conditioning. In a more recent study, Krosnick, Betz, Jussim, and Lynn (1992) asked students to watch slides depicting a target person engaged in various ambiguous activities. Depending on experimental condition, these slides were immediately preceded by briefly flashed pictures of positive (e.g. a bridal couple) or negative primes (e.g. a werewolf). This variation influenced the students' attitudes toward the stimulus person, while additional measures demonstrated that participants were unable to detect the affective connotation of the primes.

As a second difference to classical conditoning, evaluative conditioning seems rather resistant to extinction (Baeyens, Eelen, van den Bergh, & Crombez, 1989). Consequently, evaluative conditioning was explained differently from classical conditioning.[2] According to Martin and Levey (1994), individuals do not learn an if–then relationship between the conditioned and unconditioned stimulus. Instead the evaluation of the unconditioned stimulus is simply transferred to the conditioned stimulus. Note that in many instances a single pairing of the stimuli is sufficient to elicit such a transfer, as when music was paired with pens. Other studies showed that evaluative conditioning may be rather long lasting. For example, one study investigated the long-term effects of conditioned attitudes toward a brand and paired favourable images with a fictitious brand of mouthwash (Grossman & Till, 1998). Conditioning effects were observed even three weeks after the exposure.

Learning by reinforcement

Stimulus contiguity is one manner in which responses to a stimulus may be conditioned. Another is to increase the frequency of a particular response by reinforcement, which means that the response is followed by positive consequences, or to decrease its frequency by punishment, i.e. negative consequences. These mechanisms are referred to as *operant* or **instrumental conditioning**. Inspired by Skinner's (1957) account of verbal behaviour as a result of operant conditioning, several researchers applied principles of reinforcement to attitudes. Note that it is not necessary that people experience reinforcement themselves; they can also learn from observing others being reinforced or punished. Sometimes this variant of learning is referred to as **vicarious conditioning**.

Remember that in chapter 1 we described how an attitude may serve social identity functions. People may hold a particular attitude in order to fit into a desired group. It is easy to imagine that if every time one expresses a particular attitude one's peers signal support or sympathy one will be more likely to express this attitude again. Social reinforcement or punishment is usually seen as central to the operant conditioning of attitudes, but one may also imagine that an attitude gets reinforced if holding that attitude makes us feel good about ourselves. If it feels unpleasant to hold this attitude we may change it (see also chapter 8 on dissonance theory).

Typical studies on operant conditioning of attitudes involve an experimenter who interviews a participant on his or her attitudes. Unlike well-trained interviewers in professional attitude surveys, this experimenter signals agreement or disagreement by nodding, frowning or some verbal cues (e.g. "good"). Participants are later— in some studies much later—again asked to report their opinions. In one study (Insko, 1965), students at the University of Hawaii were interviewed over the telephone about their opinions on initiating an "Aloha Springtime Festival". Several questions were asked, and half of the students were reinforced by the interviewer saying "good" every time they responded favourably, whereas the other half were similarly reinforced for unfavourable responses. When the students were again asked about their attitudes toward the festival one week later in a rather different setting, this time using a paper-and-pencil survey, an effect of the conditioning could still be detected: The students who had been reinforced for unfavourable statements still reported a less positive attitude than those students who had been reinforced for favourable statements.

Again we need to ask for the reason behind this effect. And again, awareness plays a crucial role. The fact that in many studies the conditioning effect covaried with participants' reports of having been aware of the reinforcement points to deliberative cognitive processing as a mediator rather than a direct unmediated response. But which cognitive processes are instigated by attitude reinforcement? Reinforcement may reassure an individual that he or she holds correct attitudes and may consequently strengthen these attitudes. In this respect, reinforcement may represent **informational social influence**. This influence should be particularly strong for attitudes serving a utilitarian function. In contrast, as mentioned above, social reinforcement may also represent **normative social influence** (for the distinction of normative and informational influence, see Deutsch & Gerard, 1955). It may signal the individual that he is in agreement with the reinforcer. Whether this strengthens an attitude or not depends on how much a person wants to be in agreement. One may expect that normative social influences should be particularly strong for attitudes serving social identity functions, in particular for people high in self-monitoring (see chapter 1). Also in that case, reinforcement should be more successful when coming from socially attractive sources.

Somewhat related to this idea, Insko and Butzine (1967) conducted a study in which the experimenters either flattered or insulted the participants before the attitude reinforcement trial. They found that conditioning was more successful when administered after flattery than after offence. Note, however, that offending participants did not wipe out the reinforcement effects. Even participants who had been offended showed reinforcement-induced attitude change as compared to control participants who had not been reinforced. This points to the fact that in addition to reinforcement representing normative social influence, other processes may also be at work, such as informational social influence or automatic, nondeliberative processes. Likewise, several other experiments confirmed that both processes, normative and informational influence, contribute to the effect of verbal conditioning (see also Cialdini & Insko, 1969), even though they may not be necessary mediators.

Learning by observation

Parents may deliberately reinforce their children for expressing attitudes that the parents themselves approve of. But parents may also unintentionally influence the attitudes of their children by providing a model (see Figure 4.3). Much of observational learning or social learning theory has been based on imitated behavioural patterns, for example the famous studies on the imitation of aggressive behaviour by Bandura (1965), but equally children may acquire their parents' attitudes, values or prejudices by observing and imitating them. A child growing up amidst the tensions and prejudices of ethnic or

Figure 4.3.
Observational learning
may shape attitudinal
responses.

religious conflicts, as for example in former Yugoslavia or Northern Ireland, is likely to observe and acquire her caregiver's attitudes about the respective out-group. These processes of learning by observation and imitation may contribute to perpetuating such conflicts over many generations.

One may easily imagine that modelled behaviour will in turn be reinforced if it meets the expectation of the social environment, or punished if it violates the respective social norms. Assimilating to others' attitudes is an ongoing process that continues throughout a person's life-span and is certainly not restricted to childhood, nor is it simply a process of imitation. One of the most influential studies in this area was conducted at a U.S. liberal women's college, Bennington, in the 1930s. In this study, young women were observed over the four years they attended Bennington. During this time, they became continuously more liberal in their views, and this adoption of the college's values was greater the more they identified with the college (Newcomb, 1943).[3] Other researchers have observed that newcomers to an organisation gradually accept its predominant values and attitudes over time. For example, American police recruits became more authoritarian (Carlson & Sutton, 1974), and White police officers became more anti-Black, as they progressed through the police academy (Teahan, 1975). Because these studies could not tightly monitor social interactions we do not know to what extent such attitude shifts are due to mere imitation, reinforcement, explicit persuasion, pressure to conform, role taking, changes in the belief system through new experiences and information, or to any other factors. We suppose that each of these factors does contribute to changes in people's attitudes.

Concluding comment

We have reached the end of this chapter but by no means the end of what there is to know about the formation of attitudes. You may have noticed that in this chapter individuals were portrayed as very passive, simply "receiving" their attitudes. Of course this is only part of the story. In the next several chapters, we will gradually present accounts of attitude construction, formation and change that are based on more active processes, and you will see that thinking plays a prominent role in these accounts.

Chapter summary

(1) Many different processes contribute to the formation and change of attitudes. In principle, attitude formation and attitude change do not imply different cognitive mechanisms but rest on the same processes where social influences as opposed to biological influences are concerned.

(2) There is some evidence, mainly from twin studies, that attitudes may in part be genetically influenced. It is assumed that the genetic influence on attitudes is mediated by other genetically (co-)determined factors such as sensory structures (e.g. taste, hearing etc.), body chemistry, intelligence, temperament and others.

(3) Attitudes may also be acquired. In addition to environmental factors and genetic dispositions, the interaction of both may explain part of the variance in attitudes. Also, genetic dispositions and environmental factors are not necessarily independent of each other.

(4) Repeated exposure to a stimulus increases liking for that stimulus. This phenomenon is called the mere exposure effect. Mere exposure effects are stronger for more complex stimuli, for shorter exposure times including subliminal exposure, for longer delays between exposure and evaluation, and for exposure

sequences in which many other stimuli are presented as well. It is not necessary for the effect to occur that participants recognise the stimuli.

(5) It is possible to influence people's attitudes about objects by establishing a close connection in space and time between these objects and positive or negative stimuli (evaluative conditoning). It is not necessary that people are aware of the pairing, and a single pairing may be sufficient. Moreover, such evaluative conditioning is quite resistant to extinction and the conditioned attitudes may be enduring.

(6) Evaluative responses may be conditioned by reinforcement (operant conditioning). To some extent reinforcement is successful because it represents social information about the validity of one's attitude. Alternatively, reinforcement may represent social norms with which one wishes to comply. It is not necessary that an individual personally experience reinforcement; the observation of other people's attitude being reinforced may suffice (vicarious conditioning).

(7) People may acquire attitudes by imitating other people's attitudes. Such role models may be particularly influential the more one identifies with the model and the more one desires to fit into a particular group.

Exercises

(1) Try to explain what mediates a possible genetic influence on such attitudes as liking for jazz or work satisfaction.

(2) A car manufacturer has completely redesigned its models. In market research tests consumers are shown the new designs. In direct as in indirect comparisons the old models fare much better. Can you encourage the designers or is the new line really a disaster? How could one improve the test to take into account mere exposure effects?

(3) Find examples of evaluative and operant conditioned attitudes.

Notes

(1) Actually one also needs to take the interaction of both variables into account.

(2) Although cognitive psychology distinguishes between classical con-
     ditioning and evaluative conditioning as different processes, this
     distinction is not consistently made in social psychology, and evalu-
     ative conditioning is often referred to as classical conditioning.

(3) The Bennington studies have become a classic in sociology and social
     psychology because of the wealth of data in the original study, but
     even more so because the "Bennington women" were re-interviewed
     twice more in their later lives. Studies conducted approximately 25
     (Newcomb, 1967) and 50 years later (Alwin, Cohen, & Newcomb,
     1991) provided a host of insights regarding the stability and flexi-
     bility of attitudes across the life-span.

Further reading

A review of genetic influences on attitudes and a plea for closer
attention to this aspect of human experience:

Tesser, A. (1993). On the importance of heritability in psychological
    research: The case of attitudes. *Psychological Review, 100,* 129–142.

A thorough review of conditioning and mere exposure effects:

Eagly, A., & Chaiken, S. (1993). *The psychology of attitudes.* Fort Worth, TX:
    Harcourt Brace Jovanovich. (chapter 9)

Attitudes as temporary constructions 5

All of the processes covered in the preceding chapter are compatible with the classic file drawer model of attitudes. People store in memory a learned or innate response to an attitude object, and this response is then activated by the attitude object. This would imply that we would always come up with the same evaluation when encountering the same object. Clearly, this is not the case. Although we may have inherited a sweet tooth or were conditioned to associate sweet desserts with being rewarded, we evaluate a slice of apple pie quite differently when we are hungry as opposed to when we have just finished a sumptuous meal. Attitudinal responses vary across situations, a fact that caused Tesser and Martin (1996) to remark that "the three most important influences on evaluation are context, context, and context" (p. 421). That context influences attitude reports has already been shown in chapter 2; again, such context effects do not necessarily reflect measurement errors. They may as well indicate that attitudes differ depending on the situation. We like our jobs better when we think of the friendly ambience in the office rather than of the long hours, when we are in a good rather than bad mood, and when we compare the present situation to being unemployed rather than to our dream job. Because attitude reports are highly context sensitive, some scholars proposed that attitudes are constructed on the spot based on the information currently at hand (for reviews, see Schwarz & Bohner, 2001; Wilson & Hodges, 1992). Thus, attitudes depend on which information comes to mind, how it is evaluated and how it is used in judgment. We will address these three factors in turn, and as it will become obvious that context may influence each of them, the following paragraphs illustrate the context dependency and relativity of human judgment.

Context influences on information retrieval for attitude construction

In chapter 2, we already described that in order to construct an attitude people need to retrieve relevant information. Before we continue, we need to define more precisely what we mean by the buzz word "information". When we speak of information we mean *anything* that informs a person about his or her evaluation of the attitude object. For example, research evidence suggests that when asked for their attitudes toward different social categories (e.g. politicians) people retrieve exemplars of these categories (e.g. Bill Clinton), presumably because these exemplars are used for constructing the attitude (Sia, Lord, Blessum, Thomas, & Lepper, 1999). Clearly, the most prototypical information are beliefs about the attitude object, but note that a belief is hardly informative regarding the evaluation of the attitude object unless the belief itself is evaluated. Of course, everything we have said so far about how evaluations come about also applies to the evaluation of beliefs. And everything we will say in the following about situational influences on evaluations also applies. But besides evaluated beliefs, feelings evoked by the attitude object may also serve as information, as we will elaborate below. In contrast to beliefs, feelings always include an evaluative component. Another source of information is one's own behaviour (Bem, 1972). As people often infer another person's attitude from the behaviour this person shows, Bem argues that people may also observe their own behaviour to draw inferences about their own attitudes, a point we will elaborate in chapter 8. Other sources of information may be mental images, past experiences or current bodily states. Some of these will be addressed in more detail below.

When constructing a judgment people rarely retrieve all potentially relevant information; instead, they are likely to base their judgment on a subset of that information (e.g. Bodenhausen & Wyer, 1987; Wyer & Srull, 1989). Whether a particular piece of information will be retrieved and used depends on how accessible it is in memory, that is how easily it comes to mind. Accessibility in turn is influenced by a number of different factors (see Bless et al., in press, for a review). Some information may be more memorable than other because of its inherent qualities. Events or facts that stood out, were unexpected or have vivid qualities are more likely to be remembered than banal, ordinary and pallid information. For example, you will be more likely to remember that someone knocked over a glass at the

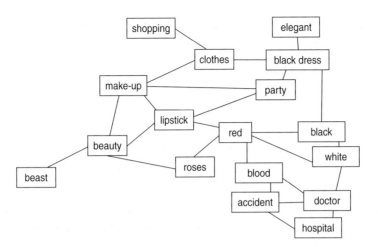

Figure 5.1. Example of a small portion of a semantic network, as postulated by the spreading activation model. Shorter lines represent stronger links.

dinner party if that glass contained red wine which spilled on an expensive white carpet than if it just contained water.

Accessibility of information also depends on how frequently it is accessed and how it is organised in memory. We can think of memory as a network containing semantic nodes that are connected via associative links, along which activation can spread between nodes (e.g. Anderson & Bower, 1973; Bower 1981, see Figure 5.1).[1]

In such models, information is being retrieved when the activation of its node exceeds a certain threshold (Anderson & Bower, 1973; Bower, 1981). The closer the activation level is to the threshold, the more likely will any additional activation cross the threshold and bring this information to mind. The activation level of each node slowly decays with time if it does not receive inputs from activation spreading through the network. The activation level of a given node thus depends on the *recency* of its last activation (i.e. the time elapsed since).

Therefore, at any given time, frequently activated information is generally close to the threshold and more likely to cross it (i.e. accessible) than information that is activated rarely, all else being equal (Higgins & King, 1981). Information that is well connected to many other nodes in memory is generally more likely to be activated than relatively isolated information. These factors, inherent salience, frequency of activation, and connectedness, amongst others, contribute to the accessibility of information independent of the particular situation (**chronic accessibility**). Representations of attitude objects and in turn attitudes depend to some extent on chronically accessible information. Linda, who defines herself as a liberal, may think of the need to strive for social equality whenever she thinks about welfare. This is because she frequently discusses social justice and equality, and as these values are very important to her, they are linked to many different concepts in her memory.

But to some degree attitudes depend on information that is accessible only in the specific situation (**temporary accessibility**; for reviews see Lord & Lepper, 1999; Schwarz & Bless, 1992; Tesser, 1978; Tourangeau & Rasinski, 1988; Wilson & Hodges, 1992). The temporary accessibility of information is mainly determined by the time since the information was last activated (i.e. its recency; Wyer & Srull, 1989). At any given time people's attitudes are likely to reflect specific information that was activated recently, in addition to chronically accessible information. In Box 2.1 (chapter 2), we reported how such recently activated information may stem from preceding questions in an attitude survey. In a survey where preceding questions had activated liberal beliefs, respondents favoured increased welfare spending more than in a survey where the preceding question had activated conservative beliefs (Tourangeau et al., 1989).

Of course the origin of temporarily accessible information is not limited to preceding questions in a survey. Experimental research has used different techniques to activate information prior to attitude assessment and has overwhelmingly shown that attitudes reflect the situationally accessible information. For example, students considered discrimination as a more pressing problem in society when a well-liked minority exemplar (e.g. Michael Jordan) had been activated in a previous "unrelated" experiment (Bodenhausen, Schwarz, Bless, & Wänke, 1995). Outside of the laboratory, people are more concerned with issues that get coverage in the media, and frequently or recently covered issues have a large impact on how people evaluate politicians (for a review see Iyengar & Kinder, 1987). Imagine for example a public opinion poll on attitudes toward using trains rather than private cars. You are one of the people asked. When assessing your attitude toward taking the train you immediately think that trains are inconvenient and expensive. Consequently, you will arrive at a quite unfavourable opinion. Imagine, however, that just the day before you had watched a TV programme on carbon-dioxide emission and global warming. Because this information was acquired quite recently you can still remember it and with this piece of information your evaluation of train use becomes a little more favourable. Had the programme been broadcast a month ago, you may not have recalled this information, at least not immediately without expending some effort thinking about the issue (see also Figure 5.2).

This example also demonstrates that the more you think about an issue, the more information you will generate. Given that the evaluative implications of the information varies, different judgments would result at different points of the thought process. That is why "mere thought", that is simply thinking about an issue without receiving any external information, may instigate attitude change. Attitudes may become more extreme if the thoughts are evaluatively consistent (Tesser, 1978; see also chapter 6), and they may become less extreme if the thoughts are inconsistent (Chaiken & Yates, 1985).

Moreover, introducing an interesting twist to the research on self-generated thought in the construction of attitudes, Timothy Wilson and his colleagues have presented an impressive research programme on how self-exploring the reasons for one's attitudes may change these attitudes (e.g. Wilson et al., 1989; Wilson, Hodges, & LaFleur, 1995). In one study (Wilson, Lisle, Schooler, Hodges, Klaaren, & LaFleur, 1993) research participants were shown several posters, some of them reproductions of impressionist paintings, the others humorous posters. When merely asked to evaluate these posters and choose the one they liked best, 95% of the participants selected one of the impressionist posters. In the group that was asked to analyse why they felt the way they did about the posters, only 64% subsequently chose an impressionist poster. Wilson and colleagues argue that analysing reasons for one's attitude produces different kinds of thoughts than would otherwise be accessible. Note that in the studies by Wilson and his colleagues participants retrieved *reasons* for their attitudes. Insofar this research is a special case of the more general principle that the retrieval of any additional thoughts that differ in their evaluative implications from those retrieved otherwise cause shifts in attitudes.

Taken together, these findings that thinking about an attitude object may change its evaluation also indicate that judgments may be constructed based on current thoughts rather than simply retrieved. Because the temporary accessibility of thoughts about the attitude object will vary over situations, attitudinal judgments are also likely to vary.[2] It should be noted, however, that so far we have treated the evaluation of each piece of information as given. In our train example, we presupposed that reducing carbon-dioxide in the atmosphere is a good thing. In the following, we will be concerned instead with contextual influences on *how we evaluate* attitude objects and information about them.

(a)

(b)

Context influences on evaluations

Of course, evaluation is not entirely dependent on context. As we have discussed above, some evaluations may be genetically influenced or may have been acquired. However, this section will show that situational conditions may also contribute to how we evaluate a particular object. We will review some of the context factors that bear on evaluation and show how they operate.

Goals

The example at the beginning of this chapter of how a slice of apple pie acquires a different significance depending on one's state of hunger illustrates a basic mechanism regarding the evaluation of objects. While stimuli are hardly inherently good or bad, favourable or unfavourable, they acquire their evaluative meaning by how they relate to a person's current goals (see the section on attitude functions in chapter 1). Whatever brings us closer to our goals is clearly desirable, whatever obstructs goal attainment will be evaluated unfavourably. As Carver and Scheier (1990; Carver, Lawrence, & Scheier, 1996) argued, progress toward goals, however, is itself seen as relative. Even though an individual may progress, he may still experience negative affect if his progress is not as fast as he had anticipated. And vice versa, things that make a person progress faster than anticipated will be associated with positive affect.

The emphasis here is on currently activated goals. People usually have quite a number of goals they would eventually like to reach, but these are not all equally relevant or accessible in different situations. When revising for an exam, you may be less concerned about meeting a potential dating partner as compared to when you are at a party. Because different goals may be activated at different times, how people evaluate an attitude object may vary depending on how it advances their currently salient goals. This was nicely demonstrated in a study by Brendl, Higgins, Markman, and Messner (as cited in Brendl & Markman, in press). Students were either approached at the university's cafeteria or while they stood in line at the bursar's office waiting to pay their tuition fees. All students were offered tickets for a lottery. At the two locations, half of the participants were told that the lottery could win them $1000 in cash. The other half were told that the lottery could win them a $1000 tuition waiver. In spite of the

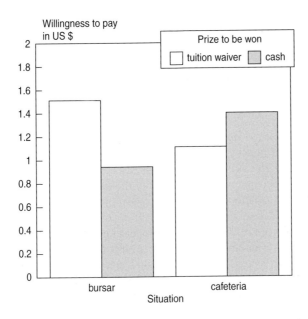

Willingness to pay in US $

Figure 5.3. Current goals affect attitudes: Amount of US dollars participants were willing to pay for a lottery ticket depending on the framing of the prize to be won (tuition waiver or cash of same amount) and the situation where the ticket was offered (bursar's office or cafeteria). (Data from Brendl & Markman, in press.)

fact that the objective value is the same for both groups, the tuition waiver provides a more direct means toward the goal of paying tuition. Indeed those students who waited at the bursar's office (for whom the goal of paying tuition was temporarily highly salient) were willing to spend more money on a lottery that offered to win a tuition waiver than were students in the cafeteria. By contrast, students in the cafeteria were more interested in cash than in a tuition waiver (see Figure 5.3).

In another study (Shavitt et al., 1994), participants either rated a list of behaviours according to whether they would make a good or bad impression on others, or they rated different tastes and smells according to their pleasantness. This procedure had been shown to activate either the goal of making a good impression or to find hedonic pleasure (Shavitt & Fazio, 1991). Afterwards, participants were shown an advert for a restaurant that showed either rather unattractive guests or rather attractive guests endorsing the restaurant. Going to a restaurant that is frequented by rather dull and boring people may be seen as detrimental to one's image, but how strongly this affects one's evaluation of the restaurant and intention to visit the restaurant should depend on how salient the goal is of making a good impression to others. As expected, participants evaluated the restaurant less favourably when impression concerns had been activated rather than concerns about the taste of the food. Note that because people may have conflicting goals, and, moreover, what is advancing one goal may obstruct another, people may experience ambivalent attitudes toward an attitude object (Kaplan, 1972).

Mood

It does not take a degree in psychology to suspect that our current mood state influences how we evaluate things. Folk wisdom refers to rose-coloured glasses when happiness tints our evaluations in a more favourable hue than would usually be the case. When psychologists explored this phenomenon more systematically, they accumulated abundant evidence showing that attitude objects are indeed evaluated more favourably in a happy mood than in a less happy mood. For example, consumers who were given a small unexpected gift when entering a shopping centre, which put them in a happy mood, subsequently reported higher satisfaction with a range of products they owned compared to other consumers who had not received a gift (Isen, Shalker, Clark, & Karp, 1978). Job applicants received higher ratings when the interviewer was in a good mood (Baron, 1993). Psychologists also provided explanations of why this phenomenon occurs and examined its boundary conditions (for a review see Clore, Schwarz, & Conway, 1994).

Originally, it had been suggested that mood, just like any other incoming information, activates related nodes and thus facilitates access to related categories in the semantic network of memory (Bower, 1981; Isen, 1987). In other words, mood would prime evaluatively similar contents. Indeed, in several studies participants were more likely to recall happy memories when they were happy rather than sad and vice versa (for a review see Blaney, 1986). If people remember the happy times of their lives in a good mood and subsequently rely on those memories for their overall evaluation of life, people would be more likely to report higher life satisfaction in a good mood than in a bad mood.

One problem with the mood-priming explanation was that the evidence for mood-congruent recall is not as strong as one might expect. Apparently many other factors moderate the effect (for reviews see Clore et al., 1994; Fiedler & Bless, 2000). Altogether it is a rather fragile phenomenon and is unlikely to account for all of the widely documented mood effects on evaluative judgment.

Schwarz and Clore (1983) proposed a different explanation why good mood makes us evaluate things more favourably. According to these authors, an economic strategy of making an evaluative judgment is to rely directly on one's feelings that are caused by the presence of the attitude object. After all, things we like tend to evoke positive feelings, and things we dislike cause us to feel bad—so why not use these affective responses as a shortcut to an evaluative judgment? When we laugh at a joke, we probably find it funny; when the mere thought of a person elicits tense feelings we probably don't like that person. Interestingly, however, it is not always easy to discriminate between feelings elicited by the attitude object and feelings one happens to experience at the time of judgment, but for irrelevant reasons. Thus, we may arrive at the conclusion that a person is dislikeable even when our negative feelings were not caused by the person but stemmed from a different source. Unless we are aware of the origin of our feelings or at least that they have nothing to do with the attitude object, we may misattribute them to the attitude object. When you think about how satisfied you are with your life and ask yourself: "How do I feel about it?", you may read your presently good mood as indicating that life is just great, while in reality your positive feelings may have been caused by an exceptionally sunny day.

Schwarz and Clore (1983) examined this "mood as information" hypothesis or "How do I feel about it?" heuristic[3] in a field experiment. By chance persons were drawn from the telephone directory, and some were called on a sunny day, whereas others were called on a rainy day. The interviewers explained that they were conducting a study on life satisfaction and asked respondents how satisfied they were with their lives. Furthermore, the interviewers pretended to be calling from another town and, within each weather condition, initially drew the attention of some respondents to the current weather by simply asking "By the way, how is the weather down there". The pattern of interviewee's responses to the life satisfaction question, which is presented in Figure 5.4, calls into question the assumption that positive or negative thoughts and memories about one's life, elicited by one's mood, are at the core of mood effects on judgment. Why is this the case? And why do the results support instead the mood-as-information hypothesis? Before reading the answer, take a look at Figure 5.4 and try to explain the observed pattern in terms of mood-congruent recall.

It can be seen that the results in one half of the study, where respondents' attention was *not* drawn to the weather as a plausible cause of their current mood, are compatible with either view. People reported higher life satisfaction when the weather was sunny rather

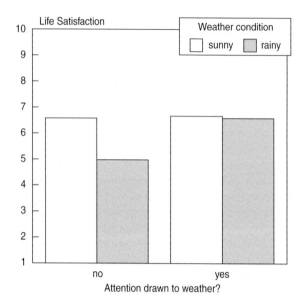

Figure 5.4. Mood as information in judgments of life satisfaction: Reported life satisfaction as a function of the weather and of whether or not respondents' attention was drawn to the weather (data from Schwarz & Clore, 1983).

than rainy. In fact, this result alone would be rather trivial and may have other explanations as well. However, if fine weather elicits good mood which in turn automatically primes positive life events, then these life events should also be recalled in the other half of the study, where people were made aware of the cause of their mood. Irrespective of whether good mood is elicited by the weather (or receiving a cookie or other sources), good mood would make happy life events more accessible. Thus, according to this perspective we would not expect different results whether or not people were made aware of the true cause of their mood. On the other hand, if we assume that people misattribute their happy moods to their (presumably happy) lives, then being made aware of the weather as the source of mood should undermine this process. In turn, we would not expect higher life satisfaction in a happy mood than in a sad mood, which is exactly what Schwarz and Clore's (1983) data show.

While these results lend support to the mood-as-information hypothesis, they do not rule out that mood-congruent recall may at times mediate mood biases on judgment. Forgas (1995) proposed an "affect infusion model" model that integrates both approaches. In essence, Forgas argues that under limited cognitive processing (e.g. time pressure etc.) mood may affect our judgment in the direct way of the "How do I feel about it?" heuristic, whereas under conditions of more extensive processing affect may be "infused" into cognition and may bias judgments by eliciting the retrieval—and fostering the construction—of mood-congruent information.

Does good mood always elevate evaluations, all else equal?

Answers to this question can be found in the theoretical approaches we discussed. One important aspect is perceived relevance. We have just seen that mood will not be used as information if it is deemed irrelevant for the judgment at hand. If I know that I am feeling good because the sun is shining, my mood obviously is not a representative indicator of my life satisfaction in general (or of my attitude toward any other object that needs to be evaluated, apart from the current weather).

Another factor is the amount of information available. If we assume that mood operates as information, its impact should depend on how much other information we have. Accordingly, consumers showed mood effects in their evaluation of unfamiliar products but not of familiar ones (Srull, 1984), and mood was shown to influence ratings of ill-defined, complex targets, such as satisfaction with one's life in general, more than ratings of well-defined and specific targets, such as satisfaction with one's income (Schwarz, Strack, Kommer, & Wagner, 1987). How much other information we have also depends on the *motivation* and *ability* to retrieve more information from memory, a point we will elaborate on in chapter 7. Indeed, more pronounced mood effects on judgments of life satisfaction were observed when individuals had less mental capacity available for making their judgment because they were distracted or under time pressure (Siemer & Reisenzein, 1998). Note, however, that effects caused by mood-congruent recall should be stronger under more effortful processing simply because the recall of information requires capacity (for a detailed review see Forgas, 1995). Thus, when we want to assess how a particular variable such as time pressure, target complexity or personal involvement—to name only a few— moderates the influence of mood on judgment, we need to take into account how mood is mediated in this particular condition.

Moreover, while mood can be used as information, how this information is used may depend on other factors. (In general, the impact of information depends on how it is used; we will explore this more deeply later in this chapter.) When you laugh about a comedian, this indicates that you are amused. Probably you think the comedian is quite good. But when you laugh while watching a performance of

Romeo and Juliet, this probably indicates that the particular performance was rather poor if it fails to move you to tears regarding Romeo's tragic and unnecessary death. Similarly, Martin, Abend, Sedikides, and Green (1997) asked participants to grade happy and sad stories while in a happy or a sad mood. The participants were asked how effective the story had been in inducing the intended mood, how much they liked it and what grade they would award. Presumably because the first question drew their attention toward the story's ability to create the intended mood, participants evaluated happy stories more favourably in a happy as compared to sad mood, but sad stories received higher ratings in a sad mood. Apparently, participants reasoned that a supposedly sad story which fails to induce sad mood is not a good story. Thus, participants again inferred their evaluation from their mood. However, they took the circumstances into account in interpreting what their mood indicated.

In addition to directly influencing judgment, mood plays a second role in attitude formation and change inasfar as mood seems to influence the intensity with which incoming or retrieved information is processed. We will return to this in chapter 7.

Bodily states

Please do us a favour and read the following chapter smiling. Research suggests that you will like this chapter better if you do. People smile when they like something and frown when they dislike something, and we have seen in chapter 2 that recordings of minute movements of the smiling and frowning muscles can serve as measures of attitude. Apparently, the relationship between facial muscle contraction and evaluation also works the other way. Several studies suggest that the contraction of specific facial muscles produces corresponding affective reactions. James Laird (1974) told research participants that he was interested in measuring facial muscle activity and, apparently for this purpose, attached electrodes between participants' eyebrows, at the corners of their mouth and on their jaws. Participants were instructed that when a set of electrodes was touched they were to contract their muscles at these points. With this instruction Laird could induce participants to smile or frown without mentioning a specific emotion. While "smiling" or "frowning", participants also rated cartoons according to their funniness. As it turned out, they rated as funnier those cartoons that they had viewed while "smiling" as opposed to "frowning".

There are several explanations for this *facial feedback* effect. One is that people are aware that they are smiling or frowning and consciously interpret this reaction ("If I smile I must like it"). Indeed, many of these studies were criticised for the fact that participants knew that their facial muscle contractions represented a smile or a frown despite the fact that no emotion was mentioned in Laird's study. Thus, one cannot decide whether the effect on evaluative judgments is caused by (a) automatic bodily feedback from the muscle contraction per se, (b) people's knowledge that they are smiling and its attribution to the target of evaluation, or (c) demand effects, i.e. participants knowing and complying with how they think they were expected to behave.

Strack, Martin, and Stepper (1988) set out to clarify matters by manipulating the contraction of the zygomaticus (smiling) muscles in a truly unobtrusive fashion, thereby disguising the notion of smiling. Their study nicely illustrates that sometimes social psychologists come up with rather weird—and very clever—experiments to test their ideas. Students were asked to rate cartoons according to their funniness. To manipulate facial muscles, they were asked to hold the pen with which they indicated their ratings in their mouths. This was done under the pretext of testing the usability of answering scales for disabled persons who had lost the ability of using their hands. Some of the participants were asked to hold the pen between their teeth, without the lips touching it (Figure 5.5a). Others were asked to hold the pen between their lips but not with their teeth (Figure 5.5b). You may try both conditions to get a feeling for what participants in the study experienced. You may notice that the teeth condition facilitates a smile whereas the lips condition prevents a smile. However, would you have been aware of this as a participant in Strack and colleagues' study, given the elaborate cover story? Probably not. Nevertheless, participants in the original study rated the cartoons as funnier when they held the pen between their teeth than when they held it with their lips.

These findings rule out that the effect of facial muscle contractions on evaluative responses is either a demand effect or even requires conscious interpretation of one's facial expression, e.g. as a smile. They are more compatible with the assumption of a direct, nonconscious path from muscle contractions to evaluative responses. It has been suggested that the different facial contractions regulate the blood flow to the brain and thus affect the temperature in certain brain regions which in turn is linked to affective reactions (Zajonc, Murphy, & Inglehart, 1989).

(a)

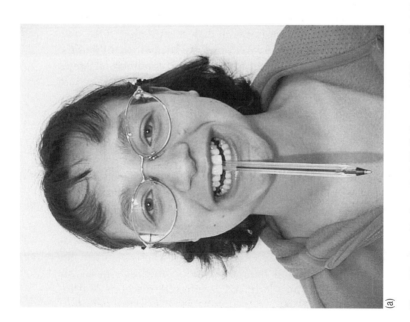

(b)

Figure 5.5. An unobtrusive method of facilitating versus inhibiting a smile: Asking participants to hold a pen between their teeth (a) or between their pursed lips (b), as in Strack, Martin, and Stepper (1988).

However, influences of muscle contractions on attitudes have also been observed for other body parts. Some researchers proposed that affective responses are conditioned responses to particular body movements. For example, when we reach out to grasp a desirable object, arm flexion is more closely coupled in time with the object's consumption than is arm extension. In the pain-flexor reflex, arm extension is temporarily coupled with the onset of an aversive stimulus whereas flexion is associated with its offset. As a consequence one may expect that flexion is associated with approach reactions and extension with avoidance reactions. To test this assumption, Cacioppo, Priester, and Berntson (1993) presented research participants with Chinese ideographs (characters of Chinese writing), which were originally neutral. While the stimuli were presented, participants either pressed their lower arm down on a table (extension) or up against the underside of a table (flexion). Later participants indicated how much they liked each ideograph. The results indicate that arm flexion while viewing increased liking compared to arm extension while viewing.

Intriguing results regarding the power of movements on later evaluations also come from another study. Participants listened to a persuasive communication (either supporting or contradicting participants' prior attitudes) presented via headphones (Wells & Petty, 1980). Under the pretext of testing the functionality of these headphones when walking or dancing, some participants were told to move their heads horizontally (shake), others vertically (nod) while listening to the tape. When participants were later asked about their attitudes, those who had nodded while listening to the message reported more favourable attitudes than those who had been shaking their heads. This effect of body movement was independent of their prior attitudes.

Although at present we lack a convincing theory that accounts for all the different phenomena—and indeed different phenomena may be based on different processes—there is a host of evidence showing that not only do attitudes influence physical reactions but that the reverse is also true: Proprioceptive feedback from both facial and body muscles may directly and unconsciously influence attitudes.

Standards

All evaluations are relative. One main reason for this relativity is that we evaluate stimuli with regard to a particular standard. Change the standard and you change the evaluation. This phenomenon is documented in a wide range of studies. For example, being exposed to highly attractive women decreased men's attractiveness ratings of other women, including their own wives (Kenrick, Gutierres, & Goldberg, 1989). Men and women rate themselves as less attractive after viewing a highly attractive person of the same sex (Brown, Novick, Lord, & Richards, 1992). Participants in one study rated themselves as more satisfied with their lives when they had previously heard a person suffering from kidney malfunction talk about his problems (Strack, Schwarz, Chassein, Kern, & Wagner, 1990).

This demonstrates that the standard of comparison induces a contrast effect. Similar to Gulliver, who appeared as a giant among the diminutive inhabitants of Lilliput but as a midget among the huge people of Brobdingnag,[4] a moderate stimulus will be evaluated more favourably against a negative rather than positive standard. In other words, the standard induces a shift in the target evaluation away from the standard. Depending on the valence of the standard of comparison used, our evaluations of a stimulus will vary. Needless to say that which standard we use depends on which information is (chronically and temporarily) accessible. In the above studies on attractiveness, participants were deliberately exposed to highly attractive standards. While you may have certain people with whom you usually compare your attractiveness, say your best friend or your class mates, thumbing through a fashion magazine may activate professional models as a standard of comparison, and you are likely to come away feeling fat and ugly. A glance around you at the supermarket or the bus may prove helpful in this situation by introducing less extreme standards of comparison.

How the judgment is put together: Context influences on information use

When we speak of attitude construction, it is not enough to list potential building blocks; we must also consider how these building blocks are put together. So far you may have inferred that whether or not a piece of information is used in judgment merely depends on whether it comes to mind at the time of judgment. But things are more complicated. Firstly, judgments do not only depend on *what* comes to mind but also on *how* it comes to mind. Secondly, the impact of a particular piece of information depends on how it is used (for a review see Martin, Strack, & Stapel, 2001). Identical information may result in opposite effects, depending on the situation. We will address both issues in the following sections.

Ease of retrieval may moderate the impact of retrieved content

From what you have learned so far you would conclude that judgments reflect the evaluative implications of the temporarily accessible information. For example, one would expect that individuals report more favourable attitudes toward an issue after they have retrieved favourable arguments as compared to unfavourable arguments. Indeed this assumption is central to most judgment models (for reviews see e.g. Higgins, 1989; Wilson & Hodges, 1992; Wyer & Srull, 1989; see also chapter 6). Recent research, however, shows that attitude judgments are not only influenced by *what* comes to mind, but also by *how* it comes to mind. More precisely, the *subjective experience* during the retrieval of information may moderate the relationship between the retrieved information and the attitude judgment. Numerous studies found that retrieved information had a stronger influence on judgment in the direction of its valence with a high **ease of retrieval**. In one study (Wänke, Bless, & Biller, 1996), participants recalled arguments either pro or contra public transportation. Half of the participants in each group were asked to recall three arguments, the other half were asked to recall seven arguments. Pretests had shown that recalling three arguments was experienced as easy whereas recalling seven arguments was experienced as difficult. If judgments merely depended on *what* comes to mind, one would expect more favourable attitudes toward public transportation after the retrieval of pro arguments. Indeed the retrieval of pro arguments led to more favourable attitudes than contra arguments. However, this occurred only in the three arguments condition, where the subjective experience of retrieval had been manipulated to feel "easy". In the seven arguments condition, where retrieval had been made to feel difficult, the impact of the valence of the retrieved information was weakened, as shown in Figure 5.6. Note that retrieving few arguments led to more attitude change than retrieving many arguments.

Other studies using the same paradigm found that self-reported assertiveness depended on the subjectively experienced ease with which examples of assertive behaviour could be recalled (Schwarz,

Figure 5.6. Ease of retrieval as information: Attitudes toward public transportation depend on whether participants had previously retrieved reasons for versus against public transportation and whether the task was easy (retrieve three reasons) versus difficult (retrieve seven reasons). (Data from Wänke et al., 1996.)

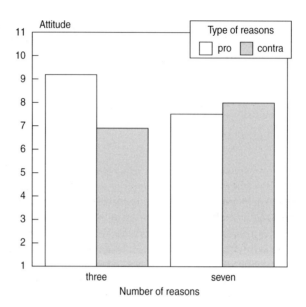

Bless, Strack, Klumpp, Rittenauer-Schatka, & Simons, 1991), that people's estimates of health risks depended on the ease with which risk-relevant behaviour could be retrieved (Raghubir & Menon, 1998), and that people liked Tony Blair better when the the retrieval of his positive characteristics was made to feel easy (Haddock, 2000). In an application to advertising, Wänke, Bohner, and Jurkowitsch (1997) presented business students with an advert that suggested retrieving reasons why to prefer a BMW over a Mercedes. When the advert suggested generating one reason to choose a BMW, which the students anticipated to be easy, they judged BMW more favourably than when the advert suggested generating ten reasons, which they anticipated to be difficult. Taken together, there is sufficient evidence to conclude that it is not only *what* comes to mind that determines the construction of judgments but also *how* it comes to mind.

The appropriateness of information may moderate its impact on judgment

Information needs to be accessible and applicable in order to be used, but this is not sufficient. Various cues can prompt individuals to use or not use a particular piece of information in a given situation.

Strack, Martin, and Schwarz (1988) summarised these cues under the term *appropriateness*—below you will find some examples. But what happens when information is deemed inappropriate? Do people simply disregard such information and ignore its implications? The data suggest otherwise. In a study on viewers' satisfaction with television (Bless & Wänke, 2000) participants were given a list of television shows and were asked to pick either two "typical" high quality shows or two "typical" low quality shows. The list contained a few good shows, a few bad shows and several shows that had been judged as neither good nor bad in pilot testing. Not too surprisingly, individuals who were asked to indicate good shows reported higher satisfaction with TV than those who had been asked to indicate poor shows. This merely reflects that different shows were temporarily accessible in the different conditions. However, in two additional conditions participants were asked to indicate "exceptionally good" or "exceptionally bad" shows. As it turned out, they indicated exactly the same good or bad shows, no matter if the instruction asked for "typical" or "exceptional" shows—after all they could only choose from the same list in either condition. But when asked later about their satisfaction with what is broadcast on TV, responses were quite different as Figure 5.7 reveals.

This example demonstrates that identical information can lead to either **assimilation** effects, which means that the judgment reflects the evaluative implications of the information, or **contrast** effects, which means that the judgment reflects a shift in the opposite direction. In the study just described, the information was seen as inappropriate to use for the judgment when it had been categorised as exceptional rather than typical. Typicality is one aspect of appro-priateness. Various other factors may indicate that the information is inappropriate to use (for a review see Schwarz & Bless, 1992). In sum, appropriate information is likely to elicit assimilation, but not all accessible information is necessarily appropriate information. Information may not really belong to the target of evaluation or may not be used for other reasons. Inappropriate information will not simply be ignored but may cause contrast.

Different models have suggested different processes how people deal with inappropriate information and why it elicits contrast. First, people may correct for any influence of inappropriate information, provided that they are motivated to judge accurately and have a subjective theory about how the information would influence their judgment (Strack, 1992; Wegener & Petty, 1997). For example they may be aware that selecting to rather good TV shows may have

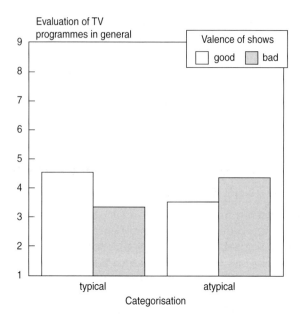

Figure 5.7. Appropriateness of information affects evaluations: General evaluation of the TV programme depending on whether participants had previously indicated in a list of TV shows which shows were typical and good, typical and bad, exceptional and good, or exceptional and bad. Importantly, within each condition of valence participants had picked the same shows as typical or exceptional (data from Bless & Wänke, 2000).

unduly biased their overall evaluation. In order to eliminate the bias they may "correct" their judgment and make it less positive. If they were accurate in their assessment of a potential inappropriate influence, then any effects of the accessible but inappropriate information should be wiped out. But often people overcorrect; then, contrast rather than no effect occurs.

Alternatively, once a person is aware that the use of the information is inappropriate, she may start anew searching for appropriate information in memory (Martin, 1986). This model is known as the set/reset model because it likens the process to the reset mode in a computer where all prior information is lost. A reset may induce contrast because when people are forced to look for different information, it is often the case that this information holds opposite implications than the one previously found. For example, when resetting they may try to retrieve other TV shows. If those are less positive than the examples previously picked the judgment will be less positive.

Third, information deemed inappropriate may be used as a standard of comparison. Respondents may think that compared to those exceptionally good shows the programme overall does not seem so appealing (for a more detailed account see Schwarz & Bless, 1992).

At present these accounts coexist and quite likely the different processes occur in different situations. What should be noted though is where the models converge. They all agree that accessible information may influence judgments in a direction opposite to its evaluative implications if the person making the judgment considers the use of the information inappropriate (for a review see Martin et al., 2001).

Attitudes as temporary constructions versus stable entities: A critical appraisal

In this chapter we documented a body of evidence showing that attitudes are highly susceptible to situational influences. All this would argue against the assumption that attitudes are concepts which are stored in memory and retrieved from there when needed. If existing attitudes were merely retrieved, situational influences should not be so pronounced. As we mentioned above, the fact that attitudes are so context dependent led many scholars to argue that attitudes are constructed on the spot based on the information that is accessible in the situation.

On the other hand, despite their malleability there is also evidence suggesting the stability of attitudes. We have already mentioned the Bennington studies, which testify to a relative stability of political attitudes over decades (Alwin et al., 1991). Moreover, we have seen that individuals are surprisingly fast in evaluating objects, while we would assume that construction processes take some time. How can we reconcile these two positions? Let us first look at each argument.

Obviously, and as we mentioned repeatedly, a retrieval model has difficulty explaining context influences. But can the construction hypothesis explain that sometimes attitudes persist over time throughout changing situational influences? We would argue that it can (see also Lord & Lepper, 1999; Schwarz & Bohner, 2001). Recall that the information which is accessible in any given situation depends on temporary factors only to some part. Some information, however, is chronically accessible and will come to mind independent of the situation. To the extent that attitudes are based on that part of the information which is chronically accessible, they will reflect stability; to the extent that they are based on temporarily accessible information they will reflect instability as long as the information accessible at time 1 and time 2 also has different evaluative implications.

Accordingly, if the proportion of chronically accessible information is large compared to the proportion of temporarily accessible information, stability of attitude will ensue. This is likely so for well-rehearsed attitudes. Moreover, one may expect that similar contexts activate similar information. So even temporarily accessible information may not vary much over time as long as the context in which the attitude is constructed does not change much. When people do not simply rely on what comes to mind easily but exhaust their memory they are likely to come up with the same information each time. Unless they learn new information this may also contribute to the stability of attitudes.

One study that investigated the stability of attitudes as a function of accessible information had participants report their attitudes toward several social groups (e.g. politicians, homosexuals etc.) at two occasions one month apart (Sia, Lord, Blessum, Ratcliff, & Lepper, 1997). In addition, participants also reported at each occasion the first exemplar for each category that came to mind. If we assume that in order to construct their attitudes toward those social groups participants retrieved exemplars of the groups (see above), participants who retrieve the same exemplar each time should show greater attitude consistency than those for whom different exemplars came to mind at the two occasions. The results clearly supported this hypothesis. Moreover, another study showed that individuals who retrieved the same exemplars across five weekly assessments were more resistant to attitude change following a counter-attitudinal message than individuals who named different exemplars (Sia, Thomas, Lord, & Lepper, 1998, as cited in Lord & Lepper, 1999). In sum, these data suggest that attitude stability is a function of the congruency of the information that comes to mind, and as such stability as well as context flexibility are compatible with the construction hypothesis.

At first glance, the speed with which attitudes can be expressed seems to be incompatible with the time-consuming construction processes described above. Note, however, that fast responses do not necessarily indicate that previously built attitudes are retrieved. New objects for which no previous attitudes exist may also elicit fast responses.

Can we completely discard the notion that attitudes are stored and can be retrieved from memory? This may well depend on how we define attitudes. According to a construction approach, information relevant to the attitude object will be retrieved and evaluated. For

computing one's attitude toward politicians one may think of different exemplars, one may retrieve further information about them, but
at some point in the hierarchy one needs to come up with an evaluation. Although it may be possible to form basic affective reactions on
the spot, research from evaluative conditioning and mere exposure
suggests that affective responses associated with objects may be
stored in memory and may be activated by the attitude object.
Conditioned evaluative responses reflect an association between an
attitude object and an evaluative response stored in memory. Such
basic affective reactions—established by conditioning or other
processes—may feed into more elaborate constructions; to this
extent they may only represent components of the final summary
evaluation. But under processing constraints they may well feed
directly into behaviour (see chapter 10).

In any case, is it reasonable to assume that attitudes function to
simplify the environment, but once formed would not be stored in
memory and retrieved when needed? If people were to construct their
attitudes anew each time they confront an attitude object, this would
hardly serve the goal of simplifying the environment. Moreover,
research from person memory suggests that people have better access
to summary judgments than to the information on which the judgment was based (Carlston, 1980). On the other hand, not taking the
respective situations into account may also prove dysfunctional. What
is needed is a framework that specifies the conditions under which
attitudes are retrieved from memory and under which they are
constructed in the respective situation. Based on such a framework
suggested by Kim and Shavitt (1993), we propose that a stored
attitude—provided that one exists—will be applied only if it is
accessible at the time of judgment. Otherwise new attitudes are
constructed. Provided that an "old" attitude is retrieved, the next
critical question is whether this attitude is adequate for the current
situation. For example, does it suit one's current goals or is there new
information that needs to be considered? Note, however, that
constructing a new attitude rather than simply relying on an old
one requires mental capacity and the motivation to expend the effort
necessary. Under time pressure, fatigue or other cognitive or motivational constraints, people may rely on old attitudes even though
they are not suitable. On the other hand, people may well have stored
an attitude but in the situation other information may be more
accessible, for example one's mood. As a consequence it is more likely
that a new attitude will be constructed rather than that the old one
will be retrieved.

This framework also allows for the retrieval and adaptation of old attitudes. The construction of attitudes does not necessarily imply construction from scratch. At this point, one may ask what happens to the old attitude once a new one is constructed. Wilson and his colleagues (2000) recently provided a "model of dual attitudes" whose complexity does not allow us to describe it in detail. We would merely like to mention two aspects. First, according to this model new and old attitudes may coexist, and be retrieved according to their accessibility and other factors. Second, old attitudes may eventually be replaced by new ones, but such replacement does not invariably happen.

Chapter summary

(1) When attitudes are constructed they are based on the currently accessible information. This includes chronically accessible information and temporarily accessible information. As a consequence attitudes are subject to contextual influences.

(2) The accessibility of information depends on its inherent qualities, its organisation in memory, the frequency of its activation and the recency of its activation. As the recency of activation varies between situations, different information may be retrieved for attitude construction at different times. Accordingly attitudes vary depending on the temporarily accessible information.

(3) The context may not only influence which information comes to mind but may also influence evaluations directly:
  (a) Attitude objects that further the attainment of a currently activated goal will be evaluated more favourably than attitude objects that hinder goal attainment.
  (b) People may use their current mood as an input to evaluating an attitude object.
  (c) People may use their bodily states as an input to evaluating an attitude object.
  (d) Evaluations are relative insofar as any evaluation depends on the standard used.

(4) Accessible information is not always used in the same manner. Accessible information that seems appropriate to use will elicit assimilation. When information is deemed inappropriate, contrast may occur. Moreover, information that comes to mind

easily has a stronger impact than information that is retrieved with difficulty.

(5) Attitudes based more on chronically accessible information than on temporarily accessible information will be more stable across contexts than attitudes that are primarily made up of temporarily accessible information. However, even attitudes primarily based on temporarily accessible information may reflect stability over time if the context remains stable over time.

(6) Once constructed, attitudes may be stored in memory and retrieved at a later point in time. However, even when stored attitudes exist, new attitudes may be constructed if old attitudes are either not accessible or not appropriate. The construction of a new attitude requires cognitive resources and the willingness to invest them. Despite the construction of new attitudes, previous attitudes may not be overwritten.

Exercises

(1) Attitude reports are highly dependent upon temporarily accessible information. What does this imply for attitude measurement, for example opinion polls etc.?

(2) Why is it that mood has a larger effect on the evaluation of new or complex stimuli rather than familiar or less complex ones?

(3) Body posture is sometimes used in psychotherapy to change people's affective responses. Can you imagine how?

(4) Suppose we knew all the information accessible to a person in a given situation. Could we exactly predict that person's attitude?

Notes

(1) More recently, social psychologists have imported a more complex variant of network models from cognitive psychology, so-called connectionist or parallel-distributed processing networks. Space does not permit us to introduce this approach in any detail. Interested readers find an accessible introduction in Smith (1996). For an application to attitudes and persuasion, see Smith and DeCoster (2000).

(2) "Not true", you may say, "some attitudes hardly vary". We will discuss this issue below when we turn to evaluating the construction hypothesis.

(3) A heuristic may be defined as a mental shortcut. Rather than systematically processing all potentially relevant information, people often use simple rules of thumb. We will extend this issue in chapters 6 and 7.

(4) We borrowed the Gulliver analogy from Brown et al. (1992).

Further reading

For reviews of the construction perspective:

Schwarz, N., & Bohner, G. (2001). The construction of attitudes. In A. Tesser & N. Schwarz (Eds.), *Blackwell handbook of social psychology: Vol. 1. Intraindividual processes* (pp. 436–457). Oxford, UK: Blackwell.

Tesser, A., & Martin, L. L. (1996). The psychology of evaluation. In E. T. Higgins & A. W. Kruglanski (Eds.), *Social psychology: Handbook of basic principles* (pp. 400–432). New York: Guilford.

Wilson, T. D., & Hodges, S. D. (1992). Attitudes as temporary constructions. In L. Martin & A. Tesser (Eds.), *The construction of social judgments* (pp. 37–65). Hillsdale, NJ: Lawrence Erlbaum Associates Inc.

A new perspective on attitudes and attitude change, based on the assumption that more than one evaluation of an object may be stored simultaneously:

Wilson, T. D., Lindsey, S., & Schooler, T. Y. (2000). A model of dual attitudes. *Psychological Review, 107,* 101–126.

Persuasion: I. From effortless judgments to complex processing

6

In chapter 4 you read about a study by Gorn showing that when a product was paired with good music, liking for it increased. But what would be more effective in changing consumers' attitudes: good music or convincing arguments? Gorn (1982) found that it depends. When simply *exposed* to adverts, recipients were more influenced by those adverts that featured good music but no information about the product. However, when recipients *expected to make a decision*, an informative advert proved more persuasive than merely playing good music. This chapter and the following one will give a detailed account of the persuasion processes that lie behind this observation.

Persuasion research addresses the questions how attitudes are formed and changed as a result of information processing, usually in response to messages about the attitude object. From the "attitudes as construals" perspective outlined in chapter 5, we can conceive of persuasion research as studying a particular subset of the situational conditions that give rise to the construal of attitude judgments. And from that perspective, whether we speak of attitude change or attitude formation does not really matter (see Schwarz & Bohner, 2001). In fact, persuasion studies often feature messages on novel or fictitious issues. This is done to eliminate any prior information that participants may have about an attitude object, so as to study the effects of situational variables in a more controlled fashion. And even though the bulk of persuasion research is more or less explicitly grounded in the "file drawer" view on attitudes, which characterises attitudes as "relatively enduring" (e.g. Petty et al., 1994, p. 70), proponents of this view also acknowledge that attitudes do change as people interact with their social environment. Thus, understanding the dynamics of persuasion is useful for basic researchers who try to explain social information processing, no matter which conceptualisation of attitude they endorse. It is vital also for practitioners in business, health, law, marketing or politics, who are interested in effective strategies of influencing people's attitudes and behaviour.

Attitude change in response to persuasive appeals has been studied from the angle of interpersonal communication within small-group settings and from an intergroup perspective (see the forthcoming volumes in this series on Social Influence and Intergroup Relations). Most studies, however, focused on persuasion processes at the level of the individual message recipient (for overviews see Chaiken, Wood, & Eagly, 1996; Petty & Wegener, 1998a). This may not be surprising, as unilateral persuasion attempts with clearly identifiable message source and recipient are almost omnipresent in our "age of advertising" (McGuire, 1985). It is this level of analysis that we emphasise in the present chapter.

Approaches to persuasion can be ordered according to the amount of cognitive effort involved in the change processes that they focus on (Petty & Cacioppo, 1981). In preceding chapters we have already discussed a number of processes influencing attitudes that require little cognitive effort, along with their associated theories: conditioning, mood as information, mere exposure, facial and bodily feedback. In this chapter, we will add to this list a few more low-effort processes that are particularly relevant to the processing of messages about an attitude object. We will then proceed to discussing persuasion approaches based on more extensive forms of processing. In chapter 7, we will discuss dual-processing models of persuasion that incorporate and integrate both low and high effort processing modes.

Persuasion processes that require little cognitive effort

The effects of mood, facial feedback and bodily states described in chapter 5 may be treated as special cases of individuals' relying on subjective experiences in attitude formation. Other examples include subjective experiences that accompany the processing of external information and codetermine the outcome of such processing.

Subjective experiences

One factor that plays an important role in persuasion is the *experienced ease* with which information can be retrieved, generated or processed to judge its evidential quality (Howard, 1997; Wänke et al., 1996, 1997). Information that can be generated and processed easily is likely to be judged as more diagnostic or valid than information that can be processed only with difficulty. For example, Howard (1997) asked students to listen to adverts that were embedded in a radio programme; depending on experimental condition, some arguments in the adverts were presented either in the form of familiar idiomatic phrases (e.g. "Don't put all your eggs in one basket") or in more literal form ("Don't risk everything on a single venture"). Under suboptimal processing conditions (e.g. when participants were distracted), students who heard the familiar phrases were more persuaded by the adverts than were students who heard the standard phrases. This seems to indicate that greater ease of processing can enhance persuasion.

While the effect just described is due to the ease with which externally presented arguments can be processed, we have already seen that the principle of **ease of processing** can affect persuasion even when no evidence is presented at all. Remember the study by Wänke and her colleagues (1997), who exposed students to a printed advertisement that suggested generating either one reason or ten reasons for choosing a BMW over a Mercedes. Students confronted with the one-reason advert anticipated generating the requested reason to be easy and judged BMW more favourably than students to whom the advert suggested generating ten reasons, which they anticipated to be difficult. Importantly, this result was independent of whether participants actually generated any reasons at all; just the *anticipated experience* of ease or difficulty seemed to be sufficient in changing the advert's persuasive effect.

Heuristic processing

The use of feelings and other subjective experiences may further be subsumed under the category of heuristic processing (e.g. Chen & Chaiken, 1999). Heuristics are simple decision rules that can be applied to a judgment. Indeed, Schwarz and Clore (1988) described the use of one's mood as information as a "how do I feel about it?" heuristic. Similarly, using experienced ease of processing may entail implicit heuristic inferences like "if generating this argument feels easy, it must be valid".

While the influence of internal states may thus be reconstructed as heuristic processing, this term was initially used to describe the application of decision rules based on *external cues* (Chaiken, 1987; Chaiken, Liberman, & Eagly, 1989). Typical examples for such persuasion cues are a message source's *expertise* and *likeability*, or the social *consensus* that is perceived for a certain attitudinal position. Thus, people may use the heuristics "experts' statements are valid", "I agree with people I like" or "the majority is usually right", which leads them to agree with experts, likeable people and majorities more than with nonexperts, dislikeable people and minorities. To do so, they must have an *applicable* heuristic available (i.e. stored in memory), and the heuristic needs to be *accessible* at the time a judgment is required, as well as subjectively *reliable* (Chaiken et al., 1989).

As with conditioning and the use of feelings as information, an individual need not be aware that she is applying a heuristic in generating an attitude judgment. Heuristics are influential even in situations where a person has little motivation or ability to engage in more extensive forms of processing (see below). Their use is guided by the "principle of least cognitive effort" (Allport, 1954; see Bohner, Moskowitz, & Chaiken, 1995).

The operation of a persuasion heuristic as well as the principle of accessibility was highlighted in experiments by Chaiken and Eagly (1983). These researchers manipulated a communicator's likeability by having participants read an interview in which the communicator either praised or ridiculed students at the participants' university. Then the communicator's message on a campus issue was presented. The modality of presentation was also varied: Depending on condition, the message was written, audiotaped or videotaped. Chaiken and Eagly assumed that the vocal and visual cues available to students in the audiotaped and videotaped versions would render the communicator's likeability more salient, and thus the likeability heuristic more accessible, as compared to the written version, where such communicator cues were not present. Indeed the results showed that in the two conditions with broadcast messages, students' attitudes were more influenced by the communicator's likeability than in the written condition.

The principle of cue reliability is exemplified in a study that Chaiken (1987, pp. 27–28) reported. In a first phase of that study, participants memorised statements that were designed to either strengthen or undermine the perceived reliability of the liking-agreement heuristic (e.g. "when people want good advice, they go to their friends" versus "best friends do not necessarily make the best advisors"). Participants in a control condition memorised unrelated statements. Later all participants took part in an apparently unrelated

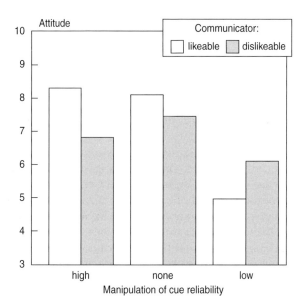

Figure 6.1. Effects of reliability of the liking-agreement rule and of communicator likeability on the attitudes of recipients low in need for cognition (data from Chaiken, 1987).

experiment in which either a likeable or a dislikeable communicator argued that people should reduce their sleep time. Participants' **need for cognition (NFC)**, a motivational disposition to think carefully (see chapter 7), was also assessed. Those participants low in NFC showed an effect of the reliability manipulation. In the high reliability condition, their attitudes toward reduced sleep time were more influenced by the likeable than by the dislikeable communicator; this effect of communicator likeability was less pronounced in the control condition; and in the low reliability condition, where the utility of the likeability rule had been negated, the effect was slightly reversed (see Figure 6.1). High NFC participants were generally unaffected by the communicator's likeability, presumably because they engaged in more extensive processing of the presented arguments, which attenuated any impact of the heuristic.

These and many other findings attest to the validity of the heuristic model of persuasion (Chaiken, 1987; for further discussion of the accessibility and reliability principles, see Eagly & Chaiken, 1993, pp. 333–336). The last study also shows that the operation of heuristics can usually be detected most clearly at low levels of processing effort. We will have to say more about this point in chapter 7. But first we will turn to approaches that focused on more effortful persuasion processes.

Persuasion through more effortful processing

Attribution

Some persuasion research was inspired by **attribution theory** (for a review, see Fincham & Hewstone, 2001). Attributional reasoning differs from heuristic processing in that it can be characterised as more "thoughtful"; an aspect similar to heuristic processing, however, is that its informational input are mainly contextual cues such as the message source or the situation in which the message is delivered. Core assumptions of the attributional approach to persuasion are that a message recipient may infer different reasons *why* a communicator presents a certain position, and that these causal inferences mediate persuasion. As Kelley (1967) noted, the recipient may conclude that a communicator's message accurately reflects external reality; in that case it is regarded valid and likely to be accepted. However, often there are other plausible causes for a communicator's statement. It may be attributed to characteristics of the communicator (her role, goals, desires etc.), to the particular situation or to the audience at which the message is targeted—including the recipient himself. Each of these attributions would lessen a statement's persuasive impact. For attitude change to occur, it is crucial that the statement be attributed to external reality. For example, we would be more likely to accept the statement that a certain product offers high quality if this statement comes from an independent testing agency rather than from the company marketing the product.

Various studies have supported this principle. Eagly, Wood, and Chaiken (1978) found that a communicator who advocated a pro-environmental policy was more likely to change recipients' attitude when his background suggested a pro-business affiliation (or when his audience were described as business people) than when he was portrayed as someone with pro-environment affiliations (or when his audience were characterised as environmentalists; see also Wood & Eagly, 1981). Thus, when either the communicator's vested interest or his concern to please the audience constituted plausible alternative reasons for the communicator's statements, external reality was *discounted* as a potential cause for his behaviour. Conversely, when the communicator's position opposed what would be expected based on his own interest or his audience, external reality was inferred with even greater confidence as the cause for the communicator's behaviour—an augmentation effect (see Fincham & Hewstone, 2001; Kelley, 1972).

Similar attribution principles seem to operate in minority influence. Research suggests that influence may be reduced via discounting if a communicator argues for a position that serves the interests of a social minority he belongs to, e.g. a gay person arguing for promoting gay rights (see Maass, Clark, & Haberkorn, 1982; for further studies applying attribution principles to minority and majority persuasion, see Bohner, Erb, Reinhard, & Frank, 1996; Bohner, Frank, & Erb, 1998; Moskowitz, 1996; Mugny & Papastamou, 1980).

On the applied side, advertisers face the problem that their marketing messages can be easily discounted by consumers, who perceive them as obviously motivated by the advertiser's self-interest. Interestingly, clever advertisers sometimes try to exploit the same attributional principle to their advantage by admitting some shortcoming of their product. They hope that this unexpected revelation will enhance the perceived validity of the overall message, which of course claims that the product is good. There is a tradeoff, however, between this enhancing effect of two-sided messages and the potential decrease in persuasion that may be caused by revealing the shortcoming at all. Therefore, if negative aspects are mentioned in adverts, they usually pertain to relatively unimportant aspects of the product. To illustrate this, Figure 6.2 shows two-sided and one-sided versions of a print advert for a restaurant that were used in research by Einwiller et al. (1997). In this study, the two-sided advert led to enhanced perceptions of communicator credibility, and ultimately to more positive attitudes toward the restaurant, than its one-sided counterpart (for more empirical evidence and a discussion of two-sided advertising strategies, see Pechmann, 1992). In sum, studies in the areas of persuasion, social influence and consumer advertising highlight the importance of attribution principles for persuasion, and the (dis)confirmation of expectancies seems to play an important role in attribution-mediated attitude change.

Processing of message content

The importance of effortful processing of message content was first emphasised by Hovland and his colleagues at Yale University in their **message-learning approach** to persuasion (Hovland, Janis, & Kelley, 1953). This approach does not represent a unitary theory; rather, it can be understood as an eclectic set of working assumptions, influenced

(a)

Ristorante *Fresco Francesco*

Fresco Francesco offers . . .

. . . many advantages . . .

Our home-made pasta and other dishes are prepared by Francesco from fresh ingredients, preserving the food's natural flavour. Therefore, our dishes are a rare treat.

Our hearty salads, also made only from fresh ingredients, are uniquely refined by Francesco's special dressing. The culinary experience is completed by a selection of five Italian wines.

You can enjoy all these delicacies in a cosy atmosphere and at reasonable prices.

. . . and only a few disadvantages . . .

Fresco Francesco's menu contains only a small selection of dishes which varies with the seasonal supply. Also, we cannot accommodate groups of more than four persons, because our guest rooms are not appropriate for larger groups.

by learning theory and other contemporary theoretical perspectives. Its proponents assumed that the learning and recall of message content mediates attitude change. Their research focused on various elements of the persuasion setting that would affect message learning. Following the guiding question "Who says what to whom through what channel with what effect?" (Smith, Lasswell, & Casey, 1946), the classes of independent variables examined by the Yale group were the message source (e.g. its expertise or trustworthiness), the message (e.g. its length and structure), recipient characteristics (e.g. self-esteem, intelligence), and the channel (or medium) of the communication (e.g. written versus spoken). Internal mediating processes that were studied include attention to the message, comprehension of

(b)   **Ristorante *Fresco Francesco***

Fresco Francesco offers . . .

   . . . many advantages . . .

Our home-made pasta and other dishes are prepared by Francesco from fresh ingredients, preserving the food's natural flavour. Therefore, our dishes are a rare treat.

Our hearty salads, also made only from fresh ingredients, are uniquely refined by Francesco's special dressing. The culinary experience is completed by a selection of five Italian wines.

You can enjoy all these delicacies in a cosy atmosphere and at reasonable prices.

its content, rehearsal of arguments, and yielding to the message position. The dependent variables assessed were changes in beliefs, attitudes and behaviour.

By structuring the persuasion process in such a way and by examining a host of interesting phenomena, the message-learning approach had a profound impact on later generations of persuasion research (for an overview of findings, see Petty & Cacioppo, 1981, chapter 3). However, due to its lack of a unifying theory, it accumulated ad hoc explanations for a variety of effects, which often conflicted with each other and could hardly be meaningfully integrated. (We will report some examples for the Yale group's research below in this section under the subheadings Role-playing and Inoculation.) Summarising the state of persuasion research in the late 1970s, Petty and Cacioppo (1986a, p. 2) noted that "existing literature supported the view that nearly every independent variable studied increased persuasion in some situations, had no effect in others, and decreased persuasion in still other contexts".

One major tenet of the message-learning approach was that attention to and comprehension (= reception) of a message would mediate persuasion. This was developed into a more comprehensive information-processing approach by McGuire (1969, 1985). As reception was assumed to be reflected in the recall of message content, high correlations of message recall and attitude change should be the rule. Empirically, however, memory for message content turned out to be a poor and inconsistent predictor of persuasion (see chapter 6 of Eagly & Chaiken, 1993, for a review).

Another general mechanism emphasised by the Yale group, also reflecting its origins in learning theory, was that the acceptance of the recommendations contained in a persuasive communication would be facilitated by *incentives* in the persuasion setting (e.g. a trustworthy communicator). The incentive concept was very loosely defined, however, and its presumed mediating role was never directly tested.

Active thought

Given the equivocal evidence for message learning as a mediator of attitude change, researchers turned their attention to other cognitive mediators of attitude change, which emphasised not the passive reception but the active transformation, elaboration and generation of arguments. Research in this direction includes the study of *role-playing* as a persuasion technique (Janis & King, 1954; King & Janis, 1956), McGuire's work on the effects of *forewarning* (McGuire & Papageorgis, 1962) and "**inoculation**" (McGuire, 1964), and the study of "**mere thought**" (Tesser, 1978). Because the idiosyncratic cognitive activity of the individual is central to these approaches, Petty and Cacioppo (1981) labelled them "self-persuasion approaches".

Role-playing

Janis and King (1954) asked participants to generate and present arguments on an issue, while other participants were instructed to listen to the same arguments. They found that participants who had actively generated arguments showed greater attitude change in the direction of these arguments than participants who merely listened to the arguments. King and Janis (1956) further showed that the crucial process mediating attitude change in role-playing was the active improvisation of arguments: Students who improvised a speech based on arguments they had previously read showed greater attitude change than others who had read externally generated arguments either into a tape recorder or silently to themselves. A process that

Figure 6.3. The effectiveness of self-generated arguments is sometimes exploited in marketing. Copyright © H. Rogers/ TRIP

seems to be at the core of this effect is what Janis (1959) called the biased scanning of evidence on one side of the issue in preparing one's speech (see also Figure 6.3).

In the light of more recent research, a caveat is in place here: Biased scanning should lead to attitude change in the direction of the position advocated mainly if generating the speech feels subjectively easy; if it is too difficult to come up with improvised arguments, the improvisation technique should backfire (Wänke et al., 1996; see Subjective experiences in the previous section). Alternative theoretical explanations why generating a message may lead to attitude change will be discussed in chapter 8.

Forewarning

McGuire and Papageorgis (1962) proposed that *forewarning* recipients of the persuasive intent of a message might help them resist persuasion by stimulating the generation of counterarguments. Various studies have supported this hypothesis. They have also shown that forewarning is only effective if there is a time delay between warning and message which enables recipients to actively generate counterarguments (e.g. Hass & Grady, 1975). Petty and Cacioppo (1977) provided direct evidence that forewarning indeed stimulated the generation of counterarguments; these authors also showed that simply instructing people to think about the issue in question was as effective as a warning in stimulating counterarguing and resistance.

Inoculation

McGuire's (1964) *inoculation theory*, with its focus on resistance to persuasion, also shed some light on the role of active thought processes. This approach was inspired by the Yale group's research on the effects of two-sided versus one-sided messages. For example, Lumsdaine and Janis (1953) observed that a message containing arguments both for and against its conclusion, conferred greater resistance to counterpersuasion than a one-sided message, which contained only arguments in favour of its conclusion. To explain this difference, they speculated that presenting the conclusion of a message in a context where opposing arguments are in evidence would "inoculate" the recipient against future attacks on that conclusion (p. 318). This biological analogy was later elaborated by McGuire (1964). A person's biological immune system can be stimulated to develop resistance against a virus by carefully applying a weak dosage of the virus. McGuire reasoned that, similarly, people's cognitive system might be immunised against a full-scale "attack" of counterattitudinal arguments by exposing them to a weak version of a counterattitudinal message.

Extending the biological metaphor, McGuire assumed that inoculation would be particularly useful in the case of beliefs that were maintained in a "germ-free" ideological environment. His inoculation studies dealt exclusively with cultural "truisms", beliefs so widely held at the time that people were unprepared and unpractised in defending them. Examples are "Mental illness is not contagious" or "Everyone should get a yearly chest X-ray to detect any signs of TB at an early stage"[1] (McGuire, 1964, p. 201). In a study by McGuire and Papageorgis (1961), participants reported their agreement with four truisms after three of these truisms had been attacked in counterattitudinal messages. Some days earlier, they had received treatments to help them resist two of these messages: an "inoculation" or "refutational defence" treatment in which counterarguments had been presented and subsequently refuted, and a "supportive defence" treatment in which arguments in favour of the truism had been presented. No defence for the third truism had been provided, and

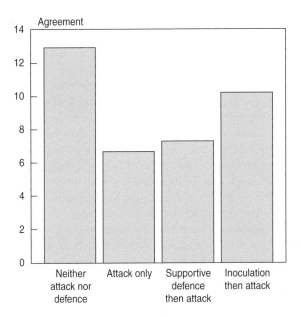

Figure 6.4. Agreement with truisms after inoculation and supportive treatments (data from McGuire & Papageorgis, 1961; adapted from a table presented by McGuire, 1964).

the fourth truism was neither defended nor subsequently attacked.[2] The results (see Figure 6.4) showed that post-message agreement was strongly affected by the counterattitudinal attack when no defence treatment had been given. Compared to the attack-only condition, a good deal of resistance was conveyed by the inoculation treatment, whereas beliefs in the supportive defence condition did not differ significantly from those in the attack-only condition.

How much did active issue-related thinking contribute to the effectiveness of inoculation? Although McGuire's research programme did not emphasise cognitive mediators as much as did later studies, two sets of findings provide suggestive evidence in this regard. Firstly, additional research addressed the question if an active form of inoculation, where participants themselves generate refutations of counterarguments, might be more effective than a passive form, where participants are simply exposed to counterarguments and refutations (McGuire, 1964). Although passive defences were superior when the attacking message followed very shortly, active defences were especially effective when there was some delay (e.g. one week) between inoculation and attack. This suggests that active defences motivated individuals to think about further arguments that could be used to bolster their truisms in the time between defence and attack. Secondly, some studies (e.g. Papageorgis & McGuire,

1961) varied the content of the inoculation treatment by either refuting exactly those counterarguments that would later be presented in the attack ("refutational-same") or refuting different counterarguments that would not be presented in the attack ("refutational-different"). The results generally showed that both types of inoculation were about equally effective. This again seems to indicate that more active thought processes may be at the core of the effect, rather than a simple reliance on externally provided information (in which case the refutational-same defence would have been superior to the refutational-different defence).

McGuire assumed that both cognitive and motivational factors were responsible for this set of findings. The cognitive aspect is that people are poorly equipped to defend truisms, as they are not practised in doing so and have little informational resources available for this task. This might explain why any effects of active defences take considerable time to unfold. At the same time, people are initially unmotivated to defend their truisms because these have never been attacked and seem self-evident. An inoculation treatment, and perhaps especially its active version, helps to overcome this motivational deficit. Inoculation theory has inspired a relatively large amount of research. It has been extended to more controversial issues other than truisms, and its predictions have been supported in at least some of those independent tests; treatments based on inoculation theory have also been successfully applied in health education programmes (see Eagly & Chaiken, 1993, pp. 565–566).

Mere thought

As a final approach highlighting the importance of active thought processes, we consider work by Tesser (1978) on the **mere thought effect**. Tesser's research revealed that even in the absence of a persuasive message, simply thinking about an attitude object can lead to more extreme attitudes. This happens because people have "naive theories" or schemata which make some attributes of an object more salient and facilitate inferences regarding related attributes. Thus schemata have a directive influence on thoughts and often produce changes in beliefs toward greater schematic consistency. As attitudes are a function of a person's beliefs, a weak initial attitude can change toward an extreme attitude under the guidance of mere thinking.

For example, Sadler and Tesser (1973) introduced research participants to a likeable or dislikeable "partner" (in fact, a tape recording). Then some participants were asked to think about their partner, while others performed a distraction task. Finally, all participants rated their partner on various scales and wrote down their thoughts about him. Compared to distracted participants, nondistracted participants evaluated the likeable partner more favourably and listed more positive thoughts about him, but rated the dislikeable partner more negatively and listed more negative thoughts about him. Further research showed that these extremisation effects are contingent upon the presence of an initial schema, e.g. a moderately positive or negative initial attitude (see Tesser, 1978).

The cognitive response approach

The accumulating evidence for the importance of active thought processes in both attitude change and resistance to change, combined with the Yale researchers' focus on message processing as a key to understanding persuasion, led to the formulation of the **cognitive response approach** to persuasion (Greenwald, 1968; Petty, Ostrom, & Brock, 1981). Its assumptions may be summarised as follows:

(1) Individuals who are exposed to a persuasive message actively relate the content of this message to their issue-relevant knowledge and pre-existing attitude toward the message topic, thereby generating new thoughts or **cognitive responses**.
(2) Attitude change is mediated by these cognitive responses.
(3) The extent and direction of attitude change are a function of the cognitive responses' valence in relation to the message's content and position. In this sense, cognitive responses can be (a) favourable, (b) unfavourable or (c) neutral.
(4) The greater the proportion of favourable responses and the smaller the proportion of unfavourable responses evoked by a message, the greater the attitude change in the direction advocated by the message should be.

The focus of the cognitive response approach, then, is on active, effortful processing (guided by the "naive scientist" metaphor of human information processing; Fiske & Taylor, 1991). To test the assumptions concerning the mediational role of cognitive responses in persuasion, a new methodology was introduced, the *thought-listing technique* (Brock, 1967; Cacioppo, Harkins, & Petty, 1981; Greenwald, 1968): Research participants are asked to list within a given time, say three minutes, any thoughts that have come to mind while they read or heard a persuasive message. These thoughts are later content-analysed and categorised according to their favourability (or other criteria; see Petty and Cacioppo, 1986a, pp. 38–40). For example, students who listened to a message that advocates the fluoridation of drinking water may list thoughts like: "The arguments concerning the reduction of tooth decay were convincing" (a favourable thought); "I don't want more chemicals in my drinking water" (an unfavourable thought); "I still need to do this reading assignment" (an irrelevant thought).

To predict the impact that a variable will have on persuasion, it is crucial to know how this variable will affect cognitive responding to the message. Any factor that increases the likelihood of counter-arguing (e.g. forewarning) should decrease persuasion, any factor that increases the likelihood of favourable responses should increase persuasion. Furthermore, if a person's dominant cognitive responses to a message can be expected to be favourable (e.g. a political party member listening to a speech of the party leader), then any factor reducing the overall amount of processing should decrease persuasion, but the opposite should hold if a person's responses can be expected to be unfavourable. As these assumptions have been incorporated and further developed in contemporary **dual-processing models of persuasion**, we will discuss related findings in the next chapter.

Chapter summary

(1) Persuasion theories deal with attitude change in reaction to messages about an attitude object. They may be ordered according to the cognitive effort involved in the processes they emphasise.

(2) Low-effort persuasion processes include affective and other subjective experiences as well as the application of heuristics.

(3) Heuristics are simple inference rules linking a heuristic cue (e.g. source expertise) to an evaluative conclusion (e.g. agreement). Heuristic processing requires the presence of a cue and the accessibility of a heuristic that is subjectively applicable and reliable.

(4) A more effortful persuasion process is attributional reasoning. It involves recipients trying to determine *why* a certain position is

forwarded. They change their attitude toward the position advocated to the extent that they infer external reality as the cause, rather than other factors (e.g. the communicator's self-interest).

(5) Effortful processing of message content was first highlighted by the message-learning approach. Although the learning of message arguments turned out to be a poor predictor of attitude change, this approach stimulated structured research efforts by differentiating components of the persuasion setting (source, message, channel and recipient factors), cognitive mediators (e.g. attention, comprehension, yielding) and outcome variables (e.g. adoption of new beliefs, attitude change).

(6) Various approaches (work on role-playing, forewarning, inoculation and mere thought) identified active thought processes as mediators of attitude change. Generating and improvising arguments produces greater attitude change than passively listening to the same arguments. Being forewarned about the persuasive intent of a message confers resistance to persuasion by prompting active counterarguing. McGuire showed that attitudes can be "inoculated" against subsequent persuasive attacks by applying a weak version of the attack, which seems to stimulate the active generation of issue-related thoughts and counterarguments. Tesser's work showed that mere thinking about an attitude object, if guided by an attitude schema, can lead to a more extreme attitude.

(7) According to the cognitive response approach, attitude change is mediated by the favourability of an individual's cognitive responses to a message. These responses are assessed by asking recipients to list the thoughts that came to mind while exposed to the message.

Exercises

(1) Sketch applications of "ease of processing" effects in advertising and political campaigning.

(2) Find examples for heuristic processing in everyday judgments.

(3) An editorial that is sponsored by the tobacco industry argues that smoking cigarettes does not lead to addiction. Why might this be ineffective in persuading the readers? What could the tobacco people do to enhance the editorial's effectiveness?

(4) Illustrate the elements of persuasion according to the message learning approach by providing examples for each.
(5) What is the unique methodological contribution of the cognitive response approach to persuasion?

Notes

(1) The second example, certainly not a truism any more, illustrates how much the particular cognitive *content* related to psychological hypotheses may depend on the socio-historic context. Still, the *concept* of truisms makes as much sense today as it did 40 years ago (and may even be applied to abstract values; see Maio & Olson, 1998), but in studying it today we would have to consider different content areas.
(2) The particular topics in each of the four conditions were counterbalanced across participants.

Further reading

A comprehensive review of the persuasion approaches discussed in this chapter (and additional theories) is presented in:

Eagly, A. H., & Chaiken, S. (1993). *The psychology of attitudes*. Fort Worth, TX: Harcourt Brace Jovanovich.

An excellent review of research guided by the message-learning approach can be found in chapter 3 of:

Petty, R. E., & Cacioppo, J. T. (1981). *Attitudes and persuasion: Classic and contemporary approaches*. Dubuque, IA: Brown.

Persuasion: II. The dual-processing approach 7

Most persuasion research since the mid-1980s has been based on theories that incorporate the assumptions of the cognitive response approach about active, effortful processing, but also include hypotheses about persuasion effects based on effortless processing. These *dual-processing theories* are the **elaboration likelihood model** (ELM; Petty & Cacioppo, 1986a,b; Petty & Wegener, 1999) and the *heuristic-systematic model* (HSM; Bohner et al., 1995; Chaiken, 1987; Chaiken et al., 1989; Chen & Chaiken, 1999). Both have been developed into comprehensive frameworks of persuasion (and beyond; see Chaiken et al., 1989; Chen & Chaiken, 1999), and both distinguish two prototypical modes of persuasion that form the poles of a continuum of processing effort. In this chapter, we present and critically compare both models and then briefly introduce a recently proposed single-process alternative.

The elaboration likelihood model

In the ELM, the two processing modes are called the *central route*, in which persuasion is mediated by effortful scrutiny of message arguments and other relevant information, and the *peripheral route*, which features the influence of peripheral cues (i.e. noncontent aspects like the message source) and includes a variety of less effortful mechanisms such as conditioning, social identification and the use of heuristics (see Figure 7.1 for an illustration). The seven basic postulates of the ELM (Petty & Cacioppo, 1986a,b) are presented in Table 7.1.

Figure 7.1. Advertisers sometimes use a dual strategy to sell a product by providing both extensive detail information and more simple cues. Copyright © The Advertising Archives.

TABLE 7.1

The seven postulates of the elaboration likelihood model (adapted from Petty & Cacioppo, 1986a)

(1) *Underlying motivation*: People are motivated to hold correct attitudes.

(2) *Variations in elaboration*: Although people want to hold correct attitudes, the amount and nature of issue-relevant elaboration in which they are willing or able to engage to evaluate a message vary with individual and situational factors.

(3) *How variables affect persuasion*: Variables can affect the amount and direction of attitude change by (a) serving as persuasive arguments, (b) serving as peripheral cues and/or (c) affecting the extent or direction of issue and argument elaboration.

(4) *Objective elaboration*: Variables affecting motivation and/or ability to process a message in an objective manner can do so by either enhancing or reducing argument scrutiny.

(5) *Biased elaboration*: Variables affecting message processing in a biased manner can produce either a positive (favourable) or a negative (unfavourable) motivational and/or ability bias to issue-relevant thoughts.

(6) *Tradeoff between argument elaboration and peripheral cues*: As motivation and/or ability to process arguments is decreased, peripheral cues become relatively more important determinants of persuasion. Conversely, as argument scrutiny is increased, peripheral cues become relatively less important determinants of persuasion.

(7) *Consequences of elaboration*: Attitude change that results mostly from processing issue-relevant arguments (central route) will show greater temporal persistence, greater prediction of behaviour and greater resistance to counterpersuasion than attitude change that results mostly from processing peripheral cues.

Determinants of the route to persuasion

The ELM assumes that people are generally motivated to hold "correct" attitudes (postulate 1 in Table 7.1). Petty and Cacioppo (1986a) use this term in a broad functional sense, equating correctness with adaptive utility (see "Knowledge organisation and regulating approach and avoidance" in chapter 1). They acknowledge that there cannot be any absolute standard of correctness; rather, people are thought to be capable of using various standards (e.g. social comparisons) for judging the adaptiveness of their attitudes (p. 6).

As people have limited time and resources in their striving for valid attitudes, they cannot elaborate the details of every persuasive message they encounter—thus, peripheral-route processes should be the default (cf. the "cognitive miser" metaphor; Taylor, 1981). Generally, elaboration likelihood varies along a continuum and is a

Figure 7.2. Interplay of processing modes in the ELM. Although central and peripheral processes may co-occur at intermediate levels of elaboration likelihood, there is a tradeoff in their assumed impact on attitudes. As the effect of central-route processing increases, the effect of peripheral processes decreases.

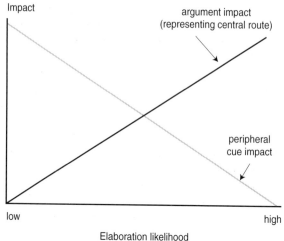

function of two factors: *motivation* and *ability* to process a given message (postulate 2). The higher the elaboration likelihood, the greater should be the impact of effortful processing of issue-relevant information, including message arguments, mediated through the favourability of the recipient's cognitive responses (as outlined in the cognitive response approach), and the lower should be the impact of peripheral cues on the formation and change of attitudes (postulate 6).

Thus, the ELM's two routes are conceived as antagonistic in their impact on persuasion outcomes. As the impact of central route processing increases, the impact of peripheral processes is bound to decrease (Petty & Cacioppo, 1986a,b; see Figure 7.2). Recently, however, Petty and colleagues have stressed that this *tradeoff* notion does not preclude that central and peripheral processes may occur simultaneously (e.g. Petty & Wegener, 1998a). This would be the case at moderate levels of elaboration likelihood (i.e. the middle range of the elaboration continuum in Figure 7.2), although the exact nature of such simultaneous occurrence has not been specified in the ELM.

Multiple roles of persuasion variables

The ELM assigns three basic roles to variables in the persuasion process (postulate 3): serving as arguments, serving as peripheral cues, or affecting the amount or direction of elaboration. Furthermore, variables are thought to be capable of playing "multiple roles" (for discussion, see chapter 8 of Petty & Cacioppo, 1986a) depending on the overall elaboration likelihood. This may be exemplified by the potential effects of source attractiveness. The attractiveness of a model who promotes a skin care product in a television advert may serve as a *peripheral cue* if elaboration likelihood is low, affecting attitudes to the product directly through a peripheral mechanism (e.g. evaluative conditioning); the model's attractiveness may serve as a *message argument* if elaboration likelihood is high, increasing persuasion through issue-relevant cognitive responses ("If I use this product, my skin will look as smooth as hers"); and finally, the model's attractiveness may *enhance the motivation* to centrally process the message if the elaboration likelihood is not constrained at a high or low level by other factors, i.e. in the middle range of the elaboration continuum (see Petty & Wegener, 1998a).

In most empirical tests of the ELM, however, source and context variables have been used to operationalise peripheral cues (e.g. expertise, attractiveness, number of sources), whereas variations in message content have been used to assess central route processing.

Varying argument quality as a methodological tool

The systematic variation of argument quality to study how variables influence the degree of message processing (postulate 4) is an important methodological tool that Petty and his colleagues introduced (e.g. Petty, Wells, & Brock, 1976). It is done by pilot-testing diverse arguments in favour of a certain issue and selecting arguments to be included in strong and weak message versions based on the kind of thoughts they evoke when carefully scrutinised. Strong arguments are those that evoke predominantly favourable cognitive responses and result in more positive attitudes; whereas weak arguments produce mainly unfavourable thoughts and lead to less positive attitudes (see chapter 2 of Petty & Cacioppo, 1986a). Examples for strong and weak arguments, used in a study by Bohner, Erb & Crow (1995), are given in Box 7.1.

If argument quality is used as one experimental factor, the kind of influence that another variable has in the persuasion process can be inferred from the result pattern it causes (Petty & Cacioppo, 1986a,b).

Strong and weak versions of arguments presented in a persuasive message

The following arguments favouring the fluoridation of drinking water were presented in a persuasion study by Bohner, Erb & Crow (1995).

Weak arguments	Strong arguments
In recent years, the prevalence of caries in highly developed countries has decreased only slightly, which means that an effective prevention is becoming more and more necessary. Studies . . . carried out over many weeks suggest that the provision of fluorides through the drinking water supplies is technically feasible and relatively harmless.	In recent years, the prevalence of caries in highly developed countries has increased so much that an effective prevention is becoming more and more necessary. Clinical studies . . . carried out over many years prove that the provision of fluorides through the drinking water supplies is effective and free from negative side effects.
Research participants were 31 women and men between 18 and 25 years of age. The sample included persons with prior illnesses like, for example, hayfever. On average, we observed no detrimental effects that could unequivocally be attributed to the fluoride.	Research participants were 1300 women and men between 18 and 75 years of age. The sample included persons suffering from diadetes and cardiovascular diseases. We observed no detrimental side effects or interactions with medication on any participant, while the incidence of caries was markedly reduced.
The production of suitable fluoride compounds would of course have its cost. All things considered, consumers would face an estimated increase in water bills of less than 50%. But ultimately, prices increase in all areas, so this would not be an unusual development.	Nowadays, the production of an unlimited amount of suitable fluoride compounds is possible and comes at a relatively low cost. Furthermore, we have to take into account that in the long run the costs for dental treatment will be reduced.

Possible patterns are depicted in Figure 7.3. In the next section, we illustrate this principle by discussing research on the effects of *distraction*.

Distraction may enhance or reduce persuasion

Various studies that addressed the effects of distraction on persuasion found that distraction reduces persuasion. But sometimes the opposite effect was observed, namely that recipients who were distracted while listening to an counterattitudinal message were *more* persuaded than nondistracted recipients (see Petty & Brock, 1981). The latter finding may seem surprising if one assumes that learning message content is the primary mediator of persuasion, as did

(1) No Effect

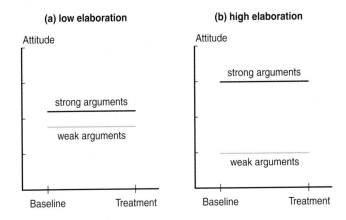

(a) low elaboration

Attitude

strong arguments

weak arguments

Baseline   Treatment

(b) high elaboration

Attitude

strong arguments

weak arguments

Baseline   Treatment

(2) Peripheral Cue Effect

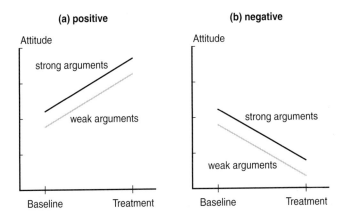

(a) positive

Attitude

strong arguments

weak arguments

Baseline   Treatment

(b) negative

Attitude

strong arguments

weak arguments

Baseline   Treatment

Figure 7.3. Possible effects of a persuasion variable according to the ELM. Panel 1 shows the basic pattern of post-message attitudes as a function of elaboration likelihood and argument quality: If elaboration likelihood is low, strong versus weak arguments should hardly make a difference; if elaboration likelihood is high, strong arguments should produce more positive attitudes than weak arguments. Panel 2 shows the typical effect of a peripheral cue: Depending on its valence, it either enhances or decreases persuasion independent of argument quality. Panel 3 shows the effect of a treatment variable that enhances or decreases elaboration (e.g. personal relevance; distraction), which results in a symmetrical interaction of that variable with argument quality. Finally, panel 4 shows the effect of a treatment variable that introduces a positive or negative bias to elaboration (e.g. forewarning), which should result in an asymmetrical interaction of that variable and argument quality.

(3) Objective Elaboration

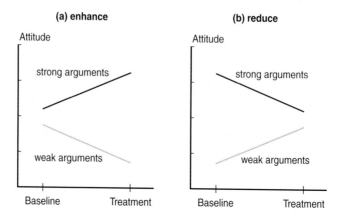

(4) Biased Elaboration

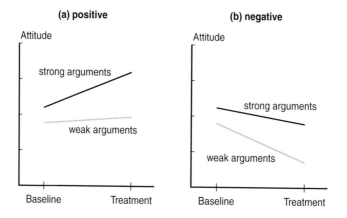

Figure 7.3. (Continued)

researchers in the Yale tradition. If so, any factor that interferes with the learning process should reduce persuasion. From the viewpoint of the ELM, however, distraction is thought to reduce recipients' ability for central route processing, thus undermining the dominant cognitive responses that the message would otherwise have elicited, whatever their valence. The dominant response to a weakly argued or counterattitudinal message should be counterarguing, and if this process is disrupted, resistance to persuasion should be weakened.

To test this disruption-of-counterarguing idea, Petty et al. (1976, Experiment 1) manipulated both distraction (at four levels, from no distraction to intense distraction) and argument quality (at two levels, strong versus weak) in a factorial design. Students were asked to listen to a tape-recorded message that advocated an increase in tuition fees at their university. The strong message included the arguments that the fee increase was recommended after a large-scale two-year investigation, that it would lead to higher quality of teaching, and that it would help to substantially increase graduates' starting salaries; the weak message featured the arguments that the recommendation of a fee increase was the result of a two-month study, that the increased fees would be used to plant more trees on campus, and that better lighting of classrooms was needed to reduce student headaches. To vary distraction, students were asked to perform a second task while listening to the message. Specifically, they had to monitor and record the position of an "X" that was briefly projected on a screen at varying time intervals. Depending on condition, the number of "X's" projected per minute was zero, four, twelve or twenty.

Petty et al. (1976) hypothesised that the strong message would be difficult to counterargue and thus distraction would reduce persuasion for this message, whereas the weak message would be easy to counterargue and thus distraction would increase persuasion. As can be seen in Figure 7.4, these hypotheses were supported. At higher levels of distraction, participants who listened to the weak message showed more agreement, and participants who listened to the strong message showed less agreement, than at lower levels of distraction. The favourability of participants' cognitive responses, which were assessed with a thought-listing technique (see Cacioppo & Petty, 1981), showed a very similar pattern: Thoughts were increasingly favourable at higher levels of distraction for the weak message, and were increasingly unfavourable at higher levels of distraction for the strong message. This overall pattern of results is incompatible with the message-learning approach, which would have predicted a general decrease in persuasion with increased distraction.

Other variables affecting the degree of elaboration

Interactions with argument quality have been observed for many variables that affect either the motivation or the ability to carefully

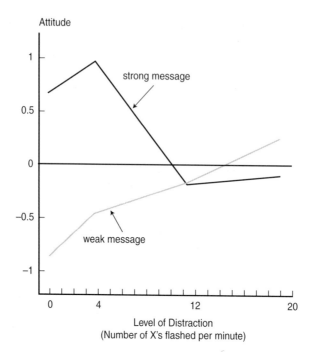

Figure 7.4. Distraction can enhance or reduce persuasion depending on argument quality (data from Petty et al., 1976).

process a message, such as message repetition, accountability for evaluating a message, the number of message sources, the functional matching of message content, recipients' mood or need for cognition (for an overview, see Petty & Wegener, 1998a). Research on some of these variables will be addressed in the following sections.

Issue involvement

Perhaps the most prominent motivational variable is issue involvement, the degree to which recipients perceive an issue as personally relevant (e.g. Petty, & Cacioppo, 1979; Petty Cacioppo, & Goldman, 1981; for a review see Johnson & Eagly, 1989). Recipients who are highly involved in an issue should be motivated to elaborate a message on this issue more than recipients who are not involved. In one experiment addressing this hypothesis, Petty, Cacioppo, and Goldman (1981) asked undergraduates to listen to a message stating that mandatory comprehensive examinations would be introduced in their area of study. Using a 2 × 2 × 2 factorial design, the authors varied three experimental factors: issue involvement, source expertise and argument strength. Adopting a technique that was introduced by

Apsler and Sears (1968) they told students in the high involvement condition that the new exam policy would take effect in the following year (and thus affect them personally), whereas students in the low involvement condition heard that it would be ten years before the policy would be implemented. To induce high versus low source expertise, the message was said to come either from "the Carnegie Commission on Higher Education" or from a local high school class. Finally, the comprehensive exam proposal was supported with either strong or weak arguments. After listening to the message, participants reported their attitude toward comprehensive exams on several items that were later combined to form a standardised index.

Petty, Cacioppo, and Goldman (1981) predicted that students for whom involvement was high would elaborate the message, which would lead them to generate mainly positive thoughts and thus report more positive attitudes after listening to strong arguments, but to generate mainly negative thoughts and thus report more negative attitudes after listening to weak arguments. Students for whom involvement was low, on the other hand, were expected not to elaborate message content but to follow the peripheral route to persuasion, i.e. to agree more with a high expertise source than with a low expertise source. The results supported these predictions, as can be seen in Figure 7.5.

Matching of message content with an attitude's functional basis

By analysing the impact that diverse variables have on message elaboration, the ELM has provided a useful framework for re-addressing topics in persuasion that had produced seemingly inconsistent findings in the past. This point is nicely illustrated by recent research on the *functional matching* hypothesis. Petty and Wegener (1998b) reframed in ELM terms the early suggestion that, in order to be effective, messages should match the functional basis of an attitude (e.g. Smith et al., 1956). They predicted that a message would be scrutinised more thoroughly if it matched the particular functional aspect of an attitude object that was most relevant to a recipient. Using an experimental paradigm similar to the one employed by Snyder and DeBono (1985; see chapter 1, Box 1.1), Petty and Wegener found support for their prediction. Replicating earlier results, strong arguments led to more persuasion when they matched rather than mismatched recipients' most central attitude function (e.g. image concerns for people high in self-monitoring); conversely,

Figure 7.5. The effect of personal involvement on persuasion showing (a) the interaction of involvement and argument quality; (b) the interaction of involvement and source expertise (adapted from Petty, Cacioppo, & Goldman, 1981).

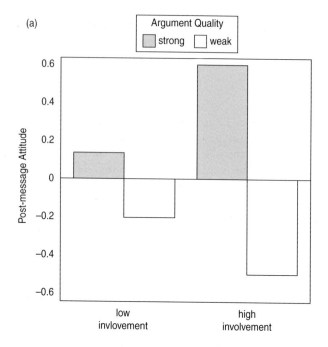

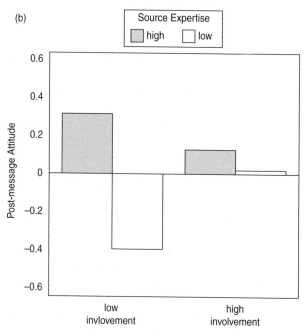

however, weak arguments were even less persuasive in the matching than nonmatching functions condition (for related findings, see Lavine & Snyder, 2000).

Mood

Another variable that can increase or decrease persuasion by affecting the degree of message scrutiny is the recipient's mood. In chapter 5 you have learned that many mood effects on attitudes are best explained by assuming that mood serves an informative function. People may form attitudes based on a "how do I feel about it" heuristic, often mistaking a pre-existing mood state for a reaction to the attitude object. You have further seen that mood may be used as input not only to a direct evaluation of the attitude object (Schwarz & Clore, 1983), but also to a decision about how much cognitive effort to invest in a task (Martin, Ward, Achee, & Wyer, 1993). The latter type of effect has been extensively studied in the persuasion domain as well. If we assume that people use their mood in a general assessment of their current situation, then a positive mood should signal a benign, unproblematic situation, whereas a negative mood should indicate a problematic state of affairs (Schwarz, 1990). Accordingly, a person who is feeling happy when confronted with a persuasive message may not feel the need to invest much effort in processing its arguments and rather rely on a salient peripheral cue—after all, her mood is telling her that things are fine. A person who is feeling bad, on the other hand, may perceive the situation as problematic or threatening, which may motivate him to invest considerable effort in message processing (cf. Bless & Schwarz, 1999).

Various studies conducted within the dual-processing framework produced results in line with these assumptions (e.g. Bless, Bohner, Schwarz, & Strack, 1990; Worth & Mackie, 1987; for a review, see Schwarz, Bless, & Bohner, 1991). In a study by Bless et al. (1990), students were asked to recall and describe either a happy or a sad life event, ostensibly to help with the construction of a life-event inventory. This task unobtrusively put them into a positive or negative mood. Later, as part of a purportedly independent second study, participants listened to a tape recorded message that contained either strong or weak arguments in favour of an increase in student services fees. To study the impact of mood states on the *spontaneous* processing of a persuasive message, participants were told that this second study was concerned with language comprehension. After listening to one of the taped messages, they reported their attitudes

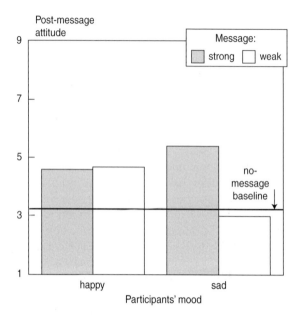

Figure 7.6. Mood effects on message scrutiny (data from Bless et al., 1990).

toward an increase in student services fees and listed their cognitive responses to the message. To obtain an attitude baseline, students in a control condition were neither exposed to a mood manipulation nor to a persuasive message, but simply reported their attitude toward the proposed increase in student services fees.

As shown in Figure 7.6, participants in a negative mood reported more favourable attitudes toward the proposed fee increase when they were exposed to strong arguments than when they were exposed to weak arguments. Participants in a positive mood, on the other hand, were not differentially affected by strong versus weak arguments, but showed a moderate degree of attitude change in comparison to the control condition regardless of message content. These results suggest that students in a happy mood were less likely to elaborate the specific content of the message than students who were in a sad mood. This conclusion was supported by the analysis of participants' cognitive responses. Participants in a sad mood reported a higher proportion of favourable thoughts and a lower proportion of unfavourable thoughts in response to strong rather than weak arguments. Thus, their cognitive responses reflected high elaboration of message content. This was not true, however, of participants in a happy mood. Neither the proportion of favourable nor the proportion of unfavourable thoughts reported by these participants differed as a function of argument strength, suggesting a low degree of message elaboration.

Interestingly, several studies show that a negative mood does not invariably increase message elaboration compared to a positive mood. As with more direct effects of mood on evaluative judgment (Schwarz & Clore, 1983), directing a person's attention to the true, judgment-irrelevant source of their mood leads to discounting of its informational value; the mood is then not interpreted as signalling a problematic or benign situation any more, and any mood differences in processing effort disappear (Sinclair, Mark, & Clore, 1994). Finally, the mood effect on message processing may even reverse in direction. Specifically, if recipients interpret a negative mood not as a reaction to the issue under consideration, but rather as a response to illegitimate pressure to change their views, it tends to reduce rather than increase message elaboration. This was shown in a series of studies by Bohner and Weinerth (2000, 2001). Without the theoretical framework provided by the dual-processing approach, these complex patterns of findings would be very difficult to explain (for additional hypotheses about mood effects on message processing, cf. Wegener & Petty, 1994; Wegener, Petty, & Smith, 1995).

Need for cognition

As a final example for factors affecting the degree of message elaboration we consider an individual difference variable, the *need for cognition* (NFC; Cacioppo & Petty, 1982; Cacioppo, Petty, Feinstein, & Jarvis, 1996). This variable is assessed by a self report measure containing items like "I am usually tempted to put more thought into a task than the job minimally requires" (Cacioppo & Petty, 1982). Individuals high in NFC tend to engage in and to enjoy effortful thinking across situations and topics, whereas individuals low in NFC are generally unwilling to expend much cognitive effort, unless forced to do so under situational pressure. High-NFC (as opposed to low-NFC) individuals have been found to show more central route processing of persuasive messages (e.g. Bless, Wänke, Bohner, Fellhauer, & Schwarz, 1994; Cacioppo, Petty, & Morris, 1983) but to be less susceptible to the impact of peripheral cues (see Chaiken's, 1987, study on the reliability of liking cues we discussed in chapter 6; Haugtvedt, Petty, & Cacioppo, 1992; Keller, Bohner, & Erb, 2000).

We have now discussed variables that seem to be very different at first sight, representing situational influences (distraction), the relationship between recipient and attitude object (involvement, attitude functions), subjective states of the recipient (mood) and enduring individual differences (NFC). Yet these variables' complex effects on persuasion can be subsumed under a common principle: They affect persuasion by enhancing or reducing motivation or ability to elaborate a message. This parsimonious explanation became possible on the basis of the dual-processing perspective, and by using its methodological tool of varying argument quality along with other factors to infer processing effort (e.g. Petty & Cacioppo, 1986b).

Biased elaboration

Variations in motivation and capacity may not only enhance or reduce the general amount of thinking (or, in ELM terminology, *objective elaboration*) as in the examples discussed above; according to the ELM's *biased elaboration* assumption (postulate 5), both cognitive and motivational factors may also facilitate specifically either positive or negative elaborations. This results in an asymmetrical interaction of the variable in question with argument quality, as shown in panel 4 of Figure 7.3.

We have already discussed Tesser's (1978) mere thought approach, which showed that schema-guided thinking may lead to a polarisation of initial attitudes (see chapter 6). Similarly, well-developed schemata and prior knowledge may enhance recipients' *ability* to elaborate externally presented arguments that are consistent with their prior attitude. To test this idea, Cacioppo, Petty, and Sidera (1982) studied the effect of proattitudinal messages on abortion that featured either religious or legalistic arguments (e.g. pointing out the sacramental quality of life versus constitutional aspects). These were presented to participants who had been identified as possessing either a legalistic or a religious self-schema. In line with the ELM's biased elaboration postulate, participants generated a greater number of mostly favourable cognitive responses, and found the message more convincing, when the arguments fitted (versus did not fit) their self-schema. In other studies, it has also been shown that extensive prior knowledge about an issue facilitates the refutation of counter-attitudinal arguments (e.g. Wood, 1982). We will have to say more about this issue in chapter 9.

On the motivational side, it has been shown that *forewarning* may motivate recipients specifically to counterargue a message (e.g. Petty & Cacioppo, 1977). Other potential sources of biased message processing are the recipient's current processing goal (motivational) and accessible persuasion heuristics (cognitive). As these factors have been conceptualised within the heuristic-systematic model, we will address them in a later section.

Consequences of elaboration

The ELM's seventh and final postulate addresses the consequences of the different routes to persuasion. Petty and Cacioppo (1986a) emphasise three characteristics of an attitude that are enhanced by central route as opposed to peripheral route processing: Attitudes formed via the central route are assumed to be more persistent, more resistant to counterpersuasion and more predictive of behaviour than those formed via peripheral mechanisms. These three aspects may be interrelated and have been conceptualised as consequences of attitude strength (see chapter 3; Petty et al., 1995).

Why should message elaboration lead to stronger attitudes? Petty and his colleagues (1995) discuss three mediating mechanisms that may operate in concert or independently. Firstly, issue-relevant thinking may increase the structural consistency of an attitude schema, because initial inconsistencies may be noticed and resolved in the process. Secondly, by elaborating a message, the attitude and associated beliefs will be activated repeatedly, thus rendering them more accessible. As you will see in chapter 10, more accessible attitudes are stronger predictors of behaviour than are less accessible attitudes. And finally, the individual may consciously perceive that she expended considerable mental effort, thereby becoming more confident in the resulting attitude.

Research on the consequences of elaboration has typically studied the effects of known antecedents of elaboration (e.g. personal relevance, need for cognition) on one or two outcome variables (e.g. resistance and persistence). To illustrate the basic paradigm, let us consider a study by Petty, Cacioppo, Haugtvedt, and Heesacker (1986; reported in Petty & Cacioppo, 1986a, pp. 175ff). Participating students listened to a message that argued for adopting comprehensive exams, either at their own university (high personal relevance) or at another university (low personal relevance). The message came in one of two versions: A positive version contained both strong arguments *and* was delivered by a prestigious, expert source; a negative version consisted of weak arguments *and* came from a low-status, inexpert source. Participants reported their attitudes immediately after the message (t1), and again about two weeks later (t2). Students in a control condition received no message but simply reported their attitudes at t1 and t2. Petty and his colleagues predicted that students in the high-relevance conditions would process via the central route, thus being influenced mainly by the content of the message, whereas students in the low-relevance conditions would process via the peripheral route and be influenced mainly by the source information. Note that because the arguments and the source cue always had identical evaluative implications (being either both positive or both negative), post-message attitudes at t1 were not expected to differ as a function of personal relevance. Indeed they were generally positive in the positive-message condition and negative in the negative-message condition, with the no-message control condition lying in between. However, whether attitudes persisted over the two-week period clearly depended on personal relevance. High-relevance participants at t2 reported attitudes that were still more positive than in the control condition when they had received the positive message/ source, and more negative when they had listened to the negative message/source. Low-relevance participants' attitudes, by contrast, did not differ from those of control participants any more at t2. These findings are in line with the ELM's prediction that individuals who process via the central route should show greater persistence of their changed attitudes over time than individuals who process via the peripheral route, although the study does not provide any direct evidence concerning the assumed mediating process.

Studies addressing the other two consequences of elaboration have also yielded results generally consistent with the ELM. When we discussed inoculation theory, we have already seen that active, issue-related processing enhances existing attitudes' resistance to counter-persuasion. Evidence for greater resistance of attitudes newly formed via the central (versus peripheral) route comes from a study by Haugtvedt and Wegener (1994). Students read two consecutive messages that contained opposing recommendations under either high or low elaboration conditions; both messages contained strong arguments. Results were consistent with the hypothesised link between elaboration and resistance: In the high-elaboration conditions, final attitudes reflected the position of the first message—a *primacy effect*—whereas in the low-elaboration conditions, the last message had a greater impact on final attitudes—a *recency effect* (see also Haugtvedt & Petty, 1992). Finally, there is some evidence that newly formed central-route attitudes are more highly correlated to behaviour than newly formed peripheral-route attitudes (for a review, see Petty et al., 1995).

ELM summary

In sum, the ELM provides a comprehensive framework of persuasion processes that can accommodate the effects of a wide range of variables and their interactions. The methodological innovation of varying argument quality to determine the kind of effect that a variable of interest has in the persuasion process has greatly advanced our understanding of persuasion processes. The ELM has been criticised, however, for a certain lack of predictive power (e.g. Eagly & Chaiken, 1993). Specifically, it is difficult to assess the level of elaboration likelihood independent of its effects (see Figure 7.3); thus, one often cannot predict a priori in which of the multiple roles featured in the ELM a variable will serve. For example, Petty and Cacioppo (1980) hypothesised that an endorser's attractiveness in an advert for shampoo would be more persuasive under low than under high involvement. When they found an equally high impact of attractiveness under both involvement conditions, they concluded that the endorser's attractiveness served as a peripheral cue under low involvement, but as a product-relevant argument under high involvement.

Furthermore, although Petty and his colleagues acknowledge that central and peripheral processes may co-occur (Petty & Wegener, 1998a), they do not specify the exact mechanisms and conditions of their interplay. Both of these issues have been addressed more directly in the other dual-processing theory of persuasion, which we will discuss next.

The heuristic-systematic model

Like the ELM, the *heuristic-systematic model* (HSM) of persuasion features two modes of processing: an effortless *heuristic* mode and a more effortful *systematic* mode (Bohner et al., 1995; Chaiken et al., 1989; Chen & Chaiken, 1999). Message recipients are thought to strike a balance between effort minimisation and achieving confidence in their attitude judgments. The model highlights three broad motivational forces: *accuracy*, *defence*, and *impression* motivation. Heuristic and systematic processing may serve either of the three motives and may co-occur in an additive or interactive manner under specified conditions.

The main similarities to the ELM lie in the HSM's assumption of a processing continuum and in the notion that processing effort varies with a perceiver's motivation and cognitive capacity. *Systematic processing* is defined in a similar way as central route processing: Chaiken et al. (1989, p. 212) "conceive of systematic processing as a comprehensive, analytic orientation in which perceivers access and scrutinise all informational input for its relevance and importance to their judgment task, and integrate all useful information in forming their judgments". The HSM differs from the ELM in the definition of its low-effort mode, its assumptions about the interplay of processing modes, and the explicitness of its motivational underpinnings. We will address these issues in turn.

The low-effort mode: Heuristic processing

The HSM's low-effort mode is a more narrow and more specific concept than the ELM's peripheral route. As we discussed in chapter 6, heuristic processing entails the application of **heuristics**, simple rules of inference like "likeable people can be trusted" or "experts' statements are correct" (whereas the ELM's peripheral route encompasses a wider range of low-effort mechanisms, e.g. conditioning). Although heuristic processing is thought to be a default mode of processing, its occurrence does require the presence of a heuristic cue (e.g. a likeable or expert source) which signals the applicability of a heuristic that is accessible in memory (see chapter 6).

Interplay of processing modes: The co-occurrence hypotheses

Systematic processing requires higher motivation and capacity than does heuristic processing. However, the HSM does not assume a general tradeoff between its processing modes. Rather, its processing continuum features a restrictive pole at its low end, where heuristic processing predominates, and a more inclusive pole at its high end, where systematic processing comes into play but does not eliminate

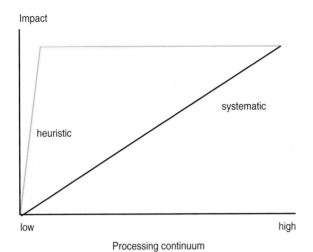

Impact

heuristic

systematic

low   high

Processing continuum
(depending on motivation and capacity)

Figure 7.7. The heuristic-systematic model's continuum of processing effort. Heuristic processing is evident at low levels of motivation and/or capacity and continues to operate at higher levels, whereas systematic processing requires higher levels of motivation and capacity. At high levels of motivation and capacity, the two modes co-occur.

the continued operation of heuristics (see Figure 7.7). Thus, at high levels of motivation and capacity, both processing modes affect persuasion either independently or in an interactive fashion. The specific types and conditions of such interplay of processing modes are described in four **co-occurrence hypotheses** (Bohner et al., 1995). These hypotheses are unique to the HSM; therefore, we present them in some detail along with pertinent research findings.

According to the *additivity hypothesis*, heuristic and systematic processing may exert independent main effects on attitude judgments. This should be the case when the outcomes of each process do not contradict each other, as for example, when an expert communicator delivers strong arguments. This hypothesis was supported in various studies (Bohner, Frank, & Erb, 1998; Chaiken & Maheswaran, 1994; Maheswaran & Chaiken, 1991). However, because systematic processing often yields more, and subjectively more relevant, information, any additional effects of heuristic processing may be obscured. This *attenuation hypothesis* has also received extensive support (e.g., Chaiken & Maheswaran, 1994; Maheswaran & Chaiken, 1991).

A statistical interaction between the two processing modes is expressed in the HSM's *bias hypothesis*: If a persuasive message is ambiguous in its implications or mixed (e.g. containing both strong and weak arguments), initial heuristic inferences may guide the interpretation of the message, leading to cognitive responses and attitudes that are in line with the valence of a heuristic cue. This has been demonstrated by Chaiken and Maheswaran (1994), who varied the content ambiguity and source credibility of a message about a (fictitious) new answer phone, the "XT-100". Participating students read product information that was unambiguously weak, unambiguously strong or ambiguous with respect to the XT-100's performance. This information was said to come from either "Consumer Reports Magazine", a prestigious independent journal specialising in product testing, or from sales staff at K-Mart, a discount retailer. Later participants reported their attitudes toward the XT-100 and listed the thoughts they had while reading the product information.

Figure 7.8 shows the valence of product-related cognitive responses of participants who were highly motivated and able to process. In the ambiguous message conditions, their cognitive responses were assimilated to the credibility cue, as predicted by the bias hypothesis; for unambiguously strong or weak messages, however, only an effect of argument strength was found, a pattern consistent with the attenuation hypothesis. Attitudes toward the product showed a highly similar pattern, and path analyses revealed that, in the ambiguous conditions, biased content-related thinking mediated the source credibility effect on attitudes (for the demonstration of similar biasing effects of consensus cues, see Erb & Bohner, 2001; Erb, Bohner, Schmälzle, & Rank, 1998).

Finally, the mirror image of assimilative bias is described in the HSM's *contrast hypothesis*: If initial heuristic-based expectancies about a message are obviously violated, then systematic evaluation of the arguments may lead to contrasting interpretations (Bohner, Moskowitz & Chaiken, 1995). Thus, positive expectancies that are disconfirmed lead to more negative cognitive responses and attitudes, whereas negative expectancies that are violated induce a positive processing bias. In line with this assumption, Bohner, Ruder & Erb (in press) found that information about high or low communicator expertise may evoke clear expectations that the message will be strong or weak. If message content obviously contradicted these expectations, a bias opposite in valence to the expectation was introduced. For example, a message ascribed to a renowned expert that contained weak arguments led to less positive cognitive responses and attitudes than the same message ascribed to a nonexpert—a contrast effect. In the case of ambiguous arguments, however, participants' expertise-based expectations led to biased assimilation of cognitive responses and attitude judgments.

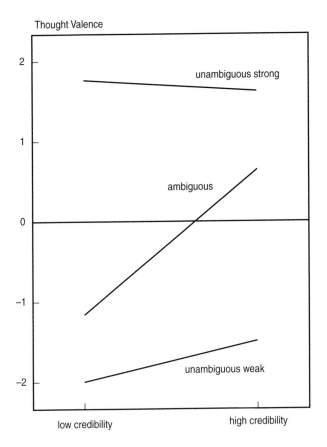

Thought Valence

unambiguous strong

ambiguous

unambiguous weak

low credibility   high credibility

Figure 7.8. Heuristic inferences may bias the processing of message content: Valenced index of product-related thoughts as a function of source credibility and message type (high importance conditions only; data from Chaiken & Maheswaran, 1994).

Conceptualising processing motivation: The sufficiency principle

More explicitly than the ELM, the HSM spells out external criteria determining the extent of processing motivation. The model's **suffi-ciency principle** states that people try to attain sufficient confidence in their attitudinal judgments. What is sufficient is defined by two constructs, the sufficiency threshold (ST), defined as the level of confidence a person would like to have, and the person's actual confidence (AC). The HSM assumes that whenever actual confidence is below the sufficiency threshold, the individual will be motivated to process (additional) information, and that larger ST–AC gaps are more likely to require systematic processing, whereas smaller gaps may be bridged by heuristic processing alone (see Eagly & Chaiken, 1993). Both ST and AC vary across persons and situations. For example, if an attitude judgment has low personal relevance, both ST and AC should be similarly low and little processing effort would be expected. If personal relevance is then temporarily heightened, the ST should be elevated and the person would be expected to engage in processing to bridge the resulting gap. Furthermore, if both ST and AC are high, a person should again expend little processing effort. The amount of processing should be stepped up, however, if the AC is temporarily lowered, for instance, by an obvious but unexpected discrepancy between heuristic cues and content information (Maheswaran & Chaiken, 1991).

Bohner, Rank, Reinhard, Einwiller, and Erb (1998) demonstrated the mediating role of the sufficiency gap. These authors varied the sufficiency threshold by inducing high or low task importance and then observed how much information participants were willing to review for upcoming social judgments. Supporting the sufficiency principle, high task importance led to the selection of greater amounts of information, and this effect was mediated through the difference between self-reported desired and actual judgmental confidence. Importantly, this research also showed that a large ST–AC gap alone was not sufficient to induce greater processing effort. Rather, this was the case only for participants who had been led to expect that they have the ability to bridge the gap by increased processing (see Figure 7.9).

Multiple motives

Finally, the HSM views the social perceiver as a "motivated tactician" (see Fiske & Taylor, 1991) by incorporating *multiple motives* that may guide information processing: *accuracy*, *defence*, and *impression* motivation. Accordingly, depending on both the situation and on individual differences, people may strive to hold attitudes that are a valid reflection of reality, but they may also seek to defend important values and self-defining beliefs, or try to adopt attitudes that serve the goals of making a good impression and "getting along" well with others. (You may notice that this feature of the HSM was influenced by early taxonomies of attitude functions, as we discussed in chapter 1.) The impact of these qualitative differences in motivation is considered to be orthogonal to those of the more quantitative sufficiency

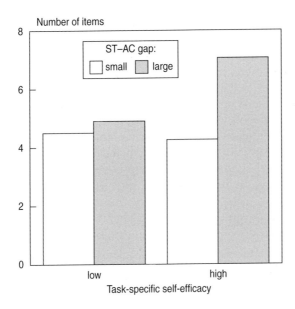

Figure 7.9. Motivational factors in systematic processing: Processing effort (number of items selected for processing) as a function of induced self-efficacy and sufficiency gap (data from Bohner, Rank, Reinhard, Einwiller, & Erb, 1998).

principle. Thus, an individual may be more or less confident with respect to any of the processing goals implied by the HSM's multiple-motive view.

Importantly, accuracy-motivated processing is thought to be relatively open-minded, whereas both defence- and impression-motivated processing tend to be selective and biased. For example, participants motivated to defend a core value may selectively ignore any information that might challenge this value, they may selectively invoke heuristics that bolster their preferred conclusion, or they may selectively counterargue any threatening information they are exposed to. Which of these strategies will be used should partly depend on their current levels of desired and actual defensive confidence (for an extended discussion and empirical evidence, see Chaiken, Giner-Sorolla, & Chen, 1996; see also chapter 9).

Concluding remarks on dual-processing accounts

Dual-processing models have had an immense impact on the field of persuasion. The ELM provides the more comprehensive framework, including effortful processing as well as a variety of low-effort processes, and allowing distinctions between these processes and the various "roles" a persuasion variable may play on an empirical basis. The HSM is more limited in its conceptualisation of low-effort processing, but at the same time makes more specific assumptions about motivational processes and the interplay of its two processing modes. Both models were generally supported in empirical tests and helped to stimulate renewed interest in persuasion processes. Recently, however, dual-processing models have been challenged by the proposal of an alternative one-process theory.

A one-process alternative?

In their "unimodel of persuasion", Kruglanski and Thompson (1999) argue that the dual-process distinction still focuses too much on *types of information* (i.e. message arguments versus contextual cues)—as did the Yale programme with its "who says what . . ." slogan—rather than conceptualising truly different *processes*. According to the unimodel, persuasion can be reduced to a single process of syllogistic reasoning about persuasive "evidence" (for other approaches that emphasised the quasi-logical nature of attitudinal processing, see McGuire, 1960, 1981; Wyer, 1970; Wyer & Hartwick, 1980). Both heuristic cues and message arguments can serve as evidence, which forms the minor premise of a syllogism. The major premise is thought to be retrieved from the recipient's memory, and the conclusion would be an attitudinal belief. For example, consider the following syllogisms:

Variant A:
Minor premise: Dr. Bloggs, an expert, says that genetically modified food weakens the immune system and should thus be prohibited.
Major premise: Anything that weakens the immune system is bad.
Conclusion: Genetically modified food is bad.

Variant B:
Minor premise: Dr. Bloggs, an expert, says that genetically modified food weakens the immune system and should thus be prohibited.
Major premise: Experts' statements are valid.
Conclusion: Genetically modified food is bad.

Note that the difference between the two variants lies in the major premise, or the particular piece of knowledge that the recipient uses to draw an attitudinal conclusion: In variant A, this is specific knowledge related to an argument; in variant B, it is a heuristic related to a source cue.

Importantly, Kruglanski and Thompson (1999) propose that the psychological process is exactly the same in both cases. To be sure, they acknowledge that processing effort varies in quantity with motivation and ability, but they deny any theoretically useful qualitative distinction between two processing modes. Thus, under conditions of low motivation or ability any information that is relatively easy to process would be processed preferentially, no matter if it is an argument or a cue, whereas under high motivation and ability processing would be more exhaustive.

We could only briefly introduce these new ideas (for related empirical evidence and theoretical discussion, see peer commentary on Kruglanski & Thompson, 1999[1]; see also Chaiken & Trope, 1999). Future theorising and empirical studies will have to show if this one-process alternative can replace the dual-process models and inspire new directions of persuasion research.

Chapter summary

(1) Dual process models—Petty's elaboration likelihood model (ELM) and Chaiken's heuristic-systematic model (HSM)—locate persuasion processes along a continuum ranging from low-effort mechanisms (peripheral route/heuristic processing) to the kind of high-effort, issue-related thinking featured in the cognitive response approach (central route/systematic processing). Both models portray high-effort processing as a function of motivation (e.g. personal relevance) and ability (e.g. time available).

(2) ELM and HSM differ in some respects. The ELM's peripheral route encompasses a broad range of mechanisms, including conditioning, affective responding, heuristic processing etc. The HSM's heuristic mode entails only heuristic processing, but specificies exactly its eliciting conditions. Whereas the ELM assumes a general tradeoff between its high and low effort modes, the HSM delineates four forms of co-occurrence: additivity, attenuation, bias and contrast.

(3) The ELM provides the benefit of accommodating a wide range of empirical phenomena. Also, it emphasises the consequences of

processing: Central (vs peripheral) route processing leads to attitudes that are more resistant, persistent and predictive of behaviour.

(4) Advantages of the HSM are its high precision concerning low-effort processing and the interplay of its processing modes. Also, it explicitly differentiates three broad processing motives: accuracy, defence and impression management.

(5) Recently, a one-process alternative to the dual-process approaches was proposed by Kruglanski and his associates. In this unimodel, any qualitative differences between a low-effort and a high-effort processing mode are denied, and the idea of a continuum of processing effort is emphasised.

Exercises

(1) An advertising agency produced two different commercials for a beer. One film shows the brewery process, describes and explains why each step is relevant for good taste and high quality. The other commercial features a group of people having fun, drinking beer at a nice place. The client tests those commercials by showing each commercial to 100 viewers. These viewers are shown the target commercial in a reel of other commercials. Later they are shown the target advert again and are asked for their impressions, their product liking and purchase intentions. Based on these results the commercial showing the brewery process wins hands down. How would you interpret this finding? Should the company go along with this commercial or is there anything that may have caused an "unrealistic" advantage for this film?

(2) How would you explain Gorn's results (see introduction to chapter 6) in terms of dual-process models?

(3) What are the main differences between the ELM and the HSM?

(4) Research has shown that health-related messages that induce fear sometimes lead to more persuasion than emotionally neutral messages on the same topic; in other studies, however, the fear-inducing messages were less effective than their neutral counterparts. Discuss some of the reasons why this variation in results may occur from a dual-process perspective.

Note

(1) Extensive peer commentary and a reply by Kruglanski and Thompson can be found in *Psychological Inquiry*, 10(1).

Further reading

The current status of the two dual-processing models of persuasion is reviewed by the model's proponents in the following chapters:

Chen, S., & Chaiken, S. (1999). The heuristic-systematic model in its broader context. In S. Chaiken & Y. Trope (Eds.), *Dual-process theories in social psychology* (pp. 73–96). New York: Guilford.

Petty, R. E., & Wegener, D. T. (1999). The elaboration likelihood model: Current status and controversies. In S. Chaiken & Y. Trope (Eds.), *Dual process theories in social psychology* (pp. 41–72). New York: Guilford.

Behaviour influences on attitudes 8

In the previous chapter we discussed how attitude change results from the processing of messages about an attitude object and of related context information. Importantly, persuasion may ultimately lead to a change in behaviour. Indeed, the practical interest of many persuasion experts lies in changing behaviour, and changing attitudes is simply a means toward that end. An advertising campaign would not be seen as a success if it simply resulted in more favourable consumer attitudes toward a product without also inducing consumers to buy the product. Conversely, the company that is marketing the product would not mind if purchasing behaviour could be enhanced directly without bothering with changing people's attitudes. In fact, many interventions in marketing, politics or health are aimed immediately at changing behaviour, through sanctions or incentives (see Stroebe & Jonas, 1996): Legislators may increase the tax on electricity to stimulate tax payers' efforts at saving energy; or a health insurance company may offer reduced rates to customers who frequent fitness programmes. Thus, changes in behaviour are initiated by changing the consequences of the behaviour. To avoid sanctions, most employees would quit smoking at work after a ban on smoking had been introduced. But would this behavioural change result in any attitude change? And if it did, would employees' attitude toward smoking become more or less favourable? In this chapter we address the question how changes in behaviour may lead to subsequent changes in attitudes.

When sanctions or incentives backfire: Reactance and overjustification

Several lines of research indicate that the direction of attitude change may be opposite to a change in behaviour that has resulted from either sanctions or positive incentives. We all have experienced that for-bidden activities or things that are unattainable often seem especially attractive. In terms of the **theory of psychological reactance** (e.g. Brehm, 1972), restricting an individual's freedom of choice among a set of alternatives motivates the individual to restore this freedom and to evaluate the eliminated alternatives more positively. Thus, sanc-tions against smoking or other unwanted behaviours may produce unintended opposite effects, and people may cherish the restricted behaviours even more as long as the restrictions are in place. This should be true especially if the sanctions are severe and the freedom to perform the restricted behaviour is highly valued.

Reactance theory has been applied to predicting the effects of censorship on people's attitudes. If a person originally believes that she has the freedom to hear or read a message on a certain issue, but then that freedom is restricted by censorship, reactance should be aroused. One way of restoring the thwarted freedom is to change one's attitude toward the position that the censored message would presumably have taken. This effect of censorship was demonstrated in experiments by Worchel and his associates. In one study (Worchel & Arnold, 1973), students were led to believe that they would hear a tape-recorded speech advocating a ban of police from university campuses—a topic hotly debated at the time of the U.S.–Vietnam war, when confrontations between protesting students and the police were not uncommon. Students who were assigned to one of the censorship conditions learned that they could not hear the tape, either because some student group had opposed to it being used in the experiment, or because the tape-recorder was broken. These students reported attitudes more in line with a ban of police from campuses than students in a control condition, who never expected that they would hear a speech (see Figure 8.1).

Later research corroborated these findings, showing that the censorship effect generalised to positions that participants initially disagreed with (Worchel, Arnold, & Baker, 1975). Interestingly, for the censorship effect to occur it does not matter much if the censor is seen to have a good reason for withholding the information, though the effect appeared somewhat weaker when the censor was liked rather than disliked.

Attitudinal consequences that are opposite to overt behaviour may also result—paradoxically—when positive incentives are offered for engaging in desired behaviours. This is true especially if those who receive the incentive have already been intrinsically motivated to show the behaviour in question (i.e. held a positive attitude toward

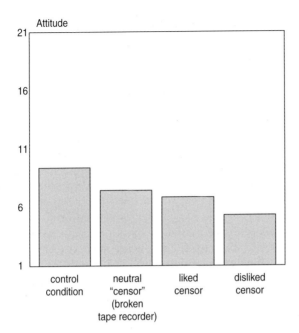

Figure 8.1. Attitudes toward allowing police forces on university campuses as a function of censorship condition. Lower values indicate attitudes more in line with the position of the censored speech (data from Worchel & Arnold, 1973).

the behaviour). Although the intensity or frequency of the behaviour may increase as long as the reward is provided, attitudes toward the behaviour may become *less* favourable and the likelihood to show the behaviour in the absence of rewards may decrease. This phenomenon has been called the **overjustification effect** (Deci, 1971; Lepper, Greene, & Nisbett, 1973). For example, Lepper et al. (1973) introduced preschool children to an enjoyable new activity: drawing with "magic markers". There were three experimental conditions: One group of children were told at the outset that they would be rewarded with a "Good Player" certificate, children in a second group received the same reward unexpectedly, and children in a third group neither expected nor received a reward. Two weeks later, the children were again given the opportunity to play with the markers during their free time, and the researchers recorded how long the children played. The result was that those children who had received the expected reward now spent only half as much time drawing than both the children who had been rewarded unexpectedly and the nonrewarded children.

These and similar findings have been explained in terms of **self-perception theory** (Bem, 1972). Bem argued that internal cues to our mental or feeling states are often weak or ambiguous. Thus, when people want to infer their own attitudes, they have to engage in attributional reasoning just like any outside observer. When I realise that I frequent an Italian restaurant once a week and always keep my freezer packed with pizza, I will infer that I must like Italian food. Generally, behaviour can have internal or external causes, and an internal cause (an attitude) will more likely be inferred to the extent that external causes or situational constraints cannot be identified (e.g. Kelley, 1972; see also chapter 6 and Fincham & Hewstone, 2001). Thus, if I go to a pizzeria because my boss has arranged a business lunch there, I am unlikely to infer anything about my food preferences from this behaviour. Similarly, those children who played with magic markers after a reward had been promised seem to have inferred that they did so *because* of the reward, and not so much because playing with the markers was fun anyway. Conversely, the children who did not expect a reward seem to have perceived themselves as enjoying the activity itself. An interesting application of self-perception principles is provided in Box 8.1.

Does this mean that providing incentives for desirable behaviour is generally useless, undermining motivation and positive attitudes toward the behaviour? Fortunately, the answer depends on the kind of incentive that is used. A recent meta-analysis (Deci et al., 1999) indicates that tangible rewards that are contingent on performance thwart intrinsic motivation, and so do threats, deadlines, and imposed external goals. In contrast, verbal performance feedback that acknowledges feelings and autonomy, as well as a secure social environment, can foster the perception of internal causality and thus enhance intrinsic motivation. People can even develop positive attitudes and an internal locus of causality for uninteresting behaviours that initially were under external control if a meaningful rationale is provided, social support is present, and the external rewards are de-emphasised (for an overview, see Ryan & Deci, 2000).

Incentives versus cognitive dissonance

We have already discussed other conditions under which the direction of attitude change is in line with a prior change in behaviour. From chapter 6 you will recall the work by Janis and King (1954; King & Janis, 1956), who showed that role playing and active improvisation in preparing a speech on an issue can lead to attitude change in the direction being advocated. Elms and Janis (1965) demonstrated that this effect can be enhanced by providing positive incentives for

A widely used application of behaviour-based change of attitudes (and subsequent behaviours) has become known as the "foot-in-the-door technique" (Freedman & Fraser, 1966). As the name suggests, the technique is often employed as a selling strategy by door-to-door salespersons, but it seems to be equally effective in eliciting donations for charities and other kinds of behaviour. How does it work? The first step is to get the target person to perform a small act in line with the influence agent's goal. Then, after some time, a larger act is requested. Various studies have shown that people who had complied with the initial request were much more likely to succumb to the subsequent request as well, compared to both people who had not initially complied and people who had not been asked the initial favour.

In a field experiment, Freedman and Fraser (1966) asked Californian homeowners if they would agree to have a large, ugly "Drive Carefully" sign erected on their front lawn. Respondents who had previously been asked to display a small and unobtrusive "Be a Safe Driver" sign in their windows were much more likely to agree than other participants who had not been previously contacted. In a study conducted in Israel, the request to sign a petition in favour of handicapped people led 92% of respondents to donate money for a similar cause when contacted two weeks later, whereas the rate of donors was only 53% for respondents who had not been contacted earlier (Schwarzwald, Bizman, & Raz, 1983). Similarly, the likelihood that blood donors actually showed up for their appointments to give blood was increased from 62% to 81% if they had been asked in a reminder call to verbally restate their commitment, rather than just being reminded (Lipsitz, Kallmeyer, Ferguson, & Abas, 1989). More examples and applications of the technique are discussed by Cialdini (1993).

What are the conditions necessary for the foot-in-the-door technique to work? Firstly, the initial request must be sufficiently large and significant so that people can infer an attitude from their behaviour. On the other hand, it must not be too burdensome, so that the target person does in fact agree to perform the behaviour in the first place. Otherwise, the technique may backfire: A person who refuses the initial request may infer a negative attitude and thus become *less likely* to perform the larger request (DeJong, 1979). Secondly, performing the initial behaviour must be perceived as genuinely voluntary. People's self-perception takes into account environmental factors (Bem, 1972). Just as intrinsic interest can be undermined by external rewards or threats (Deci, Koestner, & Ryan, 1999), so may any attitudinal inference from one's own behaviour be impeded by the perception of external causes for the behaviour.

engaging in the role playing. Furthermore, Janis and Mann (1965) provided a powerful demonstration how negative reinforcement (the anticipated removal of negative consequences) may mediate the effects of role-playing. These researchers asked heavy smokers to improvise for one hour the role of a lung cancer patient who is facing "the threat of painful illness, hospitalization, and early death" (Mann & Janis, 1968, p. 339). A control group of equally heavy smokers merely listened to a tape-recording of the role-playing session. The results showed that the role-players developed less positive attitudes toward smoking and also reported to have reduced their consumption from 24 to 14 cigarettes daily, one month after the role playing session; the reduction reported by control participants was significantly lower (22 to 17 cigarettes daily). Importantly, this effect was maintained in follow-up interviews over an 18-month period (Mann & Janis, 1968). This line of research thus suggests that vividly imagined incentives may be effective in modifying not only attitudes, but also enduring behaviour.

However, the common wisdom that higher incentives lead to more attitude change was forcefully challenged with the advent of the **theory of cognitive dissonance** (Festinger, 1957). Festinger's theory, the most famous cognitive consistency model and perhaps the most influential theory in social psychology, stimulated an enormous amount of research. An important starting point for Festinger was the observation that, in everyday life, we often find ourselves in situations where we do not act in accordance with our attitudes, but rather in line with the requirements of our roles or the social context. For example, you may recall instances in which you went along with friends who were bitching about a teacher, murmuring criticism even though you did not really agree with their negative views. An interesting question, addressed by dissonance theory, is what happens to your attitude in such a situation.

According to dissonance theory, an individual's "cognitions" (i.e. thoughts, attitudes and beliefs) may be consonant, dissonant or irrelevant (i.e. unrelated) to each other. Holding dissonant cognitions creates *cognitive dissonance*, an unpleasant state of arousal that motivates the individual to reduce the dissonance. This can be done by adding, subtracting or substituting cognitions. For example, the cognition "I never smoke at work" would be dissonant with the attitude "I like to smoke" because, subjectively, the opposite of one follows from the other (Festinger, 1957). This dissonance can be reduced by adding further cognitions to make the cognitive system more consistent overall. The cognition "If I smoked at work I would lose my job" should reduce the dissonance and thus allow the person to maintain a positive attitude toward smoking. Refraining from smoking at work in spite of a positive attitude would now be sufficiently justified by the sanctions attached to smoking in this particular setting.

Insufficient justification

But what would happen if the person realised that she *freely chose* to refrain from smoking, perhaps after a polite request from a colleague? Now the person would have *insufficient justification* for showing attitude-discrepant behaviour; she would be likely to reduce dissonance by substituting the dissonant attitude with another cognition that is more consonant, e.g. "After all, I do not *really* like to smoke that much". In short, the person might change her attitude to subjectively justify her change in behaviour.

This kind of attitude change was first shown experimentally by Festinger and Carlsmith (1959). In their study, male students were asked to perform some extremely dull motor tasks, for instance turning a series of pegs a quarter turn clockwise, using one hand only. After about one hour of such boring activities, the participants should have developed a somewhat negative attitude toward the experiment. Later, some participants were subtly induced to tell a lie about their experience. Specifically, they were told that part of the study was to assess the impact of previous expectations on performance. They were then asked to "step in" for an assistant who allegedly had failed to turn up and whose job was to describe the experiment to a prospective participant as enjoyable, fun and interesting. The students were asked if they would take the assistant's role now and occasionally in the future, should the assistant be unavailable. Most participants agreed to do so. They then met "the next participant"—in fact a female confederate—who initially pretended that she had not yet decided whether she should participate, but finally agreed to do so, apparently as a result of the positive things that the participant had told her. The purpose of this **induced compliance** procedure was to create two dissonant cognitions: (a) "I think this experiment is boring" and (b) "I just described the experiment to the other student as if it were interesting."

The crucial experimental manipulation involved the reward that the participants expected to be paid for complying with the experimenter's request. Students in one condition were promised the large sum of twenty dollars; in another condition, the promised reward was only one dollar.[1] Students in a third condition served as a control group; they were never asked to tell a lie or promised a reward. Festinger and Carlsmith hypothesised that students in the one-dollar condition would experience a high degree of cognitive dissonance, because they did not have a sufficient external justification for engaging in the attitude-discrepant behaviour. In the twenty-dollar condition, however, the researchers predicted that the high reward would keep the level of cognitive dissonance low. (Participants in this condition might have reasoned, "OK, I've told a little lie—but for twenty dollars, who wouldn't?") As a result, students in the one-dollar condition would be likely to change their attitude toward the

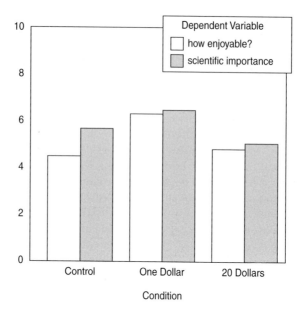

Figure 8.2. Judgments of enjoyability and scientific importance of a boring experiment, as a function of expected reward for publicly stating that the experiment was fun (data from Festinger & Carlsmith, 1959).

experiment in a positive direction, to align it with their behaviour and thus reduce the dissonance; students in the twenty-dollar condition, however, would not change their attitude. When students' attitudes toward the experiment were later assessed by a different experimenter, the "one-dollar liars" indeed evaluated the experiment more favourably compared to both the "twenty-dollar liars" and students in the control condition (see Figure 8.2). Thus, insufficient justification for a consequential behaviour was shown to cause a change in attitude (for another illustration of this effect, see Figure 8.3).

After this initial demonstration, a huge number of studies provided further evidence for dissonance effects on attitudes (see Möntmann & Irle, 1957/1978). This research also delineated more clearly the processing steps that must occur for attitude-discrepant actions to cause attitude change (for a review, see Cooper & Fazio, 1984; cf. Joule & Beauvois, 1998).

Processing steps in dissonance-induced attitude change

The first condition identified as necessary was that the person must perceive *negative consequences* of her behaviour. In the original

Dilbert by Scott Adams

Figure 8.3. Dissonance theory: An application.

Festinger and Carlsmith study, participants did perceive their attitude-discrepant behaviour as having negative consequences for a fellow student. After all, the confederate first pretended that she had not made up her mind about participating and thus seemed to be misled into wasting an hour of her time by the false information the participant had given her. In subsequent studies, the consequences of the behaviour were systematically varied (e.g. by including conditions in which the confederate remained unconvinced), and the inverse relation of incentive magnitude and attitude change was typically only found when negative consequences were present (e.g. Cooper & Worchel, 1970; Stroebe & Diehl, 1981).

Secondly, it seemed necessary that the individual must take *personal responsibility* for the behaviour. In the Festinger and Carlsmith study, the experimenter's request was staged in a way that set it apart from the experiment proper, so that participants could in principle refuse to comply (and some did). Linder, Cooper, and Jones (1967) experimentally varied participants' perception of free choice. Students were either *asked* or *required* to write a "forceful and convincing essay" (p. 247) in favour of an unpopular law that restricted freedom of speech. For doing so, they received either a low reward ($0.50) or a high reward ($2.50). It was found that students in the free-choice conditions changed their attitudes toward the position taken in the essay if they received a low reward but not if the reward was high, as predicted by dissonance theory. Importantly, however, students in the no-choice conditions showed an opposite pattern: They did not change their attitudes when the reward was low, and tended to change in the direction of the essay when the reward was high (see Figure 8.4).

Finally, it has been posited that the person needs to *feel unpleasant arousal* and to *attribute this arousal to the attitude-discrepant behaviour*. In several studies, researchers directly assessed physiological indicators of arousal (e.g. skin conductance responses) and showed that voluntarily engaging in attitude-discrepant behaviour indeed increases an individual's arousal (e.g. Croyle & Cooper, 1983; Elkin & Leippe, 1986; Losch & Cacioppo, 1990). Furthermore, in so-called misattribution experiments, the apparent cause of such arousal was manipulated. In a famous study by Zanna and Cooper (1974), participants wrote a counterattitudinal essay under high- or low-choice conditions. Furthermore, they were informed about the alleged side effects of a (placebo) pill they had taken in an earlier study. Depending on experimental condition, they were led to believe either that the pill would make them feel tense, or that it would make them

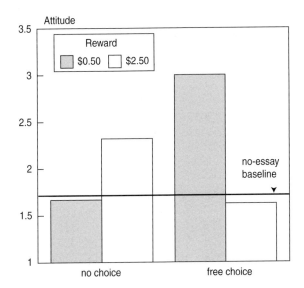

Figure 8.4. Attitude change after writing a counterattitudinal essay as a function of reward magnitude and freedom of choice (data from Linder et al., 1967). Higher bars represent attitudes more in line with the position of the essay. The horizontal baseline represents the attitude of control participants who did not write an essay.

feel relaxed, or that it would have no "side effects". The results of this study are shown in Figure 8.5. Control participants showed the classic dissonance effect, changing their attitudes toward the counterattitudinal position they had advocated more under high choice than under low choice. For participants who could attribute their arousal to an unrelated event (having taken the pill), no difference between high-choice and low-choice conditions was found; however, for those participants who felt aroused although they expected the pill to be relaxing, the dissonance effect was even more pronounced than in the control condition.

In concert with a number of conceptual replications (for a review, see Fazio & Cooper, 1983), these results established the arousal-like nature of cognitive dissonance. They also point to the importance of subjective experience; dissonance reduction seems to require that individuals interpret the arousal as negative affect caused by the counterattitudinal behaviour. However, this subjective component of cognitive dissonance had not been researched as thoroughly as its physiological aspects. More recently, Elliot and Devine (1994) conducted a couple of studies in which they assessed both negative affect (via self-report) and attitudes at various points in the hypothetical "dissonance-arousal-to-reduction" sequence. In two high-choice induced compliance conditions, both affect and attitude were assessed either *after participants had committed themselves to writing a counterattitudinal essay* (but before they had started writing), or *after*

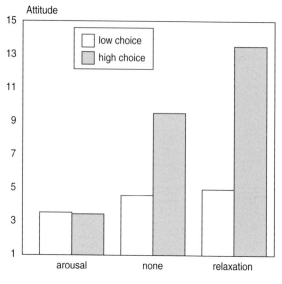

Figure 8.5. Attitudes as a function of level of choice and attribution of arousal in an induced-compliance situation (data from Zanna & Cooper, 1974).

they had completed the counterattitudinal essay. In a *baseline* condition, measures of affect and attitude were taken before participants had agreed to write an essay and after they had completed the essay under low choice, respectively. The results (see Figure 8.6) are in line with dissonance theory: Agreeing to perform a counterattitudinal behaviour initially creates negative affect but does not immediately lead to attitude change; once the behaviour has been performed, however, dissonance seems to be reduced, i.e. attitudes change in line with the behaviour whereas the level of negative affect reverts to baseline.

Generality of dissonance effects

In the course of rigorous empirical scrutiny, not only were the limiting conditions for dissonance effects outlined more clearly. Festinger's theory was also applied to situations other than those in which people show attitude-discrepant behaviour. The **effort-justification hypothesis** explains why people sometimes come to like what they had to suffer for. Groucho Marx once remarked he did not want to belong to any club that would have him as a member.

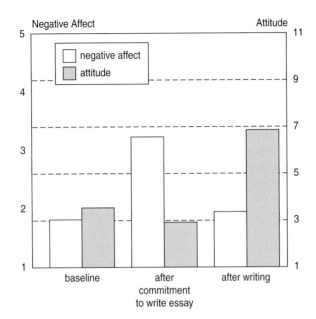

Figure 8.6. Self-reported negative affect and attitude at different stages of the dissonance-arousal-to-reduction sequence (data from Elliot & Devine, 1994).

And indeed, groups that require prospective members to undergo unpleasant initiation procedures are often liked better than groups that are easy to get into. An effort-justification account for this phenomenon was tested experimentally by Aronson and Mills (1959), who recruited female students to join a "discussion group on sex", which turned out to be a circle of students speaking in an extremely dull and boring way about secondary sexual behaviour in lower animals. To gain access to the discussion group, students in one experimental condition had to endure an embarrassing interview, which involved reading sexually explicit material to a male experimenter, whereas participants in a control condition were simply asked if they thought they could discuss sex freely before they were allowed to join the group. When asked later to evaluate the group, the former participants reported more positive attitudes than the latter. Presumably, they had justified their suffering by changing their attitude about the group (see also Wicklund & Brehm, 1976).

A highly interesting clinical application of the effort-justification paradigm was reported by Axsom and Cooper (1985). In several sessions, these researchers asked overweight women who were trying to lose weight to perform cognitive and perceptual tasks that were either difficult (high effort) or easy to perform (low effort). Apart from these pseudo interventions, which had nothing to do with any established therapy or theory of weight loss, the women were simply asked to keep track of the food they ate and were weighed at regular intervals. The results showed that women in the high-effort group lost more weight than those in the low-effort group, and this difference was maintained over a one-year period. These and other findings (e.g. Axsom, 1989) indicate that therapies which include hard work, even if this is unrelated to the therapeutic goal, seem to be more effective than therapies that are less effortful for the clients (for a review, see Draycott & Dabbs, 1998).

A further area to which dissonance theory has been successfully applied are the cognitive processes that follow decision making. If we choose one course of action over another, e.g. to study psychology rather than law, to accept a job offer in a big city rather than moving to the countryside, or buying one product rather than its competitor brand, we usually experience some degree of **postdecisional dissonance**. This is because we know about positive and negative features of the decision alternatives, and both the negative features of the chosen alternative and the positive features of the nonchosen alternatives are inconsistent with our behaviour. One way of reducing this dissonance is by magnifying our positive attitude toward the chosen alternative and decreasing our evaluation of the nonchosen alternatives (Brehm, 1956). Thus, patrons at horse races were found to feel more confident about a horse's chances of winning after they had bet money on the horse than just before they did so (Knox & Inkster, 1968). Similarly, U.S. voters felt more positive about the chances of their preferred candidate being elected president after voting for him than before (Regan & Kilduff, 1988).

Limitations and alternatives to dissonance theory

We have seen that dissonance theory has been fruitfully applied to a variety of phenomena. On the other hand, the theory has its limitations as well. Especially research in the induced-compliance paradigm has shown that quite specific conditions need to be met for counterattitudinal behaviour to produce attitude change. If the person does not perceive freedom of choice when engaging in the behaviour or does not feel responsible for any negative consequences of the behaviour, dissonance should not be aroused to begin with. And given that dissonance has been aroused, the individual may still attribute her unpleasant internal state to a salient but irrelevant cause. Finally, even if dissonance has both been aroused and attributed to the critical behaviour, there may be alternative ways of reducing dissonance that do not involve attitude change.

This becomes more obvious if we conceive of dissonance in more general terms, not as a discrepancy between a particular behaviour and a particular attitude, but rather as a state caused by a threat to a person's self concept (Aronson, 1968, 1969). Being personally responsible for aversive consequences is dissonant with viewing oneself as a responsible and decent human being. On the one hand, this view may explain why induced compliance sometimes produces attitude change if the aversive consequences are endured only by the individual himself, rather than others. For example, participants who were induced to eat fried grasshoppers under insufficient justification rated the experience as more pleasant than others who had sufficient justification for showing this behaviour (Zimbardo, Weisenberg, Firestone, & Levy, 1965). On the other hand, if dissonance is mainly a threat to the integrity of the self, then *any* opportunity to reaffirm one's integrity—not only attitude change—should help to reduce dissonance (Steele, 1988). According to Steele's **self-affirmation theory**, responses to self-threat are quite fluid, and people may engage in self-affirmation in a variety of ways, which may be unrelated to the behaviour or attitude that caused the threat to begin with. This was demonstrated in a study by Steele and Liu (1983, Study 1), in which students wrote counterattitudinal essays under high choice or low choice. Some of the high-choice participants were given an opportunity to affirm an important self-relevant value (i.e. an abstract goal that they regard as a guiding principle in their lives: Rokeach, 1973; Schwartz, 1992) by completing a value scale before their post-compliance attitudes were assessed; the remaining participants were asked to report their attitudes before they completed the value scale. Only those high choice participants who had *not* had an opportunity to reaffirm their self-worth showed dissonance-reducing attitude change, whereas the self-affirmation participants seemed to have reduced dissonance through self-affirmation: Their post-compliance attitudes did not differ from those of participants who had written the essay under low choice (and thus should not have experienced dissonance to begin with).

Although self-affirmation theory integrates induced-compliance attitude change into a wider framework of self-affirming strategies, it does not specify the conditions under which attitude change would be a more likely result of dissonance than any other cognitive or behavioural strategy. It does point to the fact, however, that in real-life situations people's opportunities to come to grips with inconsistency may be more varied than in dissonance experiments, where attitude change is often the only viable strategy (Steele, 1988). While Steele's approach mainly expands the scope of reactions to attitude-discrepant behaviour, other theorists challenged dissonance theory by explaining the same phenomena of attitude change on the basis of essentially different psychological processes. Before concluding this section, we will turn to two of the major alternative explanations.

Impression management theory

Impression management theorists (Schlenker, 1982; Tedeschi, 1981; Tedeschi, Schlenker, & Bonoma, 1971) assume that people seek to create in others an image of consistency between their attitudes and behaviours, in order to appear in a favourable light. Indeed, it has been shown that people who appear inconsistent may be evaluated negatively by others (Allgeier, Byrne, Brooks, & Revnes, 1979). The major challenge of this view to dissonance theory lies in its alternative assumptions concerning the processes that mediate attitude change. Impression management theory shares with dissonance theory the idea that a consistency motive is invoked, but now this motive is thought to operate at the public level of communicating the attitude, rather than at the level of an individual's private cognitions. In other words, participants in induced compliance studies are assumed to "fake" an attitude that is in line with their previous behaviour but not "really" to change their attitudes.

From this theoretical position, two important qualifications can be derived. Firstly, people should not report a changed attitude after attitude-discrepant behaviour if the attitude assessment is private and their responses cannot be associated with them personally. And, secondly, attitude change should also be prevented if participants believe that the experimenter has privileged access to their "true attitude", no matter what their self-report may indicate. Although precautions have been taken in many induced-compliance studies (including Festinger & Carlsmith, 1959) that participants would not report their attitudes directly to the experimenter, it cannot be completely ruled out that they still thought their responses would become known. Therefore, Tedeschi and his colleagues (e.g. Gaes, Kalle, & Tedeschi, 1978) compared induced compliance effects on attitudes under standard conditions of attitude assessment versus "bogus pipeline" conditions (see chapter 2 for a description of the bogus pipeline technique). In line with impression management theory, the classic pattern was replicated under normal conditions, but no effects of induced compliance were found in the bogus pipeline conditions. However, Stults, Messé, and Kerr (1984) did find attitude change even under bogus pipeline conditions when participants were given time to get accommodated to the fake lie-detector equipment. So the overall evidence for impression management as a mediator of attitudinal responses is mixed.

In the light of recent developments concerning the measurement of implicit attitudes, it would be interesting to explore if effects of induced compliance can be detected by more sophisticated non-reactive attitude measures like the IAT (Greenwald et al., 1998; see chapter 2). It has indeed been proposed that the organisation of implicit attitudes may be guided by principles of cognitive consistency (Greenwald et al., 2000). Interestingly, however, Wilson and his colleagues (2000) argued that what changes in an induced compliance procedure are explicit attitudes, whereas implicit attitudes may remain unchanged. They reasoned that after the process of dissonance reduction, it would take longer to retrieve the newly formed explicit attitude, whereas under suboptimal retrieval conditions (e.g. time pressure), people would be able only to retrieve and report the more accessible, unchanged implicit attitude. In line with this notion, Wilson et al. found that students who had written a counterattitudinal essay showed evidence of attitude change only if they had sufficient time to *report* their attitude. Students in another condition, who had also written a counterattitudinal essay but were asked to respond to the attitude question within five seconds, reported what seemed to be an unchanged attitude.

Importantly, this pattern was obtained even two days after the essay had been written, so the process of dissonance reduction should have been completed before the attitude question was asked (Wilson et al., 2000). From the viewpoint of impression management theory, however, one might argue that self-presentational concerns are set in motion only if and when an attitude judgment is requested; it then takes time to construct a socially acceptable attitude judgment. So the Wilson et al. data might also be interpreted as evidence for on-line impression management, which takes some time, and against a dissonance explanation.

In any case, the novel applications of cognitive consistency principles in combination with the distinction between implicit and explicit attitudes may open up interesting avenues for research. At the level of explicit attitudes, it has been argued that the accounts of cognitive dissonance and impression management may complement rather than contradict each other. Concerns for self-presentation and the striving for cognitive consistency may both contribute to attitude change in varying degrees, depending on the demands of the situation (see Tetlock & Manstead, 1985).

Self-perception theory

The most prominent challenge for dissonance theory came from self-perception theory (Bem, 1967, 1972), a perspective we already discussed in relation to the overjustification effect. As you will recall, Bem suggested that people infer their own attitudes on the basis of their behaviour and its situational constraints. Thus, when students write an essay opposing freedom of speech and do not perceive a sufficient external reward for doing so (Linder et al., 1967), they are likely to infer that they *really* believe freedom of speech should be restricted. If, however, they are paid a large sum to write the essay, they should perceive their behaviour to be under external control and thus nondiagnostic of their true attitude.

Bem (1965) showed that participants to whom the procedures of induced compliance experiments had been merely described made inferences about the true attitude of participants that replicated the actual result patterns: A genuinely positive attitude was inferred when incentives were low, but not when incentives were high. Bem concluded from these and other results (Bem, 1967) that for induced-compliance attitude change to occur it was sufficient to have *information* about the behaviour and the conditions under which it occurred, whereas a *feeling* of negative arousal was not necessary.

Although these process assumptions are more parsimonious than those of dissonance theory, they cannot accommodate later findings that misattribution of arousal to an irrelevant cause effectively undermined attitude change (e.g. Zanna & Cooper, 1974). A synthesis of dissonance and self-perception explanations was proposed by Fazio, Zanna, and Cooper (1977), who argued that self-perception theory better accounted for the effects of attitude-congruent advocacies (where the individual argues for a position close to her own prior attitude and negative arousal would not be expected), whereas dissonance theory was a better explanation for the effects of attitude-discrepant advocacies (involving positions truly opposed to the person's initial attitude). These predictions were supported by the results of a misattribution experiment (Fazio et al., 1977).

Behaviour-induced attitude change and processing effort

A more general integration of the self-perception and dissonance perspectives relies on differences in the cognitive effort involved in each process (e.g. Eagly & Chaiken, 1993; Smith & Mackie, 1995). Just as motivational concerns affect the extent of systematic processing of external messages (see chapter 7), so do they determine the effort invested in reasoning about one's own behaviour. Accordingly, if no important goals or self-relevant attitudes are at stake, people resort to relatively effortless inferences based on the self-perception of their actions. If, however, the integrity of the self is threatened (Steele, 1988) or an attitude has other important consequences, more effortful reasoning, including the rationalisation process described in dissonance theory, will ensue.

Some evidence showing that, in an induced compliance situation, people may process the same information either systematically or heuristically comes from work by Stroebe and Diehl (1981, 1988). In one study, these researchers asked students to write a counter-attitudinal essay under constantly high choice, and to be tape-recorded reading their essay. Depending on experimental condition, the consequences of this behaviour were either severe (the tape would be used to persuade another participant) or minimal (the tape would be used to compute a "voice profile"). Furthermore, social support for the participant's behaviour was varied: An attitudinally similar confederate either agreed or disagreed with the experimenter's request to write and read an essay. Stroebe and Diehl (1988) reasoned that negative consequences of counterattitudinal behaviour would motivate the person to justify her behaviour. Indeed, as shown in Figure 8.7, participants in the severe-consequences conditions seemed to take identical behaviour of a similar other as sufficient justification for their own behaviour, and showed no attitude change; if the similar other had declined to write the essay, however, attitude change in line with the essay occurred. When there were no negative consequences, however, participants seemed to use the other's behaviour as a heuristic cue ("liking-agreement"), and showed a boomerang effect when the confederate declined, i.e. changed their attitude in line with the confederate's behaviour. Although Stroebe and Diehl's analysis in terms of dual processing is suggestive, it should be noted that they did not provide any direct evidence for greater processing effort in the severe-consequences conditions of their study.

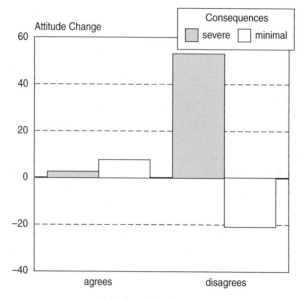

Figure 8.7. Attitude change as a function of severity of consequences of counterattitudinal essay-writing and behaviour of a similar other (data from Stroebe & Diehl, 1988).

Attitude-change processes observed in forced-compliance situations may thus include the low-effort processing of cues (e.g. social support, incentives), somewhat more effortful attributional processing of the kind emphasised in self-perception theory, and the elaborate, effortful justification of the discrepancy between behaviour and initial attitude, perhaps based on self-generated arguments. Ultimately, the amount of processing effort invested might determine both the final attitude position and the durability of its consequences (see chapters 3 and 7), but more research is needed to substantiate these speculations.

Chapter summary

(1) Changes in behaviour may lead to opposite changes in attitude if people (a) are forced to refrain from a cherished behaviour, or (b) are rewarded for engaging in a behaviour they liked to perform anyway. These phenomena have been explained by a motivation to restore a threatened freedom (psychological reactance) and the tendency to infer one's own attitudes from one's behaviour like an external observer (self-perception).

(2) Although incentives may be effective in changing attitudes, the amount of attitude change is often inversely related to the magnitude of an incentive. According to Festinger's dissonance theory, a large incentive provides sufficient justification for engaging in attitude-discrepant behaviour, whereas a small incentive does not. In the case of insufficient justification, a change in attitude is one way to re-establish consistency between attitudes and behaviour.

(3) Hundreds of studies following up on Festinger and Carlsmith's (1959) classic experiment helped to delineate the conditions necessary to create attitude change after induced compliance: aversive consequences, personal responsibility and a feeling of unpleasant arousal that is attributed to the attitude-discrepant behaviour.

(4) Dissonance theory also explains how people come to like what they have suffered for (effort justification) and how our attitudes change after decision making (postdecisional dissonance).

(5) Dissonance theory has its limitations in explaining behaviour-induced attitude change. Cognitive consistency can often be restored in ways other than changing attitudes, e.g. by affirming one's self-worth (Steele, 1988). Furthermore, alternative explanations to behaviour-induced attitude change are based on impression management and self-perception processes. Each of these approaches seems to complement dissonance theory, being applicable to different types of situation.

(6) The cognitive effort involved in attitude change based on self-perception may be lower than that involved in the reduction of cognitive dissonance. This would have consequences for the durability of each of these forms of attitude change, but further empirical corroboration is needed.

Exercises

(1) Think of ways in which the principle of psychological reactance can be used in advertising.

(2) Imagine you are asked to advise a city council on how to improve residents' attitudes toward the use of public transport: Would you recommend the use of incentives? What kind of incentive would be likely to work under what circumstances?

(3) Why do severe initiation rites work?

(4) Provide examples for the types of situations in which cognitive dissonance leads to attitude change.
(5) Under what conditions is attitude change likely to be based on a self-perception process?
(6) Design an experiment that would allow you to test the hypothesis that dissonance-based attitude change requires high processing effort.

Note

(1) Festinger and Carlsmith's participants were told at debriefing that they could not keep the reward and were asked to return it. It should be noted that such practice would not be acceptable any more under current ethical codes for psychological research (e.g., American Psychological Association, 1992; British Psychological Society, 1991).

Further reading

A highly entertaining book that illuminates everyday applications of behaviour-induced attitude change (and many other aspects of influence):

Cialdini, R. B. (1993). *Influence: The psychology of persuasion* (rev. ed.). New York: Quill/William Morrow. (chapter 3: Commitment and consistency)

A review and integration of about 25 years research on cognitive dissonance:

Cooper, J., & Fazio, R. H. (1984). A new look at dissonance theory. *Advances in Experimental Social Psychology, 17,* 229–266.

Consequences of attitudes III

In the preceding chapters, we have examined the structure, functions and origins of attitudes. In this final part of the book we turn to the consequences of holding attitudes for people's thinking (chapter 9) and overt behaviour (chapter 10). We will address attitudes' influences on information processing as well as the behavioural outcomes of such attitudinal processing. The influences of attitudes on thinking and behaviour reflect both the functions that attitudes serve (see chapter 1) and their structural properties (see chapter 3). Accordingly, both motivational and cognitive approaches have been applied to these domains. Variations in processing effort, which have been identified as an important factor in persuasion (chapters 6 and 7) and in behaviour-induced attitude change (chapter 8), will also be a recurring theme in the following two chapters on the consequences of attitudes.

Attitude influences on information processing 9

Have you ever watched a sports event in the company of supporters of *both* teams? We had this experience at a small international conference that took place during the 1998 football World Cup. In the evenings, it was interesting to see how European colleagues who watched some of the games on TV diverged in their interpretations of "their own" and other national teams' performance. The same referee's decisions would be accompanied by approving remarks from one "camp", but ridiculed by members of another (for a systematic examination of such differences, see Hastorf & Cantril, 1954; see also Figure 9.1). At the same time, American colleagues who witnessed this spectacle wondered how anybody could get so worked up about a sport that they found rather unexciting. These events provide a nice example for the fact that our attitudes may both bias our interpretation of social reality and affect the intensity of our information processing. Furthermore, these effects of attitudes may also contribute to stabilising and reinforcing our attitudes.

Theoretical assumptions guiding research on attitude-processing links: Consistency, function and structure

Much research on attitudinal effects on the processing of new information was guided by the principle of cognitive consistency (see also chapters 3 and 8). A basic tenet characterising this approach is that people attempt to maintain consistency of their cognitive structure by seeking out new information in line with their existing attitudes, and screening out new information that might challenge their attitudes (Festinger, 1957, 1964). This should result in what has been termed

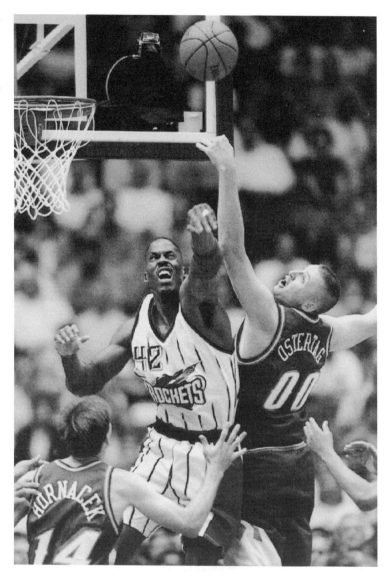

Figure 9.1. Foul or fair play? What we perceive may depend on our attitudes toward the competing teams. Copyright © Popperfoto/Reuters.

attitudinal selectivity effects at several stages of processing, including attention, elaboration and memory.

Selectivity effects can be predicted as well based on the functional analysis of attitudes with its central postulate that attitudes provide structure and inform the individual about the hedonic relevance of objects and events (see chapter 1; Maio & Olson, 2000b; Pratkanis,

Breckler, & Greenwald, 1989). From this viewpoint, an attitude may function like a cognitive **schema** (see Pratkanis, 1989). This concept was introduced into psychology by Bartlett (1932/1995) and has since been used widely in cognitive and social psychology to describe the way in which people represent certain types of memory content. Psychologists have studied schemata of persons, the self, roles, events and situations (for reviews, see chapter 4 of Fiske & Taylor, 1991; Bless et al., in press), as well as content-independent schematic structures (e.g. cognitive triads: Heider, 1958; schemata of causality: Kelley, 1972). Although different conceptualisations were proposed, we may highlight two central properties of a schema (see Fiske & Morling, 1995):

(1) A schema is *abstract*, representing general knowledge about a domain or category and emphasising the similarities between special cases, thus *simplifying reality*.
(2) A schema *affects the processing of new information* by establishing expectations, facilitating encoding and guiding inferences; a person using a schema may "go beyond the information given" in any particular situation (Bruner, 1957).

Applying these criteria to attitudes, we should expect that having an attitude both simplifies and guides information processing in predictable ways. For example, a person who strongly dislikes meat should (1) easily encode and remember information fitting his attitudinal schema (e.g. a report on cases of food poisoning caused by spoiled meat), (2) be prepared to respond negatively to any novel object he encodes as an exemplar of the meat category (e.g. an ostrich steak), and (3) make negative inferences and judgments about this object (e.g. regarding its smell, taste or nutritional value).

In line with the motivational and cognitive underpinnings of attitudinal effects on processing we may distinguish between conscious, strategic effects on the one hand (e.g. actively seeking and elaborating on attitude-consistent information) and automatic effects on the other (e.g. having one's attention involuntarily drawn towards an attitude object). Another useful distinction is related to the stage of the information processing sequence at which a particular attitudinal effect is expected to occur. Effects of attitudes on thinking have been hypothesised to occur at all stages of information processing, including (a) attention, encoding and exposure, (b) judgment and elaboration and (c) memory (see Eagly & Chaiken, 1998). In the sections to follow, we will discuss effects of attitudes on each of these stages, and within each section, we will try to differentiate between relatively automatic and more strategic consequences of attitudes.

Attitude effects on attention, encoding and exposure

Some effects of attitudes on attention and encoding happen quickly and efficiently, sometimes outside of a perceiver's conscious awareness, and may be difficult to control. Such automatic effects can be beneficial as they help individuals to notice and process objects that are of hedonic relevance, enabling them to respond appropriately without requiring much cognitive capacity (Fazio, 2000). As the number of stimuli that impinge on an individual every day is enormous, an orienting function of attitudes that helps to rapidly encode stimuli into hedonically meaningful categories as well as to attend to certain important stimuli should be highly adaptive and favoured by natural selection (see chapter 4). In ancestral times, individuals who quickly identified a perceptual object as an enemy (or a source of food, or a potential mate) and reacted to it in a proper way (e.g. by fleeing or approaching) were more likely to survive and reproduce than those who didn't. We will first discuss automatic effects of attitudes on attention and categorisation; then we turn to more strategic aspects of selective attention and exposure to information that supports existing attitudes.

Automatic attention

Until recently, experimental evidence for an "orienting value of attitudes" (Roskos-Ewoldsen & Fazio, 1992) was scarce. Some early suggestive data compatible with this idea were presented by Erdelyi and Appelbaum (1973), who demonstrated a disruptive effect of affect-laden stimuli on the processing of other stimuli. Members of a Jewish organisation were briefly shown a central item surrounded by eight other items and later asked to recall as many of those items as possible. If the central item was either a swastika or a Star of David, the Jewish participants recalled fewer of the surrounding items than if the central item was a neutral object. One explanation for this result is that the central item attracted participants' attention when it was associated with strong positive or negative affect. However, as participants had been instructed to focus their gaze on the centre of the display where the critical items appeared, it is equally possible that affective stimuli, once they are already in the focus of attention, simply disrupt further processing or make it more difficult to refocus one's attention (Erdelyi & Blumenthal, 1973).

So the question remained whether attitude objects really *attract* attention. And if they did, would this be true only for objects whose evaluation is extreme, such as the swastika in Erdelyi and Appelbaum's (1973) study? Roskos-Ewoldsen and Fazio (1992) hypothesised that attitudes would serve an orienting function to the extent that they are accessible (see chapter 2). They reasoned that, due to the strong association in memory between the attitude object and an accessible attitude, the mere presence of the object in an individual's perceptual field would activate the attitude and thus draw the individual's attention to the object. Importantly, this was predicted to happen automatically, even if the primary task that the person is engaged in could be performed better by ignoring the attitude object.

In two studies testing these hypotheses, Roskos-Ewoldsen and Fazio (1992, Experiments 1 and 2) showed their participants several pictures, each containing six objects that were arranged in a circle (e.g. a bicycle, an aeroplane, a flower, an umbrella, a purse and a squirrel). Each circular array was presented very briefly, and the participant's task was to notice as many objects as possible and to write down the objects' names immediately after each presentation. In one study, the accessibility of participants' attitudes toward each object was assessed by recording how long it took them to indicate whether they liked or disliked each object. In line with predictions, participants more frequently noticed those objects in each array that were associated with more accessible attitudes (58%) compared to objects that were associated with less accessible attitudes (54%). To test the causal role of accessibility more directly, in another study Roskos-Ewoldsen and Fazio (1992) experimentally manipulated attitude accessibility. This was done by asking participants to rehearse (= repeatedly express) their attitudes toward some randomly chosen objects. To control for frequency of exposure, other participants repeatedly judged the same objects in a nonevaluative fashion—by stating whether they are animate or inanimate. Later, participants were again asked to notice as many objects as possible in several briefly presented arrays which contained both attitude-rehearsal objects and nonrehearsal (control) objects. The results showed that repeated expression had increased the accessibility of the rehearsed attitudes, and that participants noticed a larger percentage of those objects whose associated attitudes they had rehearsed (59%) than of the control objects (54%). Although the differences in object identification in these two studies may not seem impressive, it should be noted that the associated effect sizes were quite large ($r = .62$ and .46, respectively; computed on the basis of F-tests reported by Roskos-Ewoldsen & Fazio, 1992).

These findings support the notion that accessible attitudes cause people to notice the associated attitude objects when consciously trying to notice as many stimuli as possible in their perceptual field. But would accessible attitudes also direct attention to objects when the perceiver was engaged in a completely different task? To provide a clearer test of the notion that accessible attitudes *attract* attention, Roskos-Ewoldsen and Fazio (1992, Experiment 4) conducted a study that featured a visual search task. The dependent variable was the time it took a participant to detect a target object (or to indicate that the target object was not displayed) in an array of six objects. Importantly, participants were told in advance that the target object would appear in only three out of six positions on the screen, whereas items in the remaining three positions could safely be ignored. As you may have guessed, the distractor items that appeared in the to-be-ignored positions were attitude objects, and participants had previously rehearsed their attitudes toward these objects (high accessibility items) or made nonevaluative judgments about them (control items). The main finding was that it took participants significantly longer to perform the visual search task when the distractors were high accessibility items (mean response time = 2377 ms) than when they were control items (mean response time = 2300 ms; effect size $r = .36$).

Taken together, this series of studies nicely demonstrates that strongly attitude-evoking objects automatically attract attention. This seems to be true even if a person is trying to ignore that area in her perceptual field where the attitude object appears (for a review of related evidence, see Fazio, 2000).

Automatic effects of attitudes on encoding

Another way in which attitudes may automatically affect processing is by accentuating hedonically meaningful categories for encoding a stimulus (see Fazio, 2000). Most objects can be categorised in numerous ways. For example, a car can be seen as a means of transportation or as a status symbol (Ennis & Zanna, 2000), pizza may be viewed as a tasty snack or as an unhealthy food item, and a 41-year-old White male psychologist can be categorised in terms of his age, race, sex or profession. Theories of categorisation assume that which of the possible attributes of an object is used for categorisation may depend on the allocation of attention to these attributes (e.g. Smith & Zárate, 1992). One of the factors that may control the allocation of attention to a given attribute is a person's attitude toward that attribute.

This possibility was studied by Smith, Fazio, and Cejka (1996), using triads consisting of a target object and two possible categories for that object (e.g. yoghurt: health food/dairy product). The relative accessibility of attitudes toward each alternative category was manipulated via attitude rehearsal. Participants repeatedly expressed their attitudes toward one of the two categories, whereas for the other category, they repeatedly indicated whether it was animate or inanimate. Later they were exposed to the target objects of each triad for the first time and asked to use them as recall cues for the categories that had been presented earlier. The researchers reasoned that if attitudes provide a ready aid for categorisation, then those categories that evoke accessible attitudes (the "rehearsed" ones) should show a recall advantage over the control categories. This was indeed the case. For example, if "dairy product" was the category in the attitude rehearsal task, presentation of "yoghurt" was more likely to facilitate recall of "dairy product" than of "health food", whereas the opposite result was obtained if participants had rehearsed their attitudes toward health food.

In another experiment, the same authors (Smith et al., 1996, Experiment 3) examined the impact of attitude accessibility on the time it took participants to verify the category membership of a given object (e.g. "Is yoghurt a dairy product?"). Participants had again rehearsed their attitudes toward one of two alternative categories; it was found that they were faster in verifying category membership when their attitude toward the presented category had been rehearsed rather than unrehearsed.

In a related study, Fazio and Dunton (1997) assessed similarity ratings for pairs of target persons who were depicted in photos that included cues to their occupation (e.g. a tool or a uniform). Thus, information was present on each target's sex, race and occupation. One week earlier, participants' implicit attitudes toward Black versus White people had been measured using the bona fide pipeline procedure (Fazio et al., 1995; see chapter 2). Fazio and Dunton reasoned that participants who held either strong positive or strong negative racial attitudes toward Black people, as indicated by the relative response facilitation scores in the bona fide pipeline, would be more likely to base their similarity judgments on race (as opposed to sex or occupation) compared to people with more neutral racial attitudes. This prediction was strongly supported by the results.

Comparable findings were reported by Bohner, Siebler, Sturm, Effler, Litters, Reinhard, and Rutz (1998). These researchers studied the influence of female students' rape myth acceptance on the spontaneous activation and use of the gender category. Women low in rape myth acceptance have been shown to hold positive attitudes toward victims of sexual violence, which are backed by beliefs that construe sexual violence as an intergroup phenomenon, something that men do to women. By contrast, women high in rape myth acceptance tend to derogate victims and interpret sexual violence as an interpersonal phenomenon, something that a specific perpetrator does to a particular victim (for a review, see Bohner, 1998). Bohner and his colleagues found that women low in rape myth acceptance were more likely to use the gender category in a range of social and cognitive tasks, even though nothing about gender was ever mentioned in the task instructions. For example, women low in rape myth acceptance were more likely to judge the similarity of pairs of target persons in terms of gender, and in a word-completion task spontaneously produced gender-related solutions both more frequently and more quickly compared to women who were higher in rape myth acceptance.

In sum, there is ample evidence to date that object categories for which a perceiver holds strong and accessible attitudes are more likely to be used in categorising an object or person. Moreover, these spontaneously activated, attitude-related categories may be used implicitly as input to other types of judgments, even if neither the attitude nor the category in question form part of the explicit judgment task. In the next section, we will address more deliberate decisions about the allocation of attention to attitude-related information.

Strategic effects of attitudes on attention and exposure

According to the principle of cognitive consistency, consciously considering information that challenges one's attitudes should cause an aversive state of arousal (e.g. Festinger, 1964). It follows that people should actively search for and pay close attention to information that matches their existing attitudes (*congenial* information), and should try to avoid or ignore information that is incompatible with their attitudes (*hostile* information). Numerous studies have addressed this *selective exposure* hypothesis (for a review, see Frey, 1986).

Researchers often tested an important qualification to the selective exposure hypothesis that was first introduced by Festinger (1957), namely that selectivity should be most pronounced if individuals are committed to their attitude *after* a behavioural decision (e.g. to buy a certain product) but not before a decision (cf. chapter 8). The rationale for this assumed tendency to avoid *postdecisional dissonance* is that the decision gives greater weight to the attitude; thus, the attitude becomes more resistant to change. Accordingly, changing the attitude to reduce dissonance becomes less likely and selective exposure effects become more likely.

In one study, Frey and Rosch (1984) provided students with information about a manager's job performance; later the students were asked to evaluate this performance and to decide if the manager's contract should be renewed. The main experimental manipulation was whether this decision could be reversed: It was said to be either definitive or tentative. Once participants had made their definitive or tentative decision about the manager's fate, they were given an opportunity to examine additional, new information about him. Each piece of information was clearly labelled so that the students knew whether it comprised a positive or negative evaluation (e.g. "[The manager] has done a good job and therefore his contract should be extended"). The students could choose which of five positive and five negative descriptions they wanted to read in detail. Frey and Rosch's results supported the selective exposure hypothesis (see Figure 9.2): Students who had made a final decision selected twice as many consonant than dissonant new pieces of information, whereas students who had made a reversible decision showed an almost even-handed selection of confirming and disconfirming information.

According to Frey's (1986) review, the pattern of available findings generally supports Festinger's (1957, 1964) view that selective exposure effects occur mainly for persons who have committed themselves to their initial attitude by a behavioural decision. Frey further reports that there is less clear evidence for an avoidance of hostile information than there is for exposure to congenial information. Also, selectivity is less pronounced for information that is weak or implausible. Finally, motives other than cognitive consistency

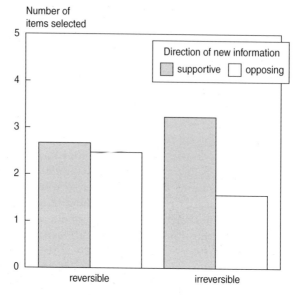

Figure 9.2. Information seeking as a function of reversibility of decision taken and direction of new information (data from Frey & Rosch, 1984).

may also have an impact on information search and avoidance. In particular, people often select information that has high utility for goal attainment, as well as unfamiliar information, irrespective of its congruence with their attitudes (Eagly & Chaiken, 1998). Thus, attitudes do affect deliberate information search and exposure, but this effect is subject to high commitment to the attitude and may be attenuated or overridden by other motivational concerns.

Attitude effects on judgment and elaboration

Once a person has attended to external information, the questions arise how that information is perceived and interpreted, and how it is used in forming a judgment. A given piece of information can usually be interpreted in more than one way, and "seeing both sides of things" can be unpleasant, as it requires high cognitive effort and may slow down decision making (see Figure 9.3 for an extreme case). By contrast, holding a positive or negative attitude may focus our view on one side of an issue and make us lean toward attitude-

consistent interpretations. In other words, attitudinal selectivity comes into play at these stages of information processing as well. Research has shown that attitudes, especially highly accessible ones, can simplify decision-making processes (Blascovich, Ernst, Tomaka, Kelsey, Salomon, & Fazio, 1993; Fazio, Blascovich, & Driscoll, 1992; Pratkanis, 1988, 1989), enhance the quality of decision making and free cognitive resources, thus facilitating coping with stressors (Fazio & Powell, 1997).

Effects of using an attitude as a heuristic

A two-fold account of attitudinal effects on information processing was proposed by Pratkanis (1989) as part of his sociocognitive model of attitude structure (see also chapter 3). According to Pratkanis, an attitude representation consists of an attitude-object category, an evaluative summary, and a supporting knowledge structure. These structural elements cause two types of information processing effects: *heuristic* and *schematic* effects. Using an attitude like a heuristic means that the link between attitude object and evaluative summary (cf. Fazio, 1995) is applied like a simple general rule for problem solving that could be paraphrased as "things I like are good". Applying this rule means that liked objects will be approached, favoured, defended etc., whereas disliked objects will be avoided, opposed, attacked etc. (Pratkanis, 1989, p. 76). This notion is similar to the cognitive functions ascribed to attitudes by early theorists (see chapter 1), such as the object-appraisal function (Smith et al., 1956) or the knowledge function (Katz, 1960).

The schematic function in Pratkanis' (1989) model refers to information-processing effects that are caused by the attitude-supporting knowledge structure. These are assumed to be more complex, as the supporting knowledge structure itself will usually be more complex than a simple summary evaluation. We will discuss some of the effects ascribed to the schematic properties of knowledge structures about an attitude object in the next section on memory. In the present section we address the more basic phenomena that Pratkanis (1989) attributed to the heuristic function of attitudes. He proposed that the operation of the attitude heuristic would affect interpretations and explanations, expectations and inferences, the formation of attitudes toward other objects and persons, as well as predictions of the future. An overview of these effects, some of which we have already talked about in earlier chapters, is given in Box 9.1. We will illustrate Pratkanis' position by discussing his research on *fact identification* in more detail.

Attitudes may affect judgments about the accuracy of factual statements. Pratkanis (1988) asked students to complete a knowledge test consisting of 16 pairs of statements about public figures as well as a scale assessing their attitudes toward these personalities. In the knowledge test, the students had to indicate which of the two statements in each pair was true, for example:

(a) Ronald Reagan maintained an "A" average at Eureka college.
(b) Ronald Reagan never achieved above a "C" average at Eureka college.

Eight pairs of statements were constructed in such a way that the true statement was the more favourable one, whereas in the other eight pairs the true statement was the less favourable one. Pratkanis reasoned that if participants used their attitudes as heuristics they would be more likely to identify as correct those statements whose evaluative implications matched their attitudes. For example, the more positive a student's attitude toward Reagan, the more likely he or she would select option (a) as the correct response in the above pair—in fact, (b) is the correct answer in this example.

The results strongly supported Pratkanis' prediction (see Figure 9.4a). While most of the students' judgments were correct in general (about 70%), the percentage of correct answers varied strongly as a function of attitude. For instance, participants were only half as likely to identify a true positive statement as correct if it pertained to a target they clearly disliked (40.7% correct) than if it pertained to a target they liked a lot (83.7% correct). Could this pattern simply reflect that in the past they had selectively attended to attitude-consistent facts about the target personalities, so that they could recall them better in the experiment? This explanation cannot be ruled out completely, although it is unlikely in the light of other measures that Pratkanis (1988) reported: When asked how confident they were about the correctness of their judgments, participants gave the highest confidence ratings for those judgments where they held the most extreme attitudes, whether these judgments were in fact correct or not (see Figure 9.4b).

Although differential recall may be an unlikely explanation, Pratkanis' (1988) findings point to the general difficulty of making a clear-cut distinction between judgment and memory. Remembering

BOX 9.1 The attitude heuristic

In a review chapter on the cognitive representation of attitudes, Pratkanis (1989) presented 11 examples of heuristic effects of attitudes. Taken together, these phenomena provide strong evidence for the power of the attitude concept in explaining social judgment.

(1) *Interpretation and explanation.* Among the things that people judge in accordance with their attitudes are the credibility of news items (Smith, 1947), events on the football field (Hastorf & Cantril, 1954) and the causes and motives for other people's actions (Regan, Straus, & Fazio, 1974).

(2) *Halo effects.* We expect that people we like possess positive characteristics, whereas people we dislike are expected to have negative traits (e.g. Lott & Lott, 1972). Survey research shows that positive events are often associated with positive expectations about the future, even in unrelated domains (Katona, 1975).

(3) *Syllogistic reasoning.* A person's attitude toward the conclusion of a syllogism may influence his judgment about the logical validity of the syllogism (Thistlethwaite, 1950; see chapter 2). This effect may be explained as a heuristic inference based on the rule "what I believe is true".

(4) *Responses to persuasive communications.* Prior attitudes can bias message recipients' cognitive responses to persuasive messages, with positive attitudes increasing favourable responses and negative attitudes increasing counterarguing (for a review, see Petty, Ostrom, & Brock, 1981).

(5) *Interpersonal attraction.* We tend to like people who hold attitudes similar to our own, and to dislike people with dissimilar attitudes (e.g. Byrne, 1971; Newcomb, 1961; Pilkington & Lydon, 1997).

(6) *Judgment of social stimuli.* Attitudes may be used as a reference point for judging social stimuli. For example, survey respondents judged the position of their preferred presidential candidate on several issues to be very similar to their own (Granberg & Jenks, 1977). However, opposite effects have also been obtained (cf. the "hostile media effect" discussed later in this chapter).

(7) *False consensus of opinion.* People often tend to overestimate the percentage of others sharing their opinions (e.g. Gilovich, 1990; Ross, Greene, & House, 1977).

(8) *Fact identification.* An attitude may be used to infer the accuracy of factual statements (Pratkanis, 1988; see discussion in this chapter) or to reconstruct past events (see section on memory in this chapter).

(9) *Estimates of own behaviour.* People often reconstruct or revise their past behaviour to fit in with their current attitudes. For example, Ross, McFarland, and Fletcher (1981) exposed participants to persuasive messages that either promoted or criticised daily toothbrushing. Later, participants who had heard the anti-toothbrushing message reported that they brushed their teeth less often than participants who had heard the pro-toothbrushing message. Interestingly, the biased reconstruction of past behaviour may contribute to people's subjective impression of their attitudes being more enduring than they actually are (Wilson & Hodges, 1992; see chapter 5).

(10) *Information error technique.* This can be seen as a variant of the fact identification effect. When asked to indicate which of two factually incorrect alternative statements is correct, people tend to select the statement whose implications correspond to their attitude (Hammond, 1948; see chapter 2).

(11) *Prediction of future events.* In chapter 8 we have seen that choice behaviour (voting, betting) results in optimistic expectations regarding related outcomes. Similarly, simply holding a particular attitude may lead to attitude-congruent predictions; this is well-documented for predictions about the results of U.S. presidential elections, where partisans usually overestimate the share of votes for their preferred party's candidate (Granberg & Brent, 1983).

(a)

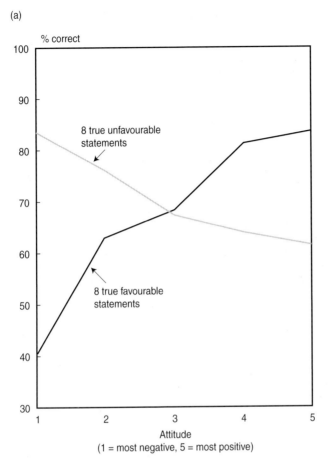

Figure 9.4. Percentage of correctly identified favourable and unfavourable facts (a), and self-reported confidence in the accuracy of fact identification (b), each as a function of attitude (data from Pratkanis, 1988).

may be seen as comprising (re-)constructive and inferential processes in a similar way as attitudinal judgments (cf. chapter 5; see also Strack & Bless, 1994). As Bartlett (1932/1995, p. 207) stated:

> When a subject is being asked to remember, very often the first thing that emerges is something of the nature of attitude. The recall is then a construction, made largely on the basis of this attitude, and its general effect is that of a justification of the attitude.

We may regard cognitive tasks as falling somewhere on a continuum that ranges from inferring or generating novel information on one end to explicit remembering of previously learned material on the

Figure 9.4. (Continued) (b)

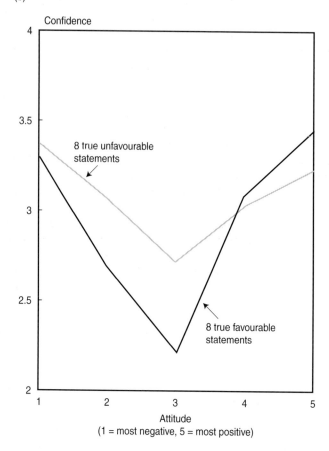

Attitude
(1 = most negative, 5 = most positive)

other. In the final section of this chapter we will address attitudinal effects on processing when the task is explicit remembering. First, however, we will consider functional aspects of attitudinal effects on decision making, as well as strategic effects of attitudes on the interpretation and elaboration of information.

Functionality of accessible attitudes for decision making: Benefits and costs

Pratkanis' (1988) results and his collection of examples regarding the attitude heuristic (Pratkanis, 1989) convincingly show that there *is* a close link between holding certain attitudes and making judgments and decisions. However, according to functional theories of attitude (see chapter 1) one should further expect that attitudes have a *beneficial* effect on processing, serving as "ready aids" in appraising an object (Smith et al., 1956). Blascovich and his colleagues addressed this issue by studying physiological indicators of stress during decision making as a function of attitude accessibility (Blascovich et al., 1993; Fazio et al., 1992). Their research was based on psycho-physiological evidence showing that tasks involving active efforts to cope with challenges cause greater increments in various indicators of autonomic arousal (e.g. heart rate, pulse transit time) than tasks involving passive endurance of noxious stimuli (e.g. Obrist, 1981). They reasoned that people who can rely on highly accessible attitudes as a basis for their decisions should show lower autonomic arousal during decision making compared to people with less accessible attitudes, who presumably have to construct their decisions on-line.

In one study, Blascovich et al. (1993) assigned students to one of three conditions: an attitude-rehearsal condition, a colour-naming control condition and a no-task control condition. In an initial phase of the study, participants in the attitude-rehearsal condition were asked to repeatedly express their attitudes toward each of 30 abstract paintings, whereas colour-naming control participants repeatedly answered questions regarding the colours present in each painting. No-task control participants were not initially exposed to the paintings. Later, all participants were presented with pairs of paintings at a rapid rate (2.5 seconds per pair) and asked to indicate which of the two paintings they liked better. The main dependent variables were changes in three measures of autonomic arousal—skin conductance response, pulse transit time and heart rate—during the pairwise preference task compared to a baseline period. Finally, all participants were given ample time to rank-order all 30 paintings from the one they personally liked best to the one they liked least.

The results supported the researchers' hypothesis. All three physiological measures indicated lower arousal in the attitude-rehearsal condition than in both the colour-naming and the no-task condition, while the latter two conditions did not differ from each other. For example, heart rate did not increase at all compared to baseline for participants who had repeatedly expressed their attitudes, whereas it did increase by about five beats per minute for participants in each of the control conditions. Furthermore, for participants in the attitude-rehearsal condition the pairwise preferences were more in line with their final rankings than for participants in each of the control conditions. Taken together, these results indicate that well-rehearsed, accessible attitudes both facilitate efficient decision making and reduce the stress experienced during decision making.

These laboratory findings are complemented by the results of a longitudinal field study conducted by Fazio and Powell (1997). Their participants, first-year college students, completed self-report questionnaires on negative life-events and mental and physical health at two points in time: during their first two weeks on campus (time 1) and again two months later (time 2). At time 1, the accessibility of the students' attitudes toward various academic issues was also assessed; the target issues included specific courses, possible majors, types of classes and academic activities (e.g. studying in the library, talking to a professor after class). Fazio and Powell hypothesised that highly accessible attitudes would serve as a stress-buffer, helping students to cope with negative life events during adjustment to college life. Their results partially supported this prediction: For those students who had reported relatively good health at time 1, health status at time 2 was less negatively affected by number of negative life events to the extent that academic attitudes were highly accessible. Students who had reported relatively poor health at time 1 showed better recovery at time 2 to the extent that their attitudes were highly accessible; however, this was only true if they also experienced few negative life events.

The studies reported in this section so far suggest that "knowing one's likes and dislikes" (Fazio & Powell, 1997) provides both short-term and long-term benefits. However, these benefits of efficient decision making and reduced stress may come at a cost. Specifically, people with accessible attitudes may be rather close-minded regarding the processing of information that is incongruent with their attitude. Furthermore, an attitude object may change over time, and relying on the automatic activation of a well-rehearsed evaluation may prevent a person from detecting such change.

This was demonstrated in a series of studies by Fazio, Ledbetter, and Towles-Schwen (2000). In part 1 of each study, their participants were repeatedly exposed to photographs of people, either rehearsing their attitudes toward each photo or performing a control task. In part 2 they were presented with both the original photos and computer-generated "morphs" of these photos that varied in their similarity to the original. Participants were told that several photos had been taken of each of the persons they had seen in part 1, and were asked to indicate in part 2 whether a photo was exactly identical to, or different from, one they had seen before. The results of two studies showed that participants in the attitude rehearsal condition needed more time to correctly identify morphs that were similar to the original as "different" and made more errors in response to such morphs. Another experiment indicated that participants with more (vs less) accessible attitudes were less likely to view a morph as a photo of a novel person and more likely to view it as a different photo of a person seen before. Thus, individuals with more accessible attitudes had greater difficulty at detecting change, and perceived relatively less change, in the attitude object than individuals with less accessible attitudes. Having considered the benefits and costs if automatically activated attitudes, we now turn to more consciously controlled effects of attitudes on the interpretation of new information.

Attitude-congruent interpretation and elaboration

Several lines of theorising allow for the possibility that a person's attitude introduces a motivational or cognitive bias into their processing of information that is related to the attitude. These approaches include cognitive consistency theories (e.g. Festinger, 1957; see chapter 8), social judgment theory (e.g. Sherif & Hovland, 1961), dual-processing models of persuasion (Chaiken & Trope, 1999; see chapter 7) and theories of motivated social cognition (e.g. Kunda, 1990).

In the section on selective exposure we have seen that people often avoid contact with information that might clash with their attitudes (Festinger, 1957; Frey, 1986). However, in everyday life, exposure to hostile information cannot always be avoided. Festinger proposed that under these conditions of "forced exposure", people would tend to distort opposing information, whereas their perception of congenial information would be more accurate. These processes would jointly minimise cognitive dissonance. Slightly different predictions were made on the basis of social judgment theory, which maintained that individuals use their own attitude as a judgmental *anchor* (e.g. Sherif & Hovland, 1961). Sherif and Hovland assumed that people represent their own attitudes as well as other attitudinal positions along an evaluative dimension that is divided into three distinct regions, called the *latitudes of acceptance, rejection, and noncommitment.*

Those positions along the evaluative continuum that a person rates as acceptable define the latitude of acceptance, those that the person judges as objectionable define the latitude of rejection, and all remaining positions constitute the latitude of noncommitment. People were thought to minimise the discrepancy between their own attitude and attitudinal positions falling within their latitude of acceptance, but to accentuate the perceived distance of positions that fall within their latitude of rejection. These accentuation effects can be reconciled with the cognitive consistency approach if one assumes that very discrepant positions can be easily dismissed as invalid and thus would be unlikely to cause a state of cognitive dissonance.

Following early observations that attitudes can severely affect people's interpretation of ambiguous events (Hastorf & Cantril, 1954; see chapter 1), several studies have provided evidence consistent with social judgment theory's predictions of assimilation and contrast effects (e.g. Dawes, Singer, & Lemons, 1972). Although it has been debated whether the reported effects are truly perceptual or just reflect attitude-dependent differences in how participants use the response scale provided (e.g. Upshaw, 1969), more recent studies indicate that at least part of the effect is due to genuine changes in perception (e.g. Judd, Kenny, & Krosnick, 1983). An interesting example of an attitude-based contrast effect in perception has been labelled the *hostile media effect*. It refers to a tendency of partisans in a political issue to judge media reports as biased *against* their own side. This was first demonstrated by Vallone, Ross, and Lepper (1985), who examined how "pro-Israeli" and "pro-Arab" students perceived TV coverage of the killing of civilians in refugee camps in Lebanon. Each group perceived the same news items as hostile to their own position and supporting the other side. This effect was replicated by Giner-Sorolla and Chaiken (1994) for attitudes toward the Middle East conflict, but findings were less consistent for attitudes toward abortion.

These complexities notwithstanding, the contrasting interpretation of positions that diverge from one's own may actually help perceivers to disparage these positions, subjectively turning them into evidence that supports their own attitude. Existing attitudes may guide the elaboration of persuasive evidence in situations where the individual is both motivated and able to invest effort in processing. They are thus one of the factors that can instigate biased processing, as featured in the ELM's biased elaboration postulate (Petty & Cacioppo, 1986b) and the HSM's assumption of defence motivation (Chaiken, Giner-Sorolla, & Chen, 1996; Chaiken et al., 1989; see

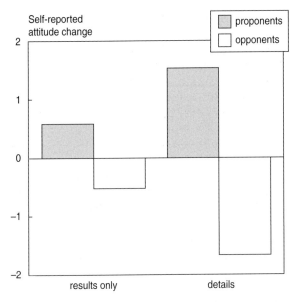

Figure 9.5. Self-reported change in U.S. students' attitudes toward capital punishment as a function of initial attitude (proponent vs opponent) and amount of "mixed" information considered. The bars on the left show change reported after considering brief descriptions of the results of two opposing studies; the bars on the right show change reported by the same students after considering the full details of these studies (data from Lord et al., 1979).

chapter 7). From this theoretical perspective, the degree of bias should increase with the amount of processing invested.

This was demonstrated in a study by Lord, Ross, and Lepper (1979). These researchers asked students who initially either opposed or favoured capital punishment to read and evaluate two (fictitious) research articles. One article supported the conclusion that the death penalty was an effective deterrent to murder, whereas the other article provided evidence favouring the opposite conclusion. Overall, the students rated the evidence that was consistent with their own attitude as more convincing than the information that questioned their attitude. More importantly, the more of the identical "two-sided" information the students had read, the more pronounced the differences between proponents' and opponents' attitudes became (see Figure 9.5). Thus, somewhat paradoxically, exposure to mixed evidence did not mitigate initial attitudes but rather led to their polarisation.

Some studies indicate that selective elaboration effects of this kind may be triggered by automatic attitude activation, as they seem to be more pronounced if the attitudes that guide perception are strong rather than weak (for a discussion of attitude strength, see chapter 3). Houston and Fazio (1989) found that the degree of pro-attitudinal bias

TABLE 9.1

Stimulus information reflecting a spurious correlation between gender and leadership ability (adapted from Schaller, 1992, Table 1, p. 64)

(a)   Aggregate data

	Good leaders	Bad leaders
Male	13	7
Female	7	13

(b)   Broken down by job category

	Executives		Office workers	
	Good leaders	Bad leaders	Good leaders	Bad leaders
Male	12	3	1	4
Female	4	1	3	12

in evaluating mixed evidence on capital punishment was greater in students whose attitudes were more accessible. Pomerantz, Chaiken, and Tordesillas (1995) further demonstrated that the degree of attitude polarisation was a direct function of attitude importance.

Outside of the persuasion domain as well, researchers have proposed that specific motives and goals may affect reasoning (for a review, see Kunda, 1990). In line with this approach, Schaller (1992) demonstrated that group-related attitudes can motivate the allocation of processing effort to statistical reasoning tasks. His participants selectively applied either simple or complex reasoning strategies depending on which of these strategies resulted in a more positive conclusion about their in-group. For instance (Experiment 1), when presented with case information about the gender, leadership ability (good or bad) and job (executive or office worker) of 40 people, as summarised in Table 9.1, female participants invested greater processing effort than male participants and were more likely to detect that a correlation between gender and leadership ability ($r = .30$ to the advantage of men) at the *aggregate* level (see Table 9.1a) was spurious. This means that it could be fully explained by correlations between gender and job (most of the office workers are women, whereas most of the executives are men, $r = .50$) and between job and leadership ability (executives are better leaders than office workers, $r = .60$). *Within* each of the two job categories, the correlation between gender and leadership ability is in fact zero (see Table 9.1b).

To test whether these findings indeed reflect a motivating effect of positive in-group attitudes, rather than greater statistical reasoning ability of women than men, Schaller (1992, Experiment 2) repeated this study with stimulus material in which the spurious correlation between gender and leadership ability was to the advantage of women. Now the men used more complex reasoning and were more likely to conclude that there is no real relation between gender and leadership, whereas the women were more likely to accept the positive correlation at face value.

The studies we reviewed in this section indicate that attitudes can lead to selective interpretation of attitude-relevant information. The processes underlying these effects may vary. They may be triggered automatically by strong and accessible attitudes and reflect relatively simple perceptual distortions, but may also involve considerable cognitive effort and elaboration. Furthermore, individuals may be content with an initial judgment based on low-effort processing if it matches their attitude-based expectations or preferences, but they may step up their processing effort if superficial processing does not yield the desired results. A similar variety of processes can be found in the domain of attitudinal effects on memory, which we will discuss in the remainder of this chapter.

Attitude effects on memory

Schematic effects of bipolar attitudes on recall

Among the first to empirically address the proposal that bipolar attitudes may serve as a schema for recall (Bartlett, 1932/1995) were Judd and Kulik (1980). They proposed that information fitting a person's attitude schema should be processed more efficiently than information not fitting the schema (see also Pratkanis, 1989). To understand what exactly this means, it is useful to take a closer look at their study, in which students read belief statements concerning several political issues (e.g. "Majority rule would only complicate the lives of most South Africans"). Participants were asked to indicate *how much they agreed* with each statement and *how favourable or unfavourable* it was. The response times for each of these judgments were measured, and at a later stage the students were asked to recall as many statements as they could. The results showed that more extreme statements, in terms of both subjective agreement and objective favourability, were both processed faster and more likely to be recalled than less extreme statements. This was equally true for statements opposed to and in line with participants' own position. Thus, information may fit an attitude schema to the extent that it is located near either pole of a bipolar evaluative continuum.

A different type of bipolarity effect was studied by Hymes (1986), who used attitudinal positions on the abortion issue to define person categories. Specifically, he presented participants who held positive, negative or neutral attitudes toward legalised abortion with positive, negative and neutral statements that had ostensibly been made by target persons who were either "pro-choice" or "anti-abortion". The statements were unrelated to the abortion issue, for example "I took two disadvantaged kids on a one-week vacation" (positive) or "I spread rumours that my roommate was dishonest" (negative). Later, participants were given a recognition test in which they had to match each statement with the target group it had come from.

Hymes (1986) tested two competing models, a selectivity hypothesis and a bipolarity hypothesis. Based on the assumption that people are motivated to see themselves and the groups they belong to in a favourable light, the selectivity hypothesis (see Howard & Rothbart, 1980) predicts that people are better at matching statements that are congruent with their attitude-based expectations (i.e. positive in-group statements and negative out-group statements) than statements that are incongruent with these expectations (i.e. negative in-group statements and positive out-group statements). By contrast, drawing on the findings of Judd and Kulik (1980) and on research into person memory (see Hastie, 1981), the bipolarity hypothesis predicts that partisans would be better at correctly categorising statements that reflect either positively or negatively on in-group and out-group members, compared to neutral statements.

The results that Hymes (1986) obtained strongly supported the bipolarity assumption. As can be seen in Figure 9.6, participants who held pro-choice or anti-abortion attitudes themselves were better at correctly matching valenced statements than neutral statements with their target categories, whereas participants with neutral abortion attitudes showed no differential sensitivity for valenced versus neutral statements. The data provided no support for the selectivity hypothesis.

The recall findings we reviewed so far are in line with schematic effects of attitudes in areas where bipolar representations seem to prevail (socio-political attitudes; see Pratkanis, 1989). Individuals

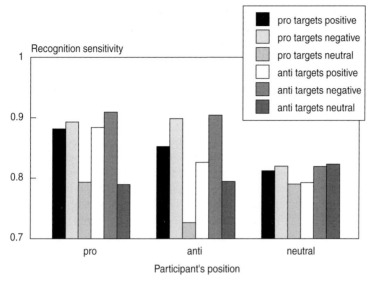

Figure 9.6. Accuracy of recognition of statements as a function of own attitude (pro, anti, neutral), attitude of target (pro, anti) and valence of statement (positive, negative, neutral). Data from Hymes (1986).

holding attitudes on either side of a bipolar continuum show a recall advantage for:

(1) information that is congruent with either side of the continuum in terms of its subjective and objective favourability (Judd & Kulik, 1980), and

(2) information that either confirms or disconfirms attitude-based expectations (Hymes, 1986),

whereas evaluatively neutral information is recalled less well. Although little evidence for attitudinal selectivity was revealed in these studies, other researchers have reported selectivity effects for a variety of issues. However, null results and findings opposite to the predictions of the selectivity hypothesis have also been reported. We will now discuss some of these findings as well as a recent meta-analysis that sheds light on the conditions and processes that contribute to attitudinal selectivity in recall.

Proattitudinal bias in recall

The idea of attitudinal selectivity, which we have discussed in relation to encoding and judgment, has also been applied to recall processes. To the extent that people selectively seek out congenial information (Frey, 1986) and use their attitudes as judgmental heuristics to generate attitude-consistent expectations and inferences (Pratkanis, 1989; see Box 9.1), it is reasonable to assume that learned material would also be recalled better if it is consistent rather than inconsistent with a person's attitude. Early research produced evidence largely consistent with this proposal. For example, Levine and Murphy (1943) presented information that was favourable or unfavourable toward the Soviet Union to communist and anti-communist participants. In several recall tests conducted over a five-week period, the anti-communists recalled the content of an anti-Soviet text passage much better than did the communists.

Later work, however, showed that the congeniality effect in recall could be reversed under certain conditions. For example, Jones and Aneshansel (1956) demonstrated that counterattitudinal information is recalled well if it can be useful for a subsequent task. Other studies failed to find a clearcut effect of attitudes on memory, or generated ambiguous findings (e.g. Brigham & Cook, 1969; Greenwald & Sakumura, 1967). Quantitative reviews of studies on selective memory (Eagly, Chen, Chaiken, & Shaw-Barnes, 1999; Roberts, 1985) indicate that, overall, there is a small but significant positive relationship between attitudes and the valence of recalled attitude-relevant information. Averaging across 65 studies, Eagly et al. (1999) reported a weighted mean effect size of $d = .23$, i.e. .23 standard deviation units difference between recall for congenial and hostile information. However, the heterogeneity of findings was considerable, with 26 of 65 studies pointing in the direction of a recall advantage for hostile information.

This prompted Eagly et al. (1999) to examine moderators of the congeniality effect. They found that the tendency for better recall of attitude-congruent information was less pronounced in more recent studies than in older ones, which may partly reflect the development and application of more sophisticated statistical techniques. More importantly, the type of attitude object studied also affected the size and direction of biases in recall. Issues high in *value-relevant involvement* (i.e. likely to be linked to important personal values) produced larger congeniality effects than issues of lower value relevance. Furthermore, for highly controversial attitude topics recall was more even-handed (e.g. Judd & Kulik, 1980; see previous section), whereas for less controversial topics it was biased towards congenial information.

These findings seem to reflect different processing strategies that people can employ to defend their attitudes. On the one hand, people may pay less attention to hostile information or try to ignore it altogether, especially if this information threatens a cherished personal value. On the other hand, people may confront and actively counterargue hostile information in an attempt to invalidate it. This should be true especially if the issue is highly controversial and the person can thus expect to be frequently exposed to opposing views by others. Whereas the more passive "defensive inattention" strategy would result in a congeniality bias, the more active "defensive counterarguing" strategy should enhance memory for hostile information (Eagly & Chaiken, 1998; Eagly et al., 1999).

It thus seems necessary for future research to pay more attention to the conditions that facilitate or inhibit the operation of more active versus more passive strategies of defence (Eagly & Chaiken, 1998). One structural condition that may explain *how* information on more or less controversial issues is processed differently is the polarity of attitude representations. As Pratkanis (1989) suggested, people can possess unipolar and bipolar attitudes, and more controversial topics are more likely to be represented in a bipolar structure (see chapter 3). It may be easier to encode and actively counterargue opposing information if the relevant attitude structure is bipolar rather than unipolar.

Furthermore, research by Eagly and her colleagues (Eagly, Kulesa, Brannon, Shaw, & Hutson-Comeaux, 2000; see also Eagly, Kulesa, Chen, & Chaiken, 2001) showed that, even when congenial and hostile information are recalled equally well, the *processing effort* devoted to each type of information may differ substantially, with greater effort invested in the encoding and retrieval of hostile than congenial information. Overall, the differentiation of an active, effortful process and a more passive, efficient process involved in attitudinal selectivity is consistent with the assumptions of dual-process models of persuasion (see chapter 7). Applying these models to the attitude-memory domain yields the prediction of a processing and recall advantage for hostile information under high motivation and ability, and an advantage for congenial information under low motivation or ability (Eagly & Chaiken, 1998). This proposition remains to be tested in future research.

Conclusion: Attitudes predict information processing

We have seen that attitudes play an important role at all stages of information processing, although their influence does not always reflect a straightforward pattern of congeniality effects. Attitude strength, structural issues as well as the perceiver's motivational goals and processing effort moderate the impact of attitudes on information processing. For didactic purposes we have discussed separate stages of processing and loosely differentiated between more automatic and more strategic processes, although it is not always easy to single out the processing stage(s) at which an effect occurs. Differences at encoding (e.g. using attitudinal positions as categories for encoding information) may lead to effects at the stage of forming a judgment or recalling information. Similarly, automatic and controlled processing may jointly influence judgments, as when a highly accessible attitude is activated automatically and then leads to biased elaboration. In sum, there is rich evidence supporting the assumption that attitudes are linked to diverse information processing effects.

Chapter summary

(1) The idea that attitudes affect information processing has its roots in cognitive consistency theory, in the functional analysis of attitudes and in theorising on attitude structure.

(2) Attitudes may influence the attention to attitude objects, the use of categories for encoding information and the interpretation, judgment and recall of attitude-relevant information. These influences tend to be more powerful for strong attitudes, which are easily accessible and based on an elaborate knowledge structure.

(3) Attitudes may guide attention and encoding automatically, even if the individual is pursuing unrelated goals. However, people may also seek out attitude-congruent information in a more strategic fashion, especially after a behavioural decision.

(4) Attitudes may affect perception and judgment in various ways. Pratkanis distinguishes between heuristic effects of attitudes, where inferences are drawn from a summary evaluation ("what I like is good"), and schematic effects of attitudes, where inferences are based on a more complex attitudinal knowledge structure.

(5) Accessible attitudes provide the benefits of efficiency and stress reduction, but come at the cost of close-mindedness. They may inhibit the detection of change in an attitude object.

(6) Forced exposure to attitude-incongruent information may lead to biased interpretation and elaboration. Processing information on both sides of an issue under the guidance of a prior attitude can result in a more extreme attitude, and people may strategically use more or less effortful reasoning strategies depending on what outcome they desire based on their attitudes.

(7) There are at least two types of attitude effects on memory: Bipolar attitudes may facilitate recall of information that fits either pole of a bipolar evaluative continuum; congeniality effects are characterised by better recall of attitude-consistent than attitude-inconsistent information. On balance, there is evidence for weak congeniality effects.

(8) The processes mediating attitudinal selectivity in processing and recall may vary both qualitatively, including selective inattention and selective counterarguing, and quantitatively along a continuum of processing effort. Dual-processing models may contribute to our understanding of selectivity phenomena.

Exercises

(1) Can you think of examples for the attention-grabbing nature of strong attitudes in everyday life?

(2) What are the similarities and differences between heuristic and schematic effects of attitudes?

(3) What is the hostile media effect, and under what conditions is it most likely to be observed?

(4) Would informing people about the potentially biasing effects of their attitudes help them in forming unbiased judgments and decisions? Why or why not?

Further reading

A narrative review of classic work on selective exposure:

Frey, D. (1986). Recent research on selective exposure to information. *Advances in Experimental Social Psychology*, 19, 41–80.

A classic study on attitudinal biases in judgment:

Lord, C. G., Ross, L., & Lepper, M. R. (1979). Biased assimilation and attitude polarization: The effects of prior theories on subsequently considered evidence. *Journal of Personality and Social Psychology*, 37, 2098–2109.

An excellent, although somewhat dated, cognitive-structural account for attitudinal effects on information processing:

Pratkanis, A. R. (1989). The cognitive representation of attitudes. In A. R. Pratkanis, S. J. Breckler, & A. G. Greenwald (Eds.), *Attitude structure and function* (pp. 71–98). Hillsdale, NJ: Lawrence Erlbaum Associates Inc.

A review of Fazio's research programme on the functionality of accessible attitudes:

Fazio, R. H. (2000). Accessible attitudes as tools for object appraisal: Their costs and benefits. In G. R. Maio & J. M. Olson (Eds.), *Why we evaluate: Functions of attitudes* (pp. 1–36). Mahwah, NJ: Lawrence Erlbaum Associates Inc.

A quantitative review of attitude effects on elaboration and memory:

Eagly, A. H., Chen, S., Chaiken, S., & Shaw-Barnes, K. (1999). The impact of attitudes on memory: An affair to remember. *Psychological Bulletin, 125,* 64–89.

Attitude influences on behaviour 10

As we stated in the introductory chapter, perhaps the major reason why attitudes are studied is the assumption that attitudes cause behaviour. On the one hand, this assumption seems obviously correct: We eat food that we like and avoid people we dislike; we vote for the political party whose aims we find most appealing, and so on. On the other hand, behaviour often seems to be at odds with attitudes: We may drive to work although we resent air pollution, practise unsafe sex although we abhor sexually transmitted diseases, or cheat on our partner although we love them (see also Figure 10.1). Quite unsurprisingly, early research trying to establish *if* a close relationship between attitudes and behaviour exists produced mixed results. It turned out that attitudes sometimes predicted behaviour quite well, whereas at other times it was hard to detect any relationship between the two. Therefore, a second generation of research was devoted to delineating the *conditions* under which attitudes predict behaviour more or less closely. And a third generation of research, which extends to the present, addresses the cognitive *processes* involved in the attitude–behaviour link (see Zanna & Fazio, 1982).

Do attitudes predict behaviour?

Early pessimism about the idea that attitudes guide behaviour was nourished in an article by LaPiere (1934). This author went on an extensive tour across the USA in the company of a Chinese couple. Given the prejudice against Asians that prevailed in the United States of the 1930s, LaPiere had expected that his Chinese travel companions would often be refused service by hotels or restaurants. To his surprise, however, this happened in only one of the 251 establishments

Behaviour often seems to be at odds with attitudes.

they visited. What is even more astonishing is the result of a mail survey that LaPiere conducted six months later. He wrote to all the hotels and restaurants visited, asking if they would accept "members of the Chinese race" as guests. In total contrast to their prior behaviour, now 118 (92%) of the 128 places who returned the questionnaire responded that they would *not* serve Chinese customers. LaPiere concluded from this enormous discrepancy between stated attitude and overt behaviour that questionnaire responses are not valid indicators of a person's true attitude. He suggested that the use of questionnaire measures of attitude, as they measure merely "symbolic" responses, should be limited to issues that remain symbolic, for example predicting voting behaviour from political attitude surveys.

Viewed in the light of contemporary methodological standards, there are, of course, a number of flaws in LaPiere's (1934) study: Respondents' attitudes were assessed long *after* the behaviour in question; it was unclear if the people who responded to the mailing were the same as those who had admitted the Chinese guests; and the attitude object, an English-speaking couple accompanied by a White American, may not have been identified as "members of the Chinese race" to begin with. However, other studies, which suffered less from methodological problems, also failed to find a high correlation between attitudes and behaviour (see Ajzen & Fishbein, 1970; Corey, 1937). These accumulated findings contributed to a generally pessimistic view on the possibility of predicting behaviour from attitudes in the 1960s and early 1970s (e.g. Wicker, 1969).

But rather than giving up the study of attitude–behaviour relations, researchers began examining the reasons why in some studies the prediction of behaviour from attitudes was quite successful (e.g. Fishbein & Coombs, 1974; Newton & Newton, 1950; for a review see Ajzen & Fishbein, 1977), whereas in others it was not (see Box 10.1 for the results of attitude–behaviour studies conducted over more than 60 years). The variability of empirical findings suggested that the question *if* attitudes predict behaviour was too broad and undifferentiated. Therefore, researchers began asking more specific questions about the conditions that need to be present in order to find a strong association between attitudes and behaviour.

When do attitudes predict behaviour?

We can differentiate two approaches to answering this question. One is mainly concerned with aspects of *measurement*, addressing how

Eckes and Six (1994) reported the most comprehensive meta-analysis of attitude–behaviour studies, covering research conducted between 1927 and 1990. Studies were categorised according to the behavioural domain that they examined, and the mean correlation between attitude and behaviour was computed separately for studies in each category. As Figure 10.2 shows, the results indicate that attitudes do predict behaviour, albeit with differing accuracy. In some domains, such as altruistic behaviour or family planning, correlations were low to moderate, whereas in other areas, for example using (both legal and illegal) drugs, the predictive power of attitudes was substantial.

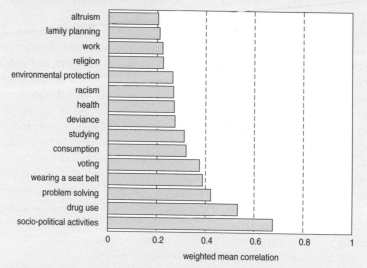

Figure 10.2. Attitude–behaviour relations in several domains of behaviour. The bars represent the weighted mean of correlation coefficients reported in studies conducted between 1927 and 1990. Only domains represented by more than five studies are shown (data from a meta-analysis reported by Eckes & Six, 1994).

Another notable finding of this quantitative review was that within domains as well, the findings varied considerably. Statistical tests of heterogeneity showed that in all but one of the areas depicted in Figure 10.2, the variability in correlation coefficients across studies was greater than would be expected by chance. Thus, it is likely that moderator variables affected the strength of the attitude–behaviour relation in varying degrees.

improvements in the assessment of attitudes and behaviour can enhance the prediction of behaviour from attitudes. The other approach involves the search for personal, situational and content variables that might *moderate* the strength of the attitude–behaviour relation: Are there certain people who are more likely to act on their attitudes than others? Do certain situations foster greater consistency between attitude and behaviour? Are there particular attitudes or behaviours that are more strongly linked than others? We address each of these approaches in the following subsections.

Level of measurement and the attitude–behaviour relation

The correspondence principle

One reason for a weak association between attitude and behaviour may lie in the lack of correspondence (or compatibility) of the two measures. Ajzen and Fishbein (1977) noted that both attitudes and behaviours can be described with respect to four characteristics:

(1) the *action element*: What behaviour is being studied—e.g. voting, donating or attending?
(2) the *target element*: What is the target of the behaviour—e.g. a political party, a charity or a lecture?
(3) the *context element*: In what context is the behaviour being performed—e.g. a totalitarian or democratic society, in public or in private, at university or evening school?
(4) the *time component*: At what point in time is the behaviour occurring—e.g. immediately or over the following year?

It is impossible to predict with accuracy any *specific* behaviour (e.g. "attending the football match of one's local team next weekend") from a *global* measure of attitude (e.g. a questionnaire on general attitudes toward football). Although this point may almost seem self-evident, it is precisely the questionable link between global attitude and specific behaviour that was examined in most early studies, with LaPiere's (1934) investigation just being one famous example.

According to Ajzen and Fishbein (1977), close relations between attitude and behaviour can be expected only if both measures agree in their degree of specification. Their review of attitude–behaviour studies supported this reasoning: The reported correlations between attitude and behaviour are indeed larger to the extent that the specification of both measures was similar. More recent reviews yielded identical conclusions (Eckes & Six, 1994; Kim & Hunter, 1993; Kraus, 1995). To illustrate the **correspondence principle**, let us consider a study by Davidson and Jaccard (1979). These researchers predicted

TABLE 10.1

Correlations of attitude measures that vary in specificity with a specific behaviour (use of birth control pills during a two-year period)

Attitude measure	Correlation with specific behaviour
Attitude toward birth control	.083
Attitude toward birth control pills	.323
Attitude toward using birth control pills	.525
Attitude toward using birth control pills during the next two years	.572

Note: Based on a sample of 244 women. Data from Davidson and Jaccard (1979).

women's contraceptive behaviours from attitudinal measures that varied in specificity. As Table 10.1 shows, the predictive power of the attitude measure increased dramatically with increasing correspondence of attitude and behaviour.

It should be noted, however, that this method of increasing the prediction of specific behaviours entails a shift on the predictor side from *attitudes toward objects* to the narrower concept of *attitudes toward behaviour*. This shift is inherent in current expectancy × value models of the attitude–behaviour relation; although other researchers have continued to use attitudes toward objects as predictors of behaviour (see below).

The aggregation principle

Although measures of general attitudes toward objects are poor predictors of single, specific behaviours, they fare better at predicting behaviour over a wider range of situations and contexts. As a complement to the strategy of maximising specificity, Fishbein and Ajzen (1974) thus proposed to assess and aggregate multiple behaviours to increase the predictive power of global attitude measures. In chapter 2 we mentioned that reliability increases with a larger number of items in a scale (Cronbach, 1951). Similarly, if we sample and aggregate a large number of behaviours—and assume that the attitude remains fairly stable over the assessment period—then any determinants of behaviour other than attitude should cancel each other out in the aggregate score. Going back to our earlier example, people differing in their global attitude toward football should also differ in predictable ways regarding a range of related behaviours taken as a whole, like playing football, attending matches, watching football programmes on television, wearing team colours and so on.

This reasoning is supported by research findings. Fishbein and Ajzen (1974) successfully predicted an aggregate measure of self-reported religious behaviours from general attitudes toward religion. Another powerful illustration of the **aggregation principle** was provided in an extensive field study by Weigel and Newman (1976). These researchers used a 16-item scale to assess town residents' general attitudes toward the environment. Then, over an extended period of time, they arranged opportunities for the residents to engage in various pro-environmental behaviours. For example, the respondents were visited in their homes and asked to sign and circulate petitions for various environmental causes; and a kerbside waste-recycling program was set up specifically for the purpose of the study. Participation in each of these activities was unobtrusively recorded, and behavioural measures at different levels of aggregation were derived from these observations. As Table 10.2 shows, the general attitude did not predict well most of the specific behaviours; however, its correlation with a fully *aggregated* measure of environmental behaviour was a remarkable .62.

Of course, as we have discussed in chapter 5, the variability of the attitude itself constrains the magnitude of the attitude–behaviour correspondence. The more the attitude itself is subject to change over the assessment period, the lower its association with behaviour should be.

In sum, the principles of correspondence and aggregation show that levels of measurement are important in determining attitude–behaviour relations. Specific attitudes predict equally specific behaviours, whereas global attitude measures predict behaviours aggregated across contexts and points in time. We now turn from methodological to more substantial moderators of the link between attitudes and behaviour.

Moderators of the attitude–behaviour relation

These moderators may be categorised into individual differences (e.g. self-monitoring), situational variables (e.g. salience of social norms), aspects of the attitude (e.g. its function), and aspects of the behaviour in question (e.g. its perceived difficulty; Ajzen, 1988). The view of attitudes as temporary constructions (see chapter 5) further suggests that all of these components may be interrelated. For example,

TABLE 10.2

General attitude as a predictor of behavioural criteria varying in generality

Correlations of environmental attitude (16-item measure) with

Single behaviours	r	Categories of behaviour	r	Fully aggregated behaviour index	r
Offshore oil	.41**				
Nuclear power	.36*	Petitioning behaviour scale (0–4)	.50**		
Auto exhaust	.39**				
Circulate petitions	.27				
Individual participation	.34*	Litter pick-up scale (0–2)	.36*		
Recruit friend	.22				
				Comprehensive behavioural index	.62***
Recycling					
Week 1	.34*				
Week 2	.57***				
Week 3	.34*				
Week 4	.33*	Recycling behaviour scale (0–8)	.39**		
Week 5	.12				
Week 6	.20				
Week 7	.20				
Week 8	.34*				

Note: Data from Weigel and Newman (1976). $N = 44$. * $p < .05$; ** $p < .01$; *** $p < .001$.

personal or situational factors may increase or decrease the accessibility of certain aspects of an attitude. To the extent that the same aspects are accessible at the time of attitude measurement and at the time of engaging in behaviour, a high attitude–behaviour correspondence should be observed. In the sections that follow, we first discuss research that addressed this situational matching hypothesis, then illustrate the moderating force of aspects of the attitude by considering some indicators of attitude strength, and finally look at individual differences that affect the attitude–behaviour correspondence.

Matching of attitude aspects

Attitudes and behaviour are more closely related if those aspects of the attitude that are highly accessible at the time of attitude measurement are also accessible at the time the behaviour is performed (Shavitt & Fazio, 1991; Tesser & Shaffer, 1990; Wilson & Dunn, 1986; Wilson et al., 1989). To test this hypothesis with respect to attitude functions, Shavitt and Fazio (1991) examined students' attitudes toward each of two brands of soft drink: "7-Up" lemonade and "Perrier" mineral water. Pilot testing had shown that attitudes toward each drink typically served distinct functions. Perrier was liked mainly because of the trendy image it imparts (social image function), whereas 7-Up was liked foremost for its taste (utilitarian function; see chapter 1). In their experiment, Shavitt and Fazio primed either image or taste before participants were asked to evaluate each drink: Specifically, some participants judged the social impression that each of 20 behaviours would create, whereas others rated 20 food items for their taste. Later, all participants reported their attitudes toward both 7-Up and Perrier along with their intentions to buy each of these drinks. Shavitt and Fazio hypothesised that attitudes would more strongly predict behavioural intention if the primed attitude function matched rather than mismatched the function that is normally associated with the attitude object. As shown in Figure 10.3, the data supported this prediction. Students' intentions to purchase Perrier were more highly correlated with attitudes toward Perrier when they had thought about social impression rather than taste just prior to attitude measurement. By contrast, students' intentions to buy 7-Up were more highly correlated with their attitudes toward 7-Up when they had previously thought about taste rather than social impression.

Other findings suggest that *thinking about the reasons why one holds a certain attitude* can either increase or decrease the attitude–behaviour

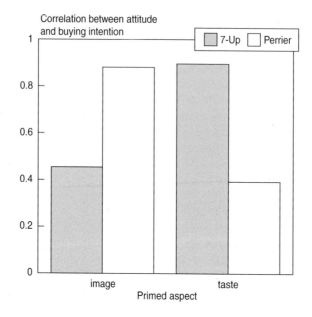

Figure 10.3. The matching of primed attitude aspects and object-bound attitude functions determines the magnitude of attitude–intention relations (data from Shavitt & Fazio, 1991).

correlation (Wilson & Dunn, 1986; Wilson et al., 1989). These results can also be understood as an instance of matching of attitude aspects. Given that thinking about *reasons* accentuates an attitude's cognitive aspects, it should elevate the attitude–behaviour correlation if mainly cognitive aspects are accessible also at the time of performing the behaviour. Conversely, the attitude–behaviour association should be weakened by introspection about reasons if the behaviour is performed in a situation where the affective attitude component is most salient (see also Millar & Tesser, 1986).

Attitude strength

As we have seen in chapter 3, research on *attitude strength* entailed the hypothesis that strong attitudes are better predictors of behaviour than weak attitudes (see Petty & Krosnick, 1995). As space does not permit to discuss all indicators of attitude strength that have been studied in this respect (for a review, see Kraus, 1995), we consider here just three indicators: *intra-attitudinal consistency*, *accessibility*, and *cognitive effort in attitude formation*.

In our discussion of attitude structure (chapter 3), we have seen that cognitive and affective components vary in their degree of *consistency* with attitude as an overall evaluation. For example, you may believe that nuclear energy has many beneficial effects, yet evaluate it negatively on the whole. Work by Rosenberg (1968) had shown that high evaluative-cognitive consistency (ECC) of an attitude is positively related to its temporal stability and resistance against persuasion attempts. Norman (1975) found support for the related hypothesis that ECC moderates the magnitude of the attitude–behaviour relation. In a series of studies, he assessed the ECC of students' attitudes toward volunteering for experiments; several weeks later, the same students were asked to sign up for an experiment that did not provide any monetary reward or course credit. Norman found that across studies, attitudes of high ECC participants strongly predicted behaviour (with correlation coefficients between .47 and .62), whereas attitudes of low ECC participants did not reliably predict behaviour (rs between $-.28$ and .24).

Work by Fazio (1986, 1990, 1995) highlighted the role of attitude *accessibility* as a moderator of the attitude–behaviour relation. Initial research within this approach addressed the role of direct experience with the attitude object. According to Regan and Fazio (1977), direct behavioural experience creates attitudes that are held with greater clarity, confidence and stability compared to attitudes formed via indirect information about the attitude object. Because of these attributes, experience-based attitudes are thought to be more accessible and, ultimately, to be more powerful determinants of future behaviour. These hypotheses were supported in numerous studies (for an overview see Fazio & Zanna, 1981). In a field study conducted by Regan and Fazio (1977), college students who had direct prior experience with a housing crisis showed greater attitude–behaviour consistency in their attempts to alleviate the crisis than did students who held similar attitudes but had no direct experience. In a related laboratory experiment, the same authors systematically varied the type of experience through which students formed attitudes to a number of intellectual puzzles: Some students gained direct behavioural experience by working through examples of the puzzles, whereas others gained only indirect experience by looking at examples of puzzles that had already been solved. Later, when the students were free to play with any of the the puzzles, attitudes toward each puzzle predicted playing behaviour more closely for students in the direct-experience condition than for those in the indirect-experience condition.

The central process assumed to mediate this effect is the attitude's accessibility, which is operationally defined as the speed with which an attitude can be expressed (Fazio, 1986). At the conceptual level, accessibility indicates the strength of association between the representation of the attitude object and its evaluation stored in memory. This evaluation can guide behaviour only if it is activated, and a stronger associative link from the attitude object increases its likelihood of being activated. Fazio and others have shown that attitudes which are based on behavioural experience are indeed more accessible (e.g. Fazio, Chen, McDonel, & Sherman, 1982); furthermore, greater attitude accessibility does go along with greater attitude–behaviour consistency (e.g. Fazio & Williams, 1986; for an application to consumer behaviour, see Kokkinaki & Lunt, 1997). In addition to direct experience, *repeated expression* of an attitude has also been shown to increase its accessibility (Fazio et al., 1982; Powell & Fazio, 1984).

Although attitude accessibility is an important mediator of attitudes' influence on behaviour, it is important to note that both direct experience and repeated expression may produce greater attitude–behaviour consistency through other mediating processes as well (Eagly & Chaiken, 1998). Direct experience has been shown to increase the temporal stability of an attitude (Doll & Ajzen, 1992), and repeated expression of an attitude can increase both its extremity (Downing, Judd, & Brauer, 1992) and its importance (Roese & Olson, 1994). Further research is thus needed to separate the effects of accessibility from those of other aspects of attitude strength in mediating the effect of attitudes on behaviour.

Cognitive effort in attitude formation

As we have discussed in chapter 7, the way in which attitudes are formed is at the core of dual-process models of persuasion (see Bohner et al., 1995; Chaiken et al., 1989; Petty & Cacioppo, 1986a,b). According to these models, high motivation and ability foster the formation of attitudes through effortful processing of all potentially relevant detail information, whereas either low motivation or low ability leads to lower processing effort and judgments based on simple rules. These different routes to attitude formation have been linked to different degrees of attitude–behaviour consistency. Within the ELM framework, Petty and Cacioppo (1986a,b) proposed that attitudes that were formed via the central route should be more predictive of behaviour than attitudes formed via the peripheral route. In line with this hypothesis, various research findings showed that the attitudes of people who processed under conditions of high personal relevance were more predictive of behaviour than those of people who processed under conditions of low relevance (Leippe &

Elkin, 1987; Petty, Cacioppo, & Schumann, 1983; Shavitt & Brock, 1986; Sivacek & Crano, 1982; for discussion see Petty et al., 1995; for applications to advertising and consumer behaviour, see Haugtvedt & Priester, 1997).

Individual differences

A number of personality traits have been linked to individual differences in attitude–behaviour consistency. We can distinguish three broad mediating processes by which these traits seem to operate: They may affect (a) *attitude strength*; they may moderate (b) the *relative importance of attitude* as opposed to other determinants of behaviour; or they may be related to (c) the *consistency of behaviour*.

We have already discussed the role of *need for cognition* (Cacioppo & Petty, 1982; Cacioppo et al., 1996; see chapter 6) in attitude formation and change. Because people high in need for cognition tend to engage in greater processing effort when forming an attitude, they should form stronger attitudes, which are highly persistent, resistant to change, and predictive of behaviour. In support of this view, Cacioppo, Petty, Kao, and Rodriguez (1986) found that the degree to which students' attitudes toward US presidential candidates predicted their voting behaviour was a direct function of these students' need for cognition.

Two traits that affect the relative importance of attitudes (versus other factors) in guiding behaviour are **self-monitoring** and *self-awareness*. People low in self-monitoring, whose social behaviour is generally more reflective of their internal states (Snyder, 1974), show higher attitude–behaviour correlations than people high in self-monitoring. High self-monitors' behaviour, on the other hand, is guided more by situational demands and the expectations of others. Part of this difference might be due to the fact that low self-monitors prefer and seek out situations in which attitudes can be openly expressed and enacted (Snyder & Kendzierski, 1982). A closer attitude–behaviour relation has also been found for persons high (as opposed to low) in self-awareness (Carver, 1975; Gibbons, 1978). Highly self-aware individuals are chronically more likely than people low in self-awareness to focus attention on their internal states, including their attitudes; thus, at any given point in time, attitudes are more likely to be accessed and used as a basis for behavioural decisions.

Finally, Bem and Allen (1974) observed that people vary in *self-consistency*, i.e. the degree to which they define themselves as consistent over situations. Only highly self-consistent people should exhibit a close link between attitude and behaviour. Indeed, Zanna, Olson, and Fazio (1980) reported evidence that individuals' past consistency over situations was related to greater correspondence between attitude and behaviour.

Attitudes and behaviour: A note on causality

In sum, the correlation between attitude and behaviour appears to be stronger the more both measures correspond in specificity or aggregation. Furthermore, if similar aspects, functions, and components of an attitude are salient at the time both attitude and behaviour are measured, greater attitude–behaviour correspondence should be detected. Various indicators of attitude strength as well as personality variables have been identified as moderators of the attitude–behaviour relation. You should be aware, however, that high *correlations* between attitude and behaviour do not provide sufficient evidence for inferring that attitudes *cause* behaviour. As we have discussed extensively in chapter 8, one alternative is that behaviour may influence attitudes. Another possibility is that third variables, such as salient context-dependent beliefs, influence both attitude reports and behaviour. To the extent that these context factors remain stable, this would result in high attitude–behaviour correlations without a direct causal link between the two constructs being present (Schwarz & Bohner, 2001; Wilson & Hodges, 1992).

How can a causal link between attitude and behaviour be established? One possibility is by experimentally manipulating the salience of an attitude before assessing a related behaviour. A causal influence of attitude on behaviour would then be indicated by a larger correlation in those conditions in which the attitude has been made salient, and thus more accessible (for a discussion of this paradigm, see Schwarz & Strack, 1981). Using this methodology, Bohner and his colleagues (Bohner, Reinhard, Rutz, Sturm, Kerschbaum, & Effler, 1998) tested the hypothesis that men's attitudes toward rape would influence their likelihood of raping a woman (e.g. Burt, 1980). Using a 20-item scale, the researchers assessed male students' attitudes toward rape either *before* or *after* these students indicated their proclivity to rape a woman. In the "before" condition, where attitudes should have been more accessible at the time of reporting rape proclivity, a higher correlation between attitudes and behavioural inclination was found than in the "after" condition. These findings suggest a causal impact of attitude on self-reported behaviour, rather than vice versa (see also Snyder & Kendzierski, 1982; Snyder & Swann, 1976).

Expectancy-value models: Attitudes toward behaviour and other determinants of behaviour

The previous sections have shown that, if measured appropriately, attitudes are a major determinant of behaviour. But researchers also recognised the importance of other influential factors, most notably social norms, but also habits, skills and abilities. They developed a family of theories in which *attitudes toward behaviour* (rather than attitudes toward targets of behaviour) are located within a network of other predictor variables (e.g. Ajzen, 1991; Bagozzi, 1992; Bentler & Speckart, 1979; Fishbein & Ajzen, 1975). These are called *expectancy-value models* (see Feather, 1982) because attitudes are defined in these models as expectancy × value products.

The theory of reasoned action

The initial model, Fishbein and Ajzen's (1975) **theory of reasoned action** (TRA), is displayed in Figure 10.4(a). According to this model, the immediate cause of behaviour is *behavioural intention*, a conscious decision to engage in a certain action. Any influences on behaviour that the theory accounts for are assumed to be mediated by this construct. The two determinants of intention are *attitude toward the behaviour* and *subjective norm*. Attitude toward the behaviour is defined as the sum of expectancy × value products. Each of these products consists of the subjective probability (= expectancy) that the behaviour has a certain consequence, multiplied by the subjective value attached to this consequence. For example, a person may expect that by studying economics she will perhaps find a prestigious, well-paid job (a very positive consequence with moderate subjective likelihood) but will have to put up with boring maths in her courses (a somewhat negative consequence with very high likelihood). These

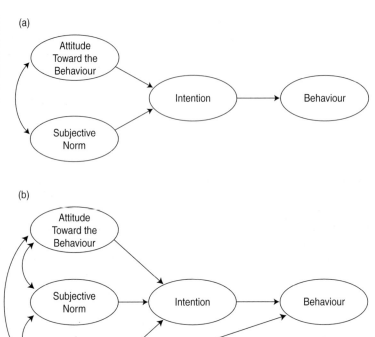

Figure 10.4. Schematic depiction of the theory of reasoned action (a) and the theory of planned behaviour (b). Adapted from Ajzen and Madden (1986).

two aspects combined would yield a moderately positive attitude toward studying economics.

The second determinant of behavioural intention is the construct of subjective norm. It is also defined as a sum of products, each product consisting of the belief that a significant "referent" (i.e. another person or group) thinks one should perform the behaviour, and the motivation to comply with this referent. For instance, a person may believe that his son thinks he should buy a motorbike, but he may not be willing to comply with his son; he may also believe that his wife would strongly disapprove of his buying the motorbike, and he may be inclined to comply with his wife. If just these two referents were considered, the resulting subjective norm would be negative and would reduce the intention of buying the motorcycle.

In the TRA, only the constructs just described were included, whereas any other, more distal variables, such as demographic variables, personality traits and even attitudes toward targets, were considered "external" to the theory. This means that they were thought to influence behaviour only indirectly, by acting upon the two proximal determinants of behavioural intention: attitude toward the behaviour and subjective norm. For example, the moderating role of self-monitoring on the attitude–behaviour relation that we discussed above can be reconstructed in terms of the TRA as an effect on the relative weighting of the attitude and subjective norm components. For low self-monitors, attitude is more important, whereas for high self-monitors, subjective norm is the major determinant of intention. A situational variable that may affect the relative importance of attitudes versus norms in a similar way is *type of self-focused attention*. This was tested in studies by Froming, Walker, and Lopyan (1982). Participants who favoured punishment as a method of teaching but thought that others would oppose it (or vice versa) were given the task of applying electric shocks to a "learner". Depending on experimental condition, participants' attention was focused either on their private self by facing a mirror, or on their public self by facing an audience. The results showed that participants' punishing behaviour was more in line with their attitudes in the former condition, but more in line with the perceived social norm in the latter.

The theory of reasoned action has been widely applied to predicting diverse behaviours, including strategy choices in laboratory games (Ajzen, 1971), health-related behaviours such as condom use (e.g. Albarracin, Fishbein, & Middlestadt, 1998) or donating blood (Pomazal & Jaccard, 1976), consumer behaviours like purchasing toothpaste (Wilson, Mathews, & Harvey, 1975), and personally significant decisions, e.g. having an abortion (Smetana & Adler, 1980). In a meta-analytic review of 87 studies, Sheppard, Hartwick, and Warshaw (1988) found an overall multiple correlation of $R = .66$ for predicting behavioural intentions from attitudes and subjective norms, and a mean correlation between intention and behaviour of $r = .53$. More recent reviews also attest to the high predictive validity of the theory of reasoned action (e.g. Sutton, 1998).

The theory of planned behaviour

The most prominent extension to the TRA was proposed by Ajzen (1991; Ajzen & Madden, 1986). His **theory of planned behaviour** (TPB) features one additional predictor variable: *perceived behavioural control* (see Figure 10.4b). This extension was assumed to enhance prediction especially for those behaviours over which a person does not have complete voluntary control, including complex behaviours that require extensive planning or preparation (e.g. running a marathon). Perceived behavioural control was conceptualised as the expected ease with which the intended behaviour can actually be performed (cf. the concept of *self-efficacy*; Bandura, 1977). It was hypothesised to affect behaviour either indirectly, via the behavioural intention, or directly, to the extent that it is an accurate reflection of the actual control a person has over the behaviour in question. For example, a person who thinks it will be difficult to run a marathon should be less likely to form a behavioural intention of doing so; in addition, once she has formed an intention to act, she may be less likely to succeed. Research on expectancy-value models is illustrated in Box 10.2.

The results of Ajzen and Madden (1986) and others suggest that the theory of planned behaviour is superior to the theory of reasoned action in predicting behavioural intentions (and behaviour) when the behaviour under study is difficult to perform. Other studies indicate that this is not true for behaviours that can easily be performed, e.g. attending a meeting (Kelly & Breinlinger, 1995). One could argue, however, that the difficult behaviour investigated in Ajzen and Madden's (1986) study, "getting an 'A' in a course", includes a *consequence* of behaviour rather than just describing the behaviour proper (i.e. studying for the course). Therefore, perceived behavioural control could be more parsimoniously subsumed in the TRA's concept of attitude, as it refers to the subjective likelihood of a behavioural consequence.

Further predictors of behaviour

Other extensions of the TRA's list of predictor variables have been proposed (see Eagly & Chaiken, 1993). Some theorists noted that behaviour is affected by *previous behaviour* or *habit*, and that these influences are not necessarily mediated by attitudes, subjective norms, or intentions (e.g. Bentler & Speckart, 1979; Triandis, 1980; cf. Ajzen, 1991). A meta-analysis (Ouellette & Wood, 1998) indicates that past behaviour does significantly contribute to the prediction of future behaviour. Interestingly, it does so along either of two mediational pathways. Well-practised behaviours that are performed in stable contexts (e.g. using a seatbelt) recur because the processing that controls them becomes automatic; the frequency of prior behaviour is then reflected in habit strength, which directly affects future

Ajzen and Madden (1986, Experiment 2) conducted a study whose aim was to demonstrate the predictive superiority of the theory of planned behaviour over the theory of reasoned action. Their participants were business students, and the target behaviour was getting an "A" (the best grade) in a course. At two points in time—both early in the semester and one week prior to final examinations— the researchers measured students' attitudes toward "receiving an 'A' in this course", students' subjective norms regarding this behaviour, and their perceived control over this behaviour. Attitude was assessed by asking students to evaluate, on a *good–bad* scale, ten salient consequences of getting an "A" (e.g. getting a sense of personal accomplishment; increasing one's grade point average), and to rate the probability of each of these consequences on a scale from *unlikely* to *likely*. A belief-based measure of attitude was then formed by summing the products of these two ratings over all ten consequences. To measure subjective norm, the students indicated how much each of five referents (e.g. the instructor; their classmates) would *approve* versus *disapprove* of their getting an "A", and how much they were willing to comply with each referent (scale from *very much* to *not at all*). A belief-based measure was formed by summing the products of these two ratings over all five referents. Finally, perceived behavioural control was assessed by summing over eight beliefs about the presence versus absence of facilitating and inhibiting factors (e.g. possessing the relevant skills; being involved in extracurricular activities).

The dependent variables were behavioural intentions, assessed with three items (e.g. "I intend to get an 'A' in this course"), and behaviour, i.e. the actual grade obtained. For each dependent variable, the researchers performed two-step hierarchical regression analyses at each time of measurement. The first step of the regression represented a test of the theory of reasoned action, and its second step provided a test of the theory of planned behaviour. Thus,

(a)   behavioural intentions were predicted from attitude and subjective norm (step 1), and then jointly from these two predictors and perceived behavioural control (step 2); and

(b)   behaviour (i.e. the grade obtained) was predicted from intention (step 1), and then jointly from intention and perceived control (step 2).

Ajzen and Madden (1986) assumed that early in the semester perceptions of behavioural control would not reflect actual control very well. The inclusion of perceived behavioural control would therefore improve the prediction of actual behaviour only indirectly, via behavioural intentions, but not directly. Late in the semester, however, the researchers hypothesised, students' perceptions of control should become more accurate as they learn more about factors facilitating or inhibiting success; this would lead to improved prediction of actual behaviour from perceived control both indirectly via intentions and directly.

Both hypotheses were supported. When measured early in the semester, attitudes and subjective norm were substantially related to behavioural intention (multiple $R = .48$), confirming the validity of the theory of reasoned action. But this multiple correlation was significantly increased (to $R = .65$) when perceived behavioural control was added as a predictor. Furthermore, intention was significantly correlated with the grade actually obtained ($R = .26$), and including perceived behavioural control as an additional predictor did not increase the magnitude of this coefficient.

When measured late in the semester, attitude and subjective norm together predicted intentions ($R = .49$); and again, this coefficient was significantly increased (to $R = .64$) when perceived behavioural control was included in the model. Finally, when measured late in the semester, perceived control also significantly improved the prediction of the actual grade obtained, from $R = .39$ when intention was the sole predictor, to $R = .45$ when intention and perceived control were used as concurrent predictors.

behaviour. However, behaviours that are less well learned or occur in unstable contexts tend to remain under conscious control; under these circumstances, past behaviour influences future behaviour indirectly via behavioural intentions.

While most studies that predict behaviour from past behaviour are correlational, Albarracín and Wyer (2000) provide the first experimental evidence for a causal impact of past behaviour. Using an elaborate cover story, they made participants believe that they had voted in favour of or against the introduction of comprehensive exams on what was said to be a subliminal measure of unconscious behavioural tendencies (in fact, no subliminal measures of voting were taken). This subjective perception of past behaviour influenced later voting behaviour via its influence on attitudes. When participants were capable of thinking about the implications of introducing comprehensive exams (i.e. engaging in the kind of outcome-related cognitions that are emphasised in the TRA/TPB), perceived past behaviour influenced attitudes both directly and also indirectly, through its impact on outcome-related cognitions. Importantly, however, past behaviour still had a direct effect on attitudes when participants were distracted from thinking about the implications of introducing comprehensive exams.

Further extensions of the expectancy × value approach include the suggestion of assessing *affective aspects* of an attitude in addition to the more rational, evaluation-based beliefs that are highlighted in the TRA and TPB (e.g. Conner & Armitage, 1998; Manstead & Parker, 1995). Other researchers have proposed to *subdivide the construct of perceived behavioural control* into the components of "self-efficacy" (the perception of own skills and ability) and "perceived control" (the perception of controllability of environmental constraints on behaviour; e.g. Armitage & Conner, 1999). Yet other proposed variables to extend the list of predictors of behaviour are *belief salience*, *moral norms*, and *self-identity* (for a review, see Conner & Armitage, 1998).

Some of these extensions are related to the more general point that the TRA and TPB are limited in scope to conscious, deliberate and "rational" behaviours, whereas they do not predict well behaviour that is not consciously intended and not based on utilitarian deliberation (e.g. Fazio, 1986). Ajzen and Fishbein (1980) disputed this criticism by emphasising that their model leaves room for the possibility that a behavioural intention has once been formed in the past, and that people may retrieve this previously formed intention rather than deliberating anew each time they engage in the behaviour in question. Furthermore, Ajzen (1991) reported that the inclusion of an affective attitude component as an additional predictor of leisure behaviours did not account for a significant increase in predictive power (but cf. Conner & Armitage, 1998).

In sum, expectancy-value theories have relegated the attitude concept to the background as one among many predictors of behaviour, focusing on a narrow definition of attitude toward behaviour. Through this increased specification they achieved considerable predictive power, especially in applied areas where deliberate behaviours are studied. An attitude–behaviour theory that is more comprehensive by including explanations for spontaneous behaviour will be discussed in the next section.

Two processes by which attitudes guide behaviour: The MODE model

To account both for situations that are characterised by conscious deliberation and for those in which people act relatively spontaneously, Fazio (1990; Fazio & Towles-Schwen, 1999) proposed a dual-process model of attitude–behaviour relations. In his **MODE model**, *attitudes toward objects* (rather than attitudes toward behaviour) are back at centre stage as antecedents of behaviour. The acronym MODE stands for "Motivation and Opportunity as Determinants" (cf. the dual-process models of persuasion presented in chapter 7). When both motivation and opportunity for conscious deliberation are low, attitudes are thought to activate behaviour immediately in an automatic fashion. This should be true mainly for highly accessible attitudes. Thus, merely encountering or considering an attitude object may trigger a behavioural response of approach or avoidance, depending on the valence of the attitude. The phenomena of selective attention and some of the effects of attitudes on information search that we discussed in chapter 9 may be subsumed under this class of attitude–behaviour processes. No deliberate reflection or reasoning about the appropriate course of action seems to be involved here; the individual may not even be aware that he is attending more closely to attitude-congruent information or criticising attitude-discrepant material. Fazio's proposal of automatic effects of attitudes on behaviour is consistent with accumulating evidence showing that social behaviour may be profoundly affected by unconscious influences (for a review, see Bargh, 1996; see also Bless et al., in press).

As an illustration of the spontaneous attitude–behaviour link proposed by Fazio, consider the results of a study by Fazio, Powell, and Williams (1989). These researchers asked participants to express their attitudes toward various products, using computerised assessment that included reaction time measures. Later, participants could choose several of the products to take home. This behavioural measure was correlated with the expressed attitude more highly the faster the attitude judgment had been given, i.e. the more accessible the attitude was. This shows that simply having an attitude may be insufficient for guiding behaviour; another important determinant of behaviour is the atitude's accessibility.

The spontaneous process of behavioural responding to accessible attitudes can be contrasted with a more deliberate process in which more detailed evidence about possible behavioural alternatives is carefully evaluated, leading to a conscious intention to act. The theory of reasoned action (Fishbein & Ajzen, 1975) and the theory of planned behaviour (Ajzen, 1991) exemplify this type of processing, but other theories of effortful processing may be considered here as well (Fazio & Towles-Schwen, 1999). The two major determinants of this more deliberate process are motivation and opportunity (e.g. time, resources, cognitive capacity).

The moderating role of motivation and opportunity has been examined by Sanbonmatsu and Fazio (1990). Their research participants received information about two department stores. One, "Brown's", was described as rather good overall but as having a poor camera department; the other, "Smith's", was portrayed quite negatively overall, but the description of its camera department was positive. Later, participants were asked to decide in which of the two stores they would buy a camera. If these decisions were based on the overall attitudes toward the stores, Brown's should have been chosen more frequently; however, if participants recalled and processed the specific attributes of each store in deriving an intention, Smith's should be chosen more often. The conditions under which participants made their decisions were varied in a 2 × 2 design, involving both motivation and opportunity to deliberate. High accuracy motivation was induced by telling participants that they would have to explain their decisions, whereas in the low motivation condition, no such instructions were given. Opportunity was varied by introducing high versus low degrees of time pressure.

Sanbonmatsu and Fazio (1990) found that participants who were both highly motivated and did *not* experience time pressure were more likely to make an attribute-based decision (choosing Smith's) than participants in any other condition. These findings support the MODE model: If either opportunity or motivation to deliberate was lacking, overall attitudes seemed to guide behaviour; but if both motivation and opportunity were present, behavioural decisions were guided by more effortful processing of relevant detail information.

In another study, Schuette and Fazio (1995) asked participants to judge the validity of studes in favour of and opposed to capital punishment, using a similar paradigm as Lord et al. (1979; see chapter 9). They varied both attitude accessibility (by asking some participants to *repeatedly* express their attitude toward capital punishment) and motivation to reach an accurate decision (in a similar way as Sanbonmatsu and Fazio had done). The results showed that the impact of prior attitudes on judgments was highest when both the attitude was highly accessible and motivation was low. However, when motivation was high, participants could overcome any biasing influences of their attitudes, even when these were highly accessible.

These and many other studies (for a review, see Fazio & Towles-Schwen, 1999) attest to the validity of the MODE model as a general framework for understanding attitude–behaviour relations. Highly accessible attitudes toward an object often directly and automatically influence our behaviour. But in situations where the accuracy of behavioural decisions is important and our capacity to deliberate is relatively unconstrained, more controlled processing may override the effect of automatic attitude activation. Then more detailed considerations of the attitude object, and also other relevant information (e.g. normative pressures), come into play, reducing the magnitude of the attitude–behaviour relation.

Conclusion: Attitudes do predict behaviour (but do they cause it?)

Our discussion has shown that, over several decades, attitude–behaviour research has greatly enhanced our understanding of the attitude–behaviour relation. Not only has it dispelled early pessimism regarding the utility of the attitude construct by introducing refined notions of measurement, it also was successful in identifying important moderators of the attitude–behaviour relation. Thus, we are now in a position to predict when attitudes will be strongly related to behaviour, and when they will not be. And finally, recent research clarified the processes by which an influence of attitudes on behaviour may occur. As in many other domains of human judgment (see Chaiken & Trope, 1999), both spontaneous, automatic mechanisms and more deliberate reasoning have been identified as the two prototypical modes of processing that mediate the well-established relationship between attitudes on behaviour.

We should reiterate, however, that attitude–behaviour consistency simply denotes a high correlation between attitude reports and observed behaviour, whereas there is still little evidence for a causal influence of behaviour on attitudes. Most of the findings that have been interpreted as indicating a guiding influence of attitudes on behaviour are just as consistent with the alternative view that people may draw on similar informational inputs when forming an attitude judgment as they do when making a behavioural decision (see chapter 5; Schwarz & Bohner, 2001).

Chapter summary

(1) A major reason why attitudes are studied is the belief that they guide behaviour. But many early studies failed to provide evidence for a close link between attitudes and behaviour, leading some scholars to suggest abandoning the attitude construct altogether.

(2) Rather than giving up on the attitude concept, researchers tried to delineate the conditions for variability in the attitude–behaviour relation. In doing so, they identified methodological as well as substantial moderators.

(3) The attitude–behaviour relation is high if both concepts are measured at the same level of specificity (the correspondence principle). General attitude measures poorly predict single behaviours, but are good predictors of aggregate measures of behaviour (the aggregation principle).

(4) Attitude–behaviour relations are stronger (a) if similar aspects of an attitude object are salient when the attitude expressed and when the behaviour is enacted; (b) if the attitude is strong and accessible; (c) for people high (vs low) in need for cognition, high (vs low) in self-awareness, and for people low (vs high) in self-monitoring.

(5) A high correlation between attitude and behaviour does not necessarily mean that attitudes cause behaviour. Only a few studies have tried to establish a causal role of attitudes by experimentally varying the accessibility of the attitude.

(6) Expectancy × value models, most notably the theory of reasoned action and the theory of planned behaviour, conceptualised

behavioural intentions as the major determinant of behaviour. Intentions are in turn thought to be influenced by attitudes toward the behaviour and subjective norms regarding the behaviour. Additional predictors have been suggested as well (e.g. perceived behavioural control; prior behaviour; affective beliefs). These models explain a substantial amount of variance in a range of deliberate and intentional behaviours.

(7) The MODE model expands the scope of attitude–behaviour relations by integrating two processes by which attitudes can guide behaviour: The deliberate formation of intentions, which requires both motivation and opportunity, and the immediate activation of behaviour through highly accessible attitudes, which may operate without intention or awareness.

Exercises

(1) For which of the following attitudes and behaviours would you expect higher correlations, and for which lower ones?
   Attitudes: (A1) toward studying at the university
                  (A2) toward the specific course "X"
   Behaviours: (B1) attending course X regularly
                  (B2) attending course X at a given day
                  (B3) attending all classes regularly
(2) What other variables have been found to influence behaviour besides attitudes?
(3) Name a few variables that moderate the attitude–behaviour link and explain why they do so.
(4) Advertisers and campaigners who aim at changing recipients' behaviour attempt to influence the favourability of attitudes. Explain why they should also try to influence the attitude's accessibility. How could they achieve this?
(5) According to the MODE model, when would attitudes affect spontaneous behaviour and when well-considered behaviour?

Further reading

A review of the theory of planned behaviour:

Ajzen, I. (1991). The theory of planned behavior. *Organizational Behavior and Human Decision Processes*, 50, 179–211.

A review of the MODE model:

Fazio, R. H., & Towles-Schwen, T. (1999). The MODE model of attitude–behavior processes. In S. Chaiken & Y. Trope (Eds.), *Dual process theories in social psychology* (pp. 97–116). New York: Guilford.

Postscript IV

In the final chapter 11, we will present some concluding remarks on the current state of the psychology of attitudes.

What's left? 11

We started out with the claim that attitudes are significant in every-day life, which makes them an important concept of social psy-chology worthwhile of being studied. You obviously believed us, otherwise you would hardly have reached the final chapter. On your way here you have seen what attitudes are, what they are good for, how they are measured, where they come from and how they influence information processing and behaviour. "Is there more to come?" you may ask, either timidly or enthusiastically depending on your interest. Our answer will satisfy both concerns: Of course there is, but not here.

The area of attitude research is so vast partly because the attitude concept is linked to so many other concepts and partly because atti-tudes pertain to so many different fields of application. Researchers who look at advertising effects, health behaviour or political cam-paigning may all have something to contribute to attitude research (for a more elaborated discussion see Shavitt & Wänke, 2001). To cover all aspects and applications of attitudes would have been almost impossible. And although it is common for authors to mention in the final chapter all the areas they have left out or have not addressed in detail, we did not want to do this. After all you have read we find it rather discouraging to tell you that there is so much more you have missed. On the contrary, we have striven to give you a thorough overview of attitude research—not just a first glimpse, but a deeper understanding and insight. As attitude issues are so pervasive in the social sciences and their applied areas, readers are bound to see many of the topics covered here return in their further studies or professional careers. We hope this book prepared the ground and readers will discover it was a useful reading.

Having said this, there is one omission we would like to mention because it reflects on the field of social psychology as a whole. In chapter 1, we emphasised the social nature of attitudes and yet throughout the whole book we focused on the individual and his or her thinking and behaviour. This was not altogether our choice but reflects the interests of attitude researchers and social psychologists in general over the last 60 years. Sure enough, the social nature of attitudes is implicitly present; after all, persuasion takes at least two parties, and the forthcoming volume on Social Influence in this series covers more on group pressure, minority and majority influence as well as related topics.

But while we referred to public opinion or Zeitgeist in chapter 1, in this final chapter we have to admit that social psychology as a field has been rather vague about (or has simply neglected) how individual attitudes turn into public opinion, social climates and social movements (of course there are exceptions; e.g. Latané and Bourgeois, 2001; Moscovici & Doise, 1994). Given the vast and detailed research on attitudes, this neglect is somewhat surprising. Of course, other disciplines of the social sciences have chosen to look at aggregate behaviour, but they also neglected the link between the individual and the aggregate. From all we know the aggregate is not simply the sum of all individual components. In our age of mass media and global exchange, the interface between individual attitudes and those of a larger social unit may be one of the most challenging questions facing attitude research. How do individual and social attitudes mutually and continuously influence each other and thus turn individuals into social beings? We end here by presenting this challenge to the reader, who in time to come may take it on and contribute as a researcher to the understanding of this issue.

Glossary

Accessibility The ease with which information (e.g. an attitude) comes to mind.

Aggregation principle Global attitudes are better predictors of aggregated behavioural measures than of any specific behaviours.

Ambivalence Holding conflicting feelings or beliefs toward one object.

Assimilation Evaluation of a stimulus is shifted towards the valence of a context stimulus.

Attitude Summary evaluation of an object of thought.

Attitude function The purpose that holding an attitude serves for an individual.

Attitude object This can be anything a person discriminates or holds in mind, e.g. things, persons, groups or abstract ideas.

Attitude strength Reflects the intensity of an individual's feelings or beliefs as manifested in attitude extremity, confidence, relevance, accessibility and other indicators.

Attitude structure Representation and organisation of different attitudes (inter-attitudinal structure) or of components belonging to one attitude (intra-attitudinal structure) in memory.

Attitudes-as-constructions perspective A theoretical orientation positing that individuals construct evaluative judgments on the basis of chronically and temporally accessible information.

Attribution theory A conceptual framework that deals with people's explanations of behaviour and events.

Balance theory A cognitive consistency theory proposed by Heider, according to which individuals strive for consistency among the relations between cognitive elements (representations of self, others and objects).

Bogus pipeline technique A procedure designed to reduce motivated response distortions in direct attitude measurement. The respondent is hooked up to fake psychophysiological machinery, which purportedly gives the experimenter access to the respondent's true attitudes.

Chronic accessibility The ease with which information comes to mind due to factors that are independent of the specific situation (chronic).

Cognitive response approach Theoretical orientation in persuasion research that conceives of attitude change as mediated by an individual's evaluative thoughts about a message or issue.

Cognitive responses Positive, negative or neutral thoughts generated in response to a persuasive message or attitude object. According to the cognitive response approach, attitude change is a function of the net valence of cognitive responses.

Contrast   Evaluation of a stimulus is shifted in a direction opposite to the valence of a context stimulus.

Co-occurrence hypotheses   A set of assumptions in the heuristic-systematic model about the interplay of its processing modes.

Correspondence principle   Attitudes best predict behaviour when both are measured at the same level of specificity.

Cronbach's alpha   A popular coefficient of reliability based on the intercorrelations of items.

Demand characteristics   Cues in a research setting that participants may use to infer how they are expected to respond or behave.

Dual-processing models of persuasion   Theories of persuasion that postulate two modes of information processing which differ in the extent to which individuals engage in effortful thought about message arguments and other specific information on an attitude object. The mode of information processing is assumed to depend on motivation and ability.

Ease of retrieval/Ease of processing   These subjective experiences may influence evaluative judgments. The more easily information comes to mind or can be processed, the higher its impact on the judgment.

Effort-justification hypothesis   The assumption that people often come to like what they had to suffer for as a result of reducing the dissonance caused by high effort invested and low attractiveness of the outcome.

Elaboration likelihood model (ELM)   Comprehensive theory positing that attitude change is mediated by two modes of information processing: central-route processing and peripheral-route processing. Elaboration denotes the extent to which an individual engages in central-route processing of issue-relevant arguments rather than being influenced by processes that characterise the peripheral route to persuasion (e.g. classical conditioning; heuristic processing). Elaboration likelihood is determined by motivation and ability.

Error-choice method   A disguised attitude measure based on forced-choice questions that ostensibly measure knowledge but are in fact designed to infer respondents' attitudes.

Evaluative conditioning   Affect felt towards one stimulus is transferred to an originally neutrally evaluated stimulus because of paired exposure.

Evolutionary psychology   Approach that conceives of human behaviour as adapted mechanisms which improve— or at one point in evolution improved— selective fitness.

Expectancy-value principle   A feature of various theories in motivation and attitude-behaviour research. It says that an individual assesses the desirability of an object (or course of action) by considering the sum of its features (or expected outcomes) weighted by their subjective probability.

File-drawer model   A theoretical perspective that characterises attitudes as enduring concepts which are stored in memory and retrieved when needed for object evaluation.

Heritability factor   Expresses which proportion of the variance of a phenotype in a population is due to genetic variance in the population.

Heuristic   Simple rule that is used to form an attitude judgment with little cognitive effort (e.g. "the majority is right" or "experts' statements are valid").

Heuristic-systematic model (HSM)   A

dual-process model of persuasion, positing that attitude change can be mediated by two modes of information processing, namely heuristic and systematic processing. When individuals are unmotivated or unable to invest much cognitive effort, they are likely to rely on heuristics in forming an attitude judgment; when motivation and ability are high, they also scrutinise message arguments and all other potentially relevant information to form a judgment.

Ideology In attitude research, this term denotes a hierarchical cognitive structure in which more specific attitudes are linked to more abstract values.

Implicit association test (IAT) A response-time based method designed to assess implicit attitudes. It measures the differential association of two target concepts (e.g. "Blacks" versus "Whites") with positive versus negative evaluations (e.g. "pleasant words" versus "unpleasant words").

Implicit attitudes Evaluations whose origin is unknown to the individual and that affect implicit responses.

Impression management The process of creating in others an image of consistency between one's attitudes and behaviours, in order to appear in a favourable light.

Induced compliance A research paradigm used in testing cognitive dissonance theory. Research participants are subtly induced to perform a counterattitudinal behaviour in order to create dissonant cognitions.

Information integration theory Approach that conceives of judgments as algebraic functions of the weighted information one holds about an object. Special cases are expectancy-value models.

Informational social influence Agreeing with others because one believes their responses are valid and correct.

Inoculation Metaphorical term describing the increase of resistance to persuasion when, prior to a persuasion attempt, other counterattitudinal arguments have been successfully refuted.

Instrumental conditioning Establishing an evaluative response to a stimulus by reinforcing the response.

Knowledge function An attitude's function of providing structure for organising and handling an otherwise complex and ambiguous environment.

Likert scale A multi-item attitude scale that consists of several evaluative statements about an object or issue. Respondents are asked to express their degree of agreement with each statement along a numerical response scale.

Lost-letter technique A behavioural measure of attitude that involves leaving addressed letters in public places, as if they had been lost, and then recording the return rate and condition of the returned letters. The attitude object studied is reflected in the address printed on the letter.

Mere exposure effect Increase in liking for an object caused by merely being exposed (repeatedly) to that object.

Mere thought effect Polarisation of an attitude caused by merely thinking about the issue without acquiring external information.

Message-learning approach Conceptual framework for studying persuasion, focusing on source, message, channel and recipient as elements of the persuasion process and on the learning of message content as the primary mediator of attitude change.

Method of equal-appearing intervals A step in the development of a Thurstone scale. Judges sort belief statements into equally spaced categories according to their favourability. A range of these items are later used to assess respondents' attitudes.

MODE model Proposal that **m**otivation and **o**pportunity **de**termine how attitudes influence behaviour. A core assumption is that attitudes can influence behaviour either via deliberate processing of the attitude's implications for behaviour, or via automatic selective processing of attitude-relevant information, depending on motivation and opportunity.

Need for cognition (NFC) An individual difference variable reflecting the extent to which a person enjoys and engages in thoughtful processing.

Nonreactive measure An indirect measure that is taken without the research participants being aware of the measurement.

Normative social influence Agreeing with others because one seeks their approval.

Overjustification effect A decrease in intrinsic motivation caused by external rewards.

Postdecisional dissonance Unpleasant state of inconsistency in beliefs arising after an individual has taken a decision, brought about by negative aspects of the chosen alternative and positive aspects of nonchosen alternatives.

Priming Increasing the accessibility of a particular concept by activating it prior to a processing task or judgment.

Projective techniques Family of indirect measures of attitude (and other constructs) that involve the presentation of unstructured or ambiguous material and an assessment of how individuals interpret this material.

Proprioceptive feedback Information that stems from an individual's perception of her own movements, muscle contractions or body posture.

Question order effect The response to a question is influenced by the questions asked previously if they bring to mind relevant information that would not have been accessible otherwise.

Random error Chance variations in measurement. A threat to reliability.

Reactivity A change in response (e.g. a reported attitude) brought about by the mere fact that a measurement is taken.

Reliability The extent to which a measure assesses a construct consistently.

Schema A cognitive structure representing an individual's knowledge (including evaluative beliefs) about an object, person, group, situation or event. Schemata are abstractions containing attributes and relationships among attributes of the object.

Self-affirmation theory A theory whose main assumption is that threats to the integrity of a person's self-concept (such as engaging in counterattitudinal behaviour) instigate a motivation to reaffirm the self.

Self-monitoring An individual difference variable. High self-monitors adjust their behaviour to fit situational cues and the expectations of others, whereas low self-monitors act more in accordance with their internal states and dispositions.

Self-perception theory Theory whose core assumption is that individuals infer their own attitudes by observing their own behaviour in context, just as they would do with other people.

Semantic differential A multi-item attitude measure consisting of several bipolar adjective scales.

Single-item measure An attitude measure consisting of a single question or statement.

Social identity function An attitude's function of serving the maintenance of social relationships.

Subliminal exposure Very brief

exposure below the threshold necessary for consciously encoding a stimulus, which may nonetheless affect subsequent responses.

Sufficiency principle Assumption in the heuristic-systematic model that individuals strike a balance between cognitive effort minimisation and the need to form a judgment with sufficient confidence.

Symbolic function Class of attitude functions that are related to the hedonic consequences of expressing a particular attitude (e.g. self-esteem maintenance).

Systematic error The extent to which a measurement is consistently influenced by constructs other than the one that is intended to be measured. A threat to construct validity.

Temporary accessibility The ease with which information comes to mind due to situational (temporary) factors.

Terror management theory An approach whose central claim is that humans' knowing about their mortality has the potential of creating fear or terror, which people cope with by emphasising their being part of a greater "immortal" cultural group. Among other things, this may result in prejudice against members of other groups.

Theory of cognitive dissonance A cognitive consistency theory positing that people who hold incongruent cognitions experience dissonance (= unpleasant arousal) and subsequently strive to reduce dissonance. This is done by changing one or more cognitions, for example attitudes.

Theory of planned behaviour (TPB) An extension of the theory of reasoned action. In addition to attitudes and subjective norms, perceived behavioural control is included as a predictor of behavioural intention and behaviour.

Theory of psychological reactance Approach whose core assumption is that individuals are motivated to restore restricted freedom by enhancing the value of "forbidden" or otherwise blocked objects or behavioural alternatives.

Theory of reasoned action (TRA) A model whose core assumption is that attitudes toward a given behaviour in combination with subjective norms influence the intention to perform that behaviour, which in turn influences behaviour.

Thurstone scale A multi-item attitude scale consisting of statements that vary in extremity along the evaluative continuum. Respondents' attitudes are inferred from those items they agree with.

Tripartite model The assumption that affective, cognitive and behavioural responses are independent elements of an attitude.

Utilitarian function An attitude's function of maximising rewards and minimising punishment.

Validity The extent to which a measure assesses the construct it is supposed to assess.

Vicarious conditioning Learning from observing others being reinforced.

References

Abelson, R. P. (1986). Beliefs are like possessions. *Journal of the Theory of Social Behavior, 16,* 223–250.

Abelson, R. P. (1995). Attitude extremity. In R. E. Petty & J. A. Krosnick (Eds.), *Attitude strength: Antecedents and consequences* (pp. 25–41). Mahwah, NJ: Lawrence Erlbaum Associates Inc.

Abelson, R. P., Aronson, E., McGuire, W. J., Newcomb, T. M., Rosenberg, M. J., & Tannenbaum, P. H. (Eds.). (1968). *Theories of cognitive consistency: A sourcebook.* Chicago: Rand-McNally.

Abelson, R. P., & Prentice, D. A. (1989). Beliefs as possessions: A functional perspective. In A. R. Pratkanis, S. J. Breckler, & A. G. Greenwald (Eds.), *Attitude structure and function* (pp. 361–381). Hillsdale, NJ: Lawrence Erlbaum Associates Inc.

Ajzen, I. (1971). Attitudinal vs. normative messages: An investigation of the differential effects of persuasive communications on behavior. *Sociometry, 34,* 263–280.

Ajzen, I. (1988). *Attitudes, personality, and behavior.* Chicago: Dorsey.

Ajzen, I. (1991). The theory of planned behavior. *Organizational Behavior and Human Decision Processes, 50,* 179–211.

Ajzen, I. & Fishbein, M. (1970). The prediction of behavior from attitudinal and normative variables. *Journal of Experimental Social Psychology, 6,* 466–487.

Ajzen, I., & Fishbein, M. (1977).

Attitude–behavior relations: A theoretical analysis and review of empirical research. *Psychological Bulletin, 84,* 888–918.

Ajzen, I., & Fishbein, M. (1980). *Understanding attitudes and predicting social behavior.* Englewood Cliffs, NJ: Prentice-Hall.

Ajzen, I., & Madden, T. J. (1986). Prediction of goal-directed behavior: Attitudes, intentions, and perceived behavioral control. *Journal of Experimental Social Psychology, 22,* 453–474.

Albarracín, D., Fishbein, M., & Middlestadt, S. (1998). Generalizing behavioral findings across times and measures: A study of condom use. *Journal of Applied Social Psychology, 28,* 657–674.

Albarracín, D., & Wyer, R. S., Jr. (2000). The cognitive impact of past behavior: Influences on beliefs, attitudes, and future behavioral decisions. *Journal of Personality and Social Psychology, 79,* 5–22.

Allgeier, A. R., Byrne, D., Brooks, B., & Revnes, D. (1979). The waffle phenomenon: Negative evaluations of those who shift attitudinally. *Journal of Applied Social Psychology, 9,* 170–182.

Allport, G. W. (1935). Attitudes. In C. Murchison (Ed.), *Handbook of social psychology* (Vol. 2). Worcester, MA: Clark University Press.

Allport, G. W. (1954). *The nature of*

prejudice. Cambridge, MA: Addison-Wesley.

Alwin, D. F., Cohen, R. L., & Newcomb, T. M. (1991). *Political attitudes over the life span: The Bennington women after fifty years*. Madison, WI: University of Wisconsin Press.

American Psychological Association (1992). *Ethical principles of psychologists and code of conduct*. [On-line] Washington, DC: American Psychological Association. Available: http://www.apa.org/ethics/code.html

Anderson, J. R., & Bower, G. H. (1973). *Human associative memory*. Washington, DC: Winston.

Anderson, N. H. (1971). Integration theory and attitude change. *Psychological Review, 78*, 171–206.

Anderson, N. H. (1981). Integration theory applied to cognitive responses and attitudes. In R. Petty, T. Ostrom, & T. Brock (Eds.), *Cognitive responses in persuasion*. Hillsdale, NJ: Lawrence Erlbaum Associates Inc.

Anderson, N. H. (Ed.). (1991). *Contributions to information integration theory* (Vols. 1, 2, and 3). Hillsdale, NJ: Lawrence Erlbaum Associates Inc.

Apsler, R., & Sears, D. O. (1968). Warning, personal involvement, and attitude change. *Journal of Personality and Social Psychology, 9*, 162–166.

Armitage, C. J., & Conner, M. (1999). The theory of planned behaviour: Assessment of predictive validity and "perceived control". *British Journal of Social Psychology, 38*, 35–54.

Aronson, E. (1968). Dissonance theory: Progress and problems. In R. P. Abelson, E. Aronson, W. J. McGuire, T. M. Newcomb, M. J. Rosenberg, & P. H. Tannenbaum (Eds.), *Theories of cognitive consistency: A sourcebook* (pp. 5–27). Chicago: Rand-McNally.

Aronson, E. (1969). The theory of cognitive dissonance: A current perspective.

Advances in Experimental Social Psychology, 4, 1–34.

Aronson, E., Ellsworth, P. C., Carlsmith, J. M., & Gonzales, M. H. (1990). *Methods of research in social psychology*. New York: McGraw-Hill.

Aronson, E., & Mills, J. (1959). The effect of severity of initiation on liking for a group. *Journal of Abnormal and Social Psychology, 59*, 177–181.

Arvey, R. D., Bouchard, T. J., Segal, N. L., & Abraham L. M. (1989). Job satisfaction: Environmental and genetic components. *Journal of Applied Psychology, 74*, 187–192.

Axsom, D. (1989). Cognitive dissonance and behavior change in psychotherapy. *Journal of Experimental Social Psychology, 25*, 234–252.

Axsom, D., & Cooper, J. (1985). Cognitive dissonance and psychotherapy: The role of effort justification in inducing weight loss. *Journal of Experimental Social Psychology, 21*, 149–160.

Baeyens, F., Eelen, P., & van den Bergh, O. (1990). Contingency awareness in evaluative conditioning: A case for unaware affective evaluative learning. *Cognition and Emotion, 4*, 3–18.

Baeyens, F., Eelen, P., van den Bergh, O., & Crombez, G. (1989). Acquired affective-evaluative value: Conservative but not unchangeable. *Behaviour Research and Therapy, 27*, 279–287.

Bagozzi, R. P. (1992). The self-regulation of attitudes, intentions, and behavior. *Social Psychology Quarterly, 55*, 178–204.

Banaji, M. R., Lemm, K. M., & Carpenter, S. J. (2001). The social unconscious. In A. Tesser & N. Schwarz (Eds.), *Blackwell handbook of social psychology: Vol. 1. Intraindividual processes* (pp. 134–158). Oxford, UK: Blackwell.

Bandura, A. (1965). Influence of model's reinforcement contingencies on the acquisition of imitative responses. *Journal of Personality and Social Psychology, 1*, 589–595.

Bandura, A. (1977). Self-efficacy: Toward a unifying theory of behavioral change. *Psychological Review, 84*, 191–215.

Bargh, J. A. (1994). The four horsemen of automaticity: Awareness, intention, efficiency, and control in social cognition. In R. S. Wyer, Jr., & T. K. Srull (Eds.), *Handbook of social cognition: Vol. 1. Basic processes* (pp. 1–40). Hillsdale, NJ: Lawrence Erlbaum Associates Inc.

Bargh, J. A. (1996). Automaticity in social psychology. In E. T. Higgins & A. W. Kruglanski (Eds.), *Social psychology: Handbook of basic principles* (pp. 169–183). New York: Guilford.

Bargh, J. A. (1997). The automaticity of everyday life. In R. S. Wyer & T. K. Srull (Eds.), *Advances in social cognition* (Vol. 10, pp. 1–61). Mahwah, NJ: Lawrence Erlbaum Associates Inc.

Bargh, J. A., Chaiken, S., Govender, R., & Pratto, F. (1992). The generality of the automatic attitude activation effect. *Journal of Personality and Social Psychology, 62*, 893–912.

Bargh, J. A., Chaiken, S., Raymond, P., & Hymes, C. (1996). The automatic evaluation effect: Unconditional automatic attitude activation with a pronunciation task. *Journal of Experimental Social Psychology, 32*, 104–128.

Baron, R. A. (1993). Interviewers' mood and evaluations of job applicants: The role of applicant qualifications. *Journal of Applied Social Psychology, 23*, 253–271.

Bartlett, F. C. (1995). *Remembering: A study in experimental and social psychology.* Cambridge, UK: Cambridge University Press. (Original work published 1932)

Bassili, J. N. (1996). Meta-judgmental versus operative indexes of psychological attributes: The case of measures of attitude strength. *Journal of Personality and Social Psychology, 71*, 637–653.

Bem, D. J. (1965). An experimental analysis of self-persuasion. *Journal of Experimental Social Psychology, 1*, 199–218.

Bem, D. J. (1967). Self-perception: An alternative interpretation of cognitive dissonance phenomena. *Psychological Review, 74*, 183–200.

Bem, D. J. (1972). Self-perception theory. *Advances in Experimental Social Psychology, 6*, 1–62.

Bem, D. J., & Allen, A. (1974). On predicting some of the people some of the time: The search for cross-situational consistencies in behavior. *Psychological Review, 81*, 506–520.

Bentler, P. M., & Speckart, G. (1979). Models of attitude–behavior relations. *Psychological Review, 86*, 452–464.

Berkowitz, L., & Knurek, D. A. (1969). Label-mediated hostility generalization. *Journal of Personality and Social Psychology, 13*, 200–206.

Blaney, P. H. (1986). Affect and memory: A review. *Psychological Bulletin, 99*, 229–246.

Blascovich, J., Ernst, J. M., Tomaka, J., Kelsey, R. M., Salomon, K. L., & Fazio, R. H. (1993). Attitude accessibility as a moderator of autonomic reactivity during decision making. *Journal of Personality and Social Psychology, 64*, 165–176.

Bless, H., Bohner, G., Schwarz, N., & Strack, F. (1990). Mood and persuasion: A cognitive response analysis. *Personality and Social Psychology Bulletin, 16*, 331–345.

Bless, H., & Schwarz, N. (1999). Sufficient and necessary conditions in dual process models: The case of mood and information processing. In S. Chaiken & Y. Trope (Eds.), *Dual process models in social cognition* (pp. 423–440). New York: Guilford.

Bless, H., Fiedler, K., & Strack, F. (in press). *Social cognition: How individuals construct social reality.* London: Psychology Press.

Bless, H., & Wänke, M. (2000). Can the same information be typical and atypical? How perceived typicality moderates assimilation and contrast in evaluative judgments. *Personality and Social Psychology Bulletin, 26*, 306–315.

Bless, H., Wänke, M., Bohner, G., Fellhauer, R., & Schwarz, N. (1994). Need for cognition: Eine Skala zur Erfassung von Engagement und Freude bei Denkaufgaben. *Zeitschrift für Sozialpsychologie, 25*, 147–154.

Bodenhausen, G. V., Schwarz, N., Bless, H., & Wänke, M. (1995). Effects of atypical exemplars on racial beliefs: Enlightened racism or generalized appraisals? *Journal of Experimental Social Psychology, 31*, 48–63.

Bodenhausen, G. V., & Wyer, R. S. (1987). Social cognition and social reality: Information acquisition and use in the laboratory and the real world. In H. J. Hippler, N. Schwarz, & S. Sudman (Eds.), *Social information processing and survey methodology* (pp. 6–41). New York: Springer.

Bohner, G. (1998). *Vergewaltigungsmythen* [Rape myths]. Landau, Germany: Verlag Empirische Pädagogik.

Bhoner, G., Erb, H.-P., & Crow, K. (1995). Priming und Persuasion: Einflüsse der Aktivierung verschiedener Persönlichkeitsdimensionen auf Prozesse der Einstellungsänderung und auf die Beurteilung des Kommunikators [Priming and persuasion: Effects of activating different personality dimensions on processes of attitude change and judgments about the communicator]. *Zeitschrift für Sozialpsychologie, 26*, 263–271.

Bohner, G., Erb, H.-P., Reinhard, M.-A., & Frank, E. (1996). Distinctiveness across topics in minority and majority influence: An attributional analysis and preliminary data. *British Journal of Social Psychology, 35*, 27–46.

Bohner, G., Frank, E., & Erb, H.-P. (1998). Heuristic processing of distinctiveness information in minority and majority influence. *European Journal of Social Psychology, 28*, 855–860.

Bohner, G., Moskowitz, G., & Chaiken, S. (1995). The interplay of heuristic and systematic processing of social information. *European Review of Social Psychology, 6*, 33–68.

Bohner, G., Rank, S., Reinhard, M.-A., Einwiller, S., & Erb, H.-P. (1998). Motivational determinants of systematic processing: Expectancy moderates effects of desired confidence on processing effort. *European Journal of Social Psychology, 28*, 185–206.

Bohner, G., Reinhard, M.-A., Rutz, S., Sturm, S., Kerschbaum, B., & Effler, D. (1998). Rape myths as neutralizing cognitions: Evidence for a causal impact of anti-victim attitudes on men's self-reported likelihood of raping. *European Journal of Social Psychology, 28*, 257–268.

Bohner, G., Ruder, M., & Erb, H.-P. (in press). When expertise backfires: Contrast versus assimilation in the interplay of heuristic and systematic processing. *British Journal of Social Psychology*.

Bohner, G., Siebler, F., Sturm, S., Effler, D., Litters, M., Reinhard, M.-A., & Rutz, S. (1998). Rape myth acceptance and accessibility of the gender category. *Group Processes and Intergroup Relations, 1*, 67–79.

Bohner, G., & Weinerth, T. (2000). Negative affect and persuasion: The role of affect interpretation. In H. Bless & J. P. Forgas (Eds.), *The message within: The role of subjective experiences in social cognition and behavior* (pp. 203–239). Philadelphia: Psychology Press.

Bohner, G., & Weinerth, T. (2001). Negative affect can increase or decrease message scrutiny: The affect interpretation hypothesis. *Personality* and *Social Psychology Bulletin, 27,* 1417–1428.

Bornstein, R. F. (1989). Exposure and affect: Overview and meta-analysis of research, 1968–1987. *Psychological Bulletin, 106,* 265–289.

Bornstein, R. F., & D'Agostino, P. R. (1994). The attribution and discounting of perceptual fluency: Preliminary tests of a perceptual fluency/attribution model of the mere exposure effect. *Social Cognition, 12,* 113–128.

Bower, G. (1981). Mood and memory. *American Psychologist, 36,* 129–148.

Breckler, S. J. (1984). Empirical validation of affect, behavior, and cognition as distinct components of attitude. *Journal of Personality and Social Psychology, 47,* 1191–1205.

Brehm, J. W. (1956). Post-decision changes in desirability of alternatives. *Journal of Abnormal and Social Psychology, 52,* 384–389.

Brehm, J. W. (1972). *Responses to loss of freedom: A theory of psychological reactance.* Morristown, NJ: General Learning Press.

Brendl, M., & Markman, A. B. (in press).

Brigham, J. C., & Cook, S. W. (1969). The influence of attitude on the recall of controversial material: A failure to confirm. *Journal of Experimental Social Psychology, 5,* 240–243.

British Psychological Society (1991). *Code of conduct, ethical principles and guidelines.* Leicester, UK: British Psychological Society.

Brock, T. C. (1967). Communication discrepancy and intent to persuade as determinants of counterargument production. *Journal of Experimental Social Psychology, 3,* 269–309.

Brown, J. D., Novick, N. J., Lord, K. A., & Richards, J. M. (1992). When Gulliver travels: Social context, psychological closeness, and self-appraisals. *Journal of Personality and Social Psychology, 62,* 717–727.

Bruner, J. S. (1957). On perceptual readiness. *Psychological Review, 64,* 123–152.

Burt, M. R. (1980). Cultural myths and supports of rape. *Journal of Personality and Social Psychology, 38,* 217–230.

Buss, D. M., & Schmitt, D. P. (1993). Sexual strategies theory: An evolutionary perspective on human mating. *Psychological Review, 100,* 204–232.

Buss, D. M., et al. (1990). International preferences in selecting mates: A study of 37 cultures. *Journal of Cross-Cultural Psychology, 21,* 5–47.

Byrne, D. (1971). *The attraction paradigm.* New York: Academic Press.

Cacioppo, J. T., Gardner, W. L., & Berntson, G. G. (1997). Beyond bipolar conceptualizations and measures: The case of attitudes and evaluative space. *Personality and Social Psychology Review, 1,* 3–25.

Cacioppo, J. T., Harkins, S. G., & Petty, R. E. (1981). The nature of attitudes and cognitive responses and their relationships to behavior. In R. Petty, T. Ostrom & T. Brock (Eds.), *Cognitive responses in persuasion.* Hillsdale, NJ: Lawrence Erlbaum Associates Inc.

Cacioppo, J. T., & Petty, R. E. (1979). Attitudes and cognitive response: An electrophysical approach. *Journal of Personality and Social Psychology, 37,* 2181–2199.

Cacioppo, J. T., & Petty, R. E. (1981). Social psychological procedures for cognitive response assessment: The thought listing technique. In T. Merluzzi, C. Glass, & M. Genest (Eds.), *Cognitive assessment.* New York: Guilford.

Cacioppo, J. T., & Petty, R. E. (1982). The need for cognition. *Journal of Personality and Social Psychology, 42,* 116–131.

Cacioppo, J. T., Petty, R. E., Feinstein, J. A., & Jarvis, W. B. G. (1996). Dispositional differences in cognitive motivation: The life and times of individuals varying in need for cognition. *Psychological Bulletin, 119,* 197–253.

Cacioppo, J. T., Petty, R. E., Kao, C. F., & Rodriguez, R. (1986). Central and peripheral routes to persuasion: An individual difference perspective. *Journal of Personality and Social Psychology, 51,* 1032–1043.

Cacioppo, J. T., Petty, R. E., Losch, M., & Crites, S. (1994). Psychophysiological approaches to attitudes. In S. Shavitt & T. C. Brock (Eds.), *Persuasion.* Boston: Allyn & Bacon.

Cacioppo, J. T., Petty, R. E., & Morris, K. J. (1983). Effects of need for cognition on message evaluation, recall, and persuasion. *Journal of Personality and Social Psychology, 45,* 805–818.

Cacioppo, J. T., Petty, R. E., & Sidera, J. (1982). The effects of a salient self-schema on the evaluation of proattitudinal editorials: Top-down versus bottom-up message processing. *Journal of Experimental Social Psychology, 18,* 324–338.

Cacioppo, J. T., Priester, J. R., & Berntson, G. G. (1993). Rudimentary determinants of attitudes: II. Arm flexion and extension have differential effects on attitudes. *Journal of Personality and Social Psychology, 65,* 5–17.

Carlson, H. M., & Sutton, M. S. (1974). The development of attitudes as a function of police roles. *Personality and Social Psychology Bulletin, 1,* 113–115.

Carlston, D. E. (1980). The recall and use of traits and events in social inference processes. *Journal of Experimental Social Psychology, 16,* 303–328.

Carver, C. S. (1975). Physical aggression as a function of objective self-awareness and attitudes towards punishment. *Journal of Experimental Social Psychology, 11,* 510–519.

Carver, C. S., Lawrence, J. W., & Scheier, M. F. (1996). A control-process perspective on the origins of affect. In L. L. Martin & A. Tesser (Eds.), *Striving*

and feeling: Interactions between goals and affect (pp. 11–52). Hillsdale, NJ: Lawrence Erlbaum Associates Inc.

Carver, C. S., & Scheier, M. F. (1990). Principles of self-regulation: Action and emotion. In E. T. Higgins & R. M. Sorrentino (Eds.), *Handbook of motivation and cognition: Foundations of social behavior* (Vol. 2, pp. 3–52). New York: Guilford.

Chaiken, S. (1987). The heuristic model of persuasion. In M. P. Zanna, J. M. Olson, & C. P. Herman (Eds.), *Social influence: The Ontario Symposium* (Vol. 5, pp. 3–39). Hillsdale, NJ: Lawrence Erlbaum Associates Inc.

Chaiken, S., & Eagly, A. H. (1983). Communication modality as a determinant of persuasion: The role of communicator salience. *Journal of Personality and Social Psychology, 45,* 241–256.

Chaiken, S., Giner-Sorolla, R., & Chen, S. (1996). Beyond accuracy: Defense and impression motives in heuristic and systematic processing. In P. M. Gollwitzer & J. A. Bargh (Eds.), *The psychology of action: Linking cognition and motivation to behavior* (pp. 553–578). New York: Guilford.

Chaiken, S., Liberman, A., & Eagly, A. H. (1989). Heuristic and systematic information processing within and beyond the persuasion context. In J. S. Uleman & J. A. Bargh (Eds.), *Unintended thought* (pp. 212–252). New York: Guilford.

Chaiken, S., & Maheswaran, D. (1994). Heuristic processing can bias systematic processing: Effects of source credibility, argument ambiguity, and task importance on attitude judgment. *Journal of Personality and Social Psychology, 66,* 460–473.

Chaiken, S., Pomerantz, E. M., & Giner-Sorolla, R. (1995). Structural consistency and attitude strength. In R. E. Petty & J. A. Krosnick (Eds.), *Attitude strength:*

Antecedents and consequences (pp. 387–412). Mahwah, NJ: Lawrence Erlbaum Associates Inc.

Chaiken, S., & Trope, Y. (Eds.). (1999). *Dual-process theories in social psychology*. New York: Guilford.

Chaiken, S., Wood, W., & Eagly, A. H. (1996). Principles of persuasion. In E. T. Higgins & A. W. Kruglanski (Eds.), *Social psychology: Handbook of basic principles* (pp. 702–742). New York: Guilford.

Chaiken, S., & Yates, S. (1985). Affective-cognitive consistency and thought-induced attitude polarization. *Journal of Personality and Social Psychology, 49,* 1470–1481.

Chen, S., & Chaiken, S. (1999). The heuristic-systematic model in its broader context. In S. Chaiken & Y. Trope (Eds.), *Dual-process theories in social psychology* (pp. 73–96). New York: Guilford.

Cialdini, R. B. (1993). *Influence: The psychology of persuasion* (rev. ed.). New York: Quill/William Morrow.

Cialdini, R. B., & Insko, C. A. (1969). Attitudinal verbal reinforcement as a function of informational consistency: A further test of the two-factor theory. *Journal of Personality and Social Psychology, 12,* 342–350.

Clark, R. D., & Hatfield, E. (1989). Gender differences in receptivity to sexual offers. *Journal of Psychology and Human Sexuality, 2,* 39–55.

Clore, G. L., Schwarz, N., & Conway, M. (1994). Affective causes and consequences of social information processing. In R. S. Wyer & T. K. Srull (Eds.), *Handbook of social cognition* (Vol. 1, 2nd ed., pp. 323–417). Hillsdale, NJ: Lawrence Erlbaum Associates Inc.

Commission of the European Community (1982). *Eurobarometer 18,* Brussels.

Commission of the European Community (1990). *Eurobarometer 33,* Brussels.

Conner, M., & Armitage, C. J. (1998). Extending the theory of planned behavior: A review and avenues for further research. *Journal of Applied Social Psychology, 28,* 1429–1464.

Conover, P. J., & Feldman, S. (1981). The origins and meanings of liberal/conservative self-identifications. *American Journal of Political Science, 25,* 617–645.

Converse, P. E. (1964). The nature of belief systems in mass publics. In D. E. Apter (Ed.), *Ideology and discontent* (pp. 206–261). New York: Free Press.

Converse, P. E. (1970). Attitudes and non-attitudes: Continuation of a dialogue. In E. R. Tufte (Ed.), *The quantitative analysis of social problems* (pp. 168–189). Reading, MA: Addison-Wesley.

Cooper, J., & Fazio, R. H. (1984). A new look at dissonance theory. *Advances in Experimental Social Psychology, 17,* 229–266.

Cooper, J., & Worchel, S. (1970). Role of undesired consequences in arousing cognitive dissonance. *Journal of Personality and Social Psychology, 16,* 199–206.

Corey, S. M. (1937). Professed attitudes and actual behavior. *Journal of Educational Psychology, 28,* 171–280.

Cosmides, L., Tooby, J., & Barkow, J. H. (1992). Evolutionary psychology and conceptual integration. In J. H. Barkow, L. Cosmides, & J. Tooby (Eds.), *The adapted mind: Evolutionary psychology and the generation of culture* (pp. 3–15). New York: Oxford University Press.

Crano, W. D. (1995). Attitude strength and vested interest. In R. E. Petty & J. A. Krosnick (Eds.), *Attitude strength: Antecedents and consequences* (pp. 131–157). Mahwah, NJ: Lawrence Erlbaum Associates Inc.

Cronbach, L. J. (1951). Coefficient alpha and the internal structure of tests. *Psychometrika, 16,* 297–334.

Crowne, D. P., & Marlowe, D. (1964). *The*

approval motive: Studies in evaluative dependence. New York: Wiley.

Croyle, R. T., & Cooper, J. (1983). Dissonance arousal: Physiological evidence. *Journal of Personality and Social Psychology, 45*, 782–791.

Cunningham, M. R. (1986). Measuring the physical in physical attractiveness: Quasi-experiments on the sociobiology of female facial beauty. *Journal of Personality and Social Psychology, 50*, 925–935.

Davidson, A. R., & Jaccard, J. J. (1979). Variables that moderate the attitude–behavior relation: Results of a longitudinal survey. *Journal of Personality and Social Psychology, 37*, 1364–1376.

Dawes, R. M., Singer, D., & Lemons, F. (1972). An experimental analysis of the contrast effect and its implications for intergroup communication and the indirect assessment of attitude. *Journal of Personality and Social Psychology, 21*, 281–295.

Dawkins, R. (1989). *The selfish gene* (2nd ed.). Oxford, UK: Oxford University Press.

Dawson, M. E., & Schell, A. M. (1987). Human autonomic and skeletal classical conditioning: The role of conscious cognitive factors. In G. Davey (Ed.), *Cognitive processes and Pavlovian conditioning in humans* (pp. 27–55). Chichester, UK: Wiley.

DeBono, K. G. (2000). Attitude functions and consumer psychology: Understanding perceptions of product quality. In G. R. Maio & J. M. Olson (Eds.), *Why we evaluate: Functions of attitudes* (pp. 195–221). Mahwah, NJ: Lawrence Erlbaum Associates Inc.

DeBono, K. G., & Harnish, R. J. (1988). Source expertise, source attractiveness, and the processing of persuasive information: A functional approach. *Journal of Personality and Social Psychology, 55*, 541–546.

DeBono, K. G., & Packer, M. (1991). The effects of advertising appeal on perceptions of product quality. *Personality and Social Psychology Bulletin, 17*, 194–200.

Deci, E. L. (1971). Effects of externally mediated rewards on intrinsic motivation. *Journal of Personality and Social Psychology, 18*, 105–115.

Deci, E. L., Koestner, R., & Ryan, R. M. (1999). A meta-analytic review of experiments examining the effects of extrinsic rewards on intrinsic motivation. *Psychological Bulletin, 125*, 627–668.

DeJong, W. (1979). An examination of self-perception mediation on the foot-in-the-door effect. *Journal of Personality and Social Psychology, 37*, 2221–2239.

DeMaio, T. J. (1984). Social desirability and survey measurement: A review. In C. F. Turner & E. Martin (Eds.), *Surveying subjective phenomena* (Vol. 2, pp. 257–281). New York: Russell Sage Foundation.

Deutsch, M., & Gerard, H. B. (1955). A study of normative and informational social influences upon individual judgment. *Journal of Abnormal and Social Psychology, 51*, 629–636.

Doll, J., & Ajzen, I. (1992). Accessibility and stability of predictors in the theory of planned behavior. *Journal of Personality and Social Psychology, 63*, 754–765.

Dovidio, J. F., Kawakami, K., & Beach, K. R. (2001). Implicit and explicit attitudes: Examination of the relationship between measures of intergroup bias. In R. Brown & S. Gaertner (Eds.), *Blackwell handbook of social psychology: Vol. 4. Intergroup processes* (pp. 175–197). Oxford, UK: Blackwell.

Downing, J. W., Judd, C. M., & Brauer, M. (1992). Effects of repeated expressions on attitude extremity. *Journal of*

Personality and Social Psychology, 63, 17–29.

Draycott, S., & Dabbs, A. (1998). Cognitive dissonance: 1. An overview of the literature and its integration into theory and practice in clinical psychology. *British Journal of Clinical Psychology, 37,* 341–353.

Eagly, A. H., & Chaiken, S. (1993). *The psychology of attitudes.* Fort Worth, TX: Harcourt Brace Jovanovich.

Eagly, A. H., & Chaiken, S. (1998). Attitude structure and function. In D. Gilbert, S. T. Fiske, & G. Lindzey (Eds.), *Handbook of social psychology* (4th ed., pp. 269–322). New York: McGraw-Hill.

Eagly, A. H., Chen, S., Chaiken, S., & Shaw-Barnes, K. (1999). The impact of attitudes on memory: An affair to remember. *Psychological Bulletin, 125,* 64–89.

Eagly, A. H., Kulesa, P., Brannon, L. A., Shaw, K., & Hutson-Comeaux, S. (2000). Why counterattitudinal messages are as memorable as proattitudinal messages: The importance of active defense against attack. *Personality and Social Psychology Bulletin, 26,* 1392–1408.

Eagly, A. H., Kulesa, P., Chen, S., & Chaiken, S. (2001). Do attitudes affect memory? Tests of the congeniality hypothesis. *Current Directions in Psychological Science, 10,* 5–9.

Eagly, A. H., Mladinic, A., & Otto, S. (1994). Cognitive and affective bases of attitudes toward social groups and social policies. *Journal of Experimental Social Psychology, 30,* 113–137.

Eagly, A. H., & Wood, W. (1999). The origins of sex differences in human behavior: Evolved dispositions versus social roles. *American Psychologist, 54,* 408–423.

Eagly, A. H., Wood, W., & Chaiken, S. (1978). Causal inferences about communicators and their effect on opinion change. *Journal of Personality and Social Psychology, 36,* 424–435.

Eaves, L. J., Eysenck, H. J., & Martin, N. G. (1989). *Genes, culture and personality: An empirical approach.* London: Academic Press.

Eckes, T., & Six, B. (1994). Fakten und Fiktionen in der Einstellungs-Verhaltens-Forschung: Eine Meta-Analyse [Fact and fiction in research on the relationship between attitude and behaviour: A meta-analysis]. *Zeitschrift für Sozialpsychologie, 25,* 253–271.

Einwiller, S., Erb, H.-P., & Bohner, G. (1997, June). *Schlussfolgerungsprozesse und die Wirkung zweiseitiger Persuasion* [Inferential processing and the effectiveness of two-sided persuasion]. Paper presented at the sixth "Tagung der Fachgruppe Sozialpsychologie", Konstanz, Germany.

Elkin, R. A., & Leippe, M. R. (1986). Physiological arousal, dissonance, and attitude change: Evidence for a dissonance arousal link and a "don't remind me" effect. *Journal of Personality and Social Psychology, 51,* 55–65.

Elliot, A. J., & Devine, P. G. (1994). On the motivational nature of cognitive dissonance: Dissonance as psychological discomfort. *Journal of Personality and Social Psychology, 67,* 382–394.

Elms, A. C., & Janis, I. L. (1965). Counter-norm attitudes induced by consonant versus dissonant conditions of role-playing. *Journal of Experimental Research in Personality, 1,* 50–60.

Ennis, R., & Zanna, M. P. (2000). Attitude function and the automobile. In G. R. Maio & J. M. Olson (Eds.), *Why we evaluate: Functions of attitudes* (pp. 395–415). Mahwah, NJ: Lawrence Erlbaum Associates Inc.

Erb, H.-P., & Bohner, G. (2000). Mere consensus in minority and majority influence. In N. K. De Vries & C. K. W. De Dreu (Eds.), *Group consensus and minority influence: Implications for innovation* (pp. 40–59). Oxford, UK: Blackwell.

Erb, H.-P., Bohner, G., Schmälzle, K., & Rank, S. (1998). Beyond conflict and discrepancy: Cognitive bias in minority and majority influence. *Personality and Social Psychology Bulletin, 24*, 620–633.

Erber, R., Hodges, S. D., & Wilson, T. D. (1995). Attitude strength, attitude stability, and the effects of analyzing reasons. In R. E. Petty & J. A. Krosnick (Eds.), *Attitude strength: Antecedents and consequences* (pp. 433–454). Mahwah, NJ: Lawrence Erlbaum Associates Inc.

Erdelyi, M. H., & Appelbaum, A. G. (1973). Cognitive masking: The disruptive effect of an emotional stimulus upon the perception of contiguous neutral items. *Bulletin of the Psychonomic Society, 1*, 59–61.

Erdelyi, M. H., & Blumenthal, D. G. (1973). Cognitive masking in rapid sequential processing: The effect of an emotional picture on preceding and succeeding pictures. *Memory and Cognition, 1*, 201–204.

Fazio, R. H. (1986). How do attitudes guide behavior? In R. M. Sorrentino & E. T. Higgins (Eds.), *Handbook of motivation and cognition* (pp. 204–243). New York: Guilford.

Fazio, R. H. (1990). Multiple processes by which attitudes guide behavior: The MODE model as an integrative framework. *Advances in Experimental Social Psychology, 23*, 75–109.

Fazio, R. H. (1995). Attitudes as object-evaluation associations: Determinants, consequences, and correlates of attitude accessibility. In R. E. Petty & J. A. Krosnick (Eds.), *Attitude strength: Antecedents and consequences* (pp. 247–282). Mahwah, NJ: Lawrence Erlbaum Associates Inc.

Fazio, R. H. (2000). Accessible attitudes as tools for object appraisal: Their costs and benefits. In G. R. Maio & J. M. Olson (Eds.), *Why we evaluate: Functions of attitudes* (pp. 1–36). Mahwah, NJ: Lawrence Erlbaum Associates Inc.

Fazio, R. H., Blascovich, J., & Driscoll, D. M. (1992). On the functional value of attitudes: The influence of accessible attitudes upon the ease and quality of decision making. *Personality and Social Psychology Bulletin, 18*, 388–401.

Fazio, R. H., Chen, J., McDonel, E. C., & Sherman, S. J. (1982). Attitude accessibility, attitude–behavior consistency, and the strength of the object–evaluation association. *Journal of Experimental Social Psychology, 18*, 339–357.

Fazio, R. H., & Cooper, J. (1983). Arousal in the dissonance process. In J. T. Cacioppo & R. E. Petty (Eds.), *Social psychophysiology: A sourcebook* (pp. 122–152). New York: Guilford Press.

Fazio, R. H., & Dunton, B. C. (1997). Categorization by race: The impact of automatic and controlled components of racial prejudice. *Journal of Experimental Social Psychology, 33*, 451–470.

Fazio, R. H., Jackson, J. R., Dunton, B. C., & Williams, C. J. (1995). Variability in automatic activation as an unobtrusive measure of racial attitudes: A bona fide pipeline? *Journal of Personality and Social Psychology, 69*, 1013–1027.

Fazio, R. H., Ledbetter, J. E., & Towles-Schwen, T. (2000). On the costs of accessible attitudes: Detecting that the attitude object has changed. *Journal of Personality and Social Psychology, 78*, 197–210.

Fazio, R. H., & Powell, M. C. (1997). On the value of knowing one's likes and dislikes: Attitude accessibility, stress, and health in college. *Psychological Science, 8*, 430–436.

Fazio, R. H., Powell, M. C., & Williams, C. J. (1989). The role of attitude accessibility in the attitude-to-behavior process. *Journal of Consumer Research, 16*, 280–288.

Fazio, R. H., Sanbonmatsu, D. M., Powell, M. C., & Kardes, F. R. (1986). On the automatic activation of attitudes. *Journal of Personality and Social Psychology, 50,* 229–238.

Fazio, R. H., & Towles-Schwen, T. (1999). The MODE model of attitude–behavior relations. In S. Chaiken & Y. Trope (Eds.), *Dual-process theories in social psychology* (pp. 97–116). New York: Guilford.

Fazio, R. H., & Williams, C. J. (1986). Attitude accessibility as a moderator of the attitude–perception and attitude–behavior relations: An investigation of the 1984 presidential election. *Journal of Personality and Social Psychology, 51,* 505–514.

Fazio, R. H., & Zanna, Mark P. (1981). Direct experience and attitude–behavior consistency. *Advances in Experimental Social Psychology, 14,* 161–202.

Fazio, R. H., Zanna, M. P., & Cooper, J. (1977). Dissonance and self-perception: An integrative view of each theory's proper domain of application. *Journal of Experimental Social Psychology, 13,* 464–479.

Feather, N. T. (Ed.). (1982). *Expectations and actions: Expectancy-value models in psychology.* Hillsdale, NJ: Lawrence Erlbaum Associates Inc.

Festinger, L. (1957). *A theory of cognitive dissonance.* Stanford, CA: Stanford University Press.

Festinger, L. (1964). *Conflict, decision, and dissonance.* Stanford, CA: Stanford University Press.

Festinger, L., & Carlsmith, J. M. (1959). Cognitive consequences of forced compliance. *Journal of Abnormal and Social Psychology, 58,* 203–210.

Fiedler, K., & Bless, H. (2000). The formation of beliefs in the interface of affective and cognitive processes. In N. Frijda, A. Manstead, & S. Bem (Eds.), *The influence of emotions on beliefs* (pp.

144–170). Cambridge, UK: Cambridge University Press.

Fincham, F., & Hewstone, M. (2001). Attribution theory and research: From basic to applied. In M. Hewstone, & W. Stroebe (Eds.), *Introduction to social psychology* (3rd ed., pp. 197–238). Oxford, UK: Blackwell.

Fishbein, M. (1967a). A behavior theory approach to the relations between beliefs about an object and the attitude toward the object. In M. Fishbein (Ed.), *Readings in attitude theory and measurement* (pp. 389–400). New York: Wiley.

Fishbein, M. (1967b). A consideration of beliefs, and their role in attitude measurement. In M. Fishbein (Ed.), *Readings in attitude theory and measurement* (pp. 257–266). New York: Wiley.

Fishbein, M., & Ajzen, I. (1974). Attitudes toward objects as predictors of single and multiple behavioral criteria. *Psychological Review, 81,* 59–74.

Fishbein, M., & Ajzen, I. (1975). *Belief, attitude, intention, and behavior.* Reading, MA: Addison-Wesley.

Fishbein, M., & Coombs, F. S. (1974). Basis for decision: An attitudinal analysis of voting behavior. *Journal of Applied Social Psychology, 4,* 95–124.

Fiske, S. T., & Morling, B. A. (1995). Schemas/schemata. In A. S. R. Manstead & M. Hewstone (Eds.), *The Blackwell encyclopedia of social psychology* (pp. 489–494). Oxford, UK: Blackwell.

Fiske, S. T., & Taylor, S. E. (1991). *Social cognition* (2nd ed.). New York: McGraw-Hill.

Florack, A., Scarabis, M., & Bless, H. (2001). When do associations matter?: The use of implicit associations towards ethnic groups in person judgments. *Journal of Experimental Social Psychology, 37,* 518–524.

Forgas, J. P. (1995). Mood and judgment:

The affect infusion model (AIM). *Psychological Bulletin, 117*, 39–66.

Fram, E. H., & Cibotti, E. (1991, December). The shopping list studies and projective techniques: A 40-year view. *Marketing Research*, 14–22.

Freedman, J. L., & Fraser, S. C. (1966). Compliance without pressure: The foot-in-the-door technique. *Journal of Personality and Social Psychology, 4*, 195–202.

Frey, D. (1986). Recent research on selective exposure to information. *Advances in Experimental Social Psychology, 19*, 41–80.

Frey, D., & Rosch, M. (1984). Information seeking after decisions: The roles of novelty of information and decision reversibility. *Personality and Social Psychology Bulletin, 10*, 91–98.

Froming, W. J., Walker, G. R., & Lopyan, K. J. (1982). Public and private self-awareness: When personal attitudes conflict with societal expectations. *Journal of Experimental Social Psychology, 18*, 476–487.

Furnham, A. (1997). *The psychology of behavior at work*. Hove, UK: Taylor & Francis.

Gaes, G. G., Kalle, R. J., & Tedeschi, J. T. (1978). Impression management in the forced compliance situation: Two studies using the bogus pipeline. *Journal of Experimental Social Psychology, 14*, 493–510.

Gibbons, F. X. (1978). Sexual standards and reactions to pornography: Enhancing behavioral consistency through self-focused attention. *Journal of Personality and Social Psychology, 36*, 976–987.

Gilovich, T. (1990). Differential construal and the false consensus effect. *Journal of Personality and Social Psychology, 59*, 623–634.

Giner-Sorolla, R., & Chaiken, S. (1994). The causes of hostile media judgments. *Journal of Experimental Social Psychology, 30*, 165–180.

Gorn, G. J. (1982). The effects of music in advertising on choice behavior: A classical conditioning approach. *Journal of Marketing Research, 46*, 94–101.

Granberg, D., & Brent, E. (1983). When prophecy bends: The preference–expectation link in U.S. presidential elections, 1952–1980. *Journal of Personality and Social Psychology, 45*, 477–491.

Granberg, D., & Jenks, R. (1977). Assimilation and contrast effects in the 1972 election. *Human Relations, 30*, 623–640.

Green, D. P., & Gerken, A. E. (1989). Self-interest and public opinion toward smoking restrictions and cigarette taxes. *Public Opinion Quarterly, 53*, 1–16.

Greenberg, J., Pyszczynski, T., Solomon, S., Rosenblatt, A., Veeder, S., Kirkland, S., & Lyon, D. (1990). Evidence for terror management theory II: The effects of mortality salience on reactions to those who threaten or bolster the cultural worldview. *Journal of Personality and Social Psychology, 58*, 308–318.

Greenberg, J., Solomon, S., & Pyszczynski, T. (1997). Terror management theory of self-esteem and cultural worldviews: Empirical assessments and conceptual refinements. *Advances in Experimental Social Psychology, 29*, 61–139.

Greenwald, A. G. (1968). Cognitive learning, cognitive response to persuasion, and attitude change. In A. Greenwald, T. Brock, & T. Ostrom (Eds.), *Psychological foundations of attitudes* (pp. 148–170). New York: Academic Press.

Greenwald, A. G. (1989). Why attitudes are important: Defining attitude and attitude theory 20 years later. In A. R. Pratkanis, S. J. Breckler, & A. G. Greenwald (Eds.), *Attitude structure and function* (pp. 429–440). Hillsdale, NJ: Lawrence Erlbaum Associates Inc.

Greenwald, A. G., & Banaji, M. R. (1995). Implicit social cognition: Attitudes, self-esteem, and stereotypes. *Psychological Review, 102,* 4–27.

Greenwald, A. G., Banaji, M. R., Rudman, L. A., Farnham, S. D., Nosek, B. A., & Rosier, M. (2000). Prologue to a unified theory of attitudes, stereotypes, and self-concept. In Forgas, J. P. (Ed.), *Feeling and thinking: The role of affect in social cognition* (pp. 308–330). New York: Cambridge University Press.

Greenwald, A. G., McGhee, D. E., & Schwartz, J. L. K. (1998). Measuring individual differences in implicit cognition: The implicit association test. *Journal of Personality and Social Psychology, 74,* 1464–1480.

Greenwald, A. G., & Nosek, B. A. (2001). Health of the implicit association test at age 3. *Zeitschrift für Experimentelle Psychologie, 48,* 85–93.

Greenwald, A. G., & Sakumura, J. S. (1967). Attitude and selective learning: Where are the phenomena of yesteryear? *Journal of Personality and Social Psychology, 7,* 387–397.

Gross, S. R., Holtz, R., & Miller, N. (1995). Attitude certainty. In R. E. Petty & J. A. Krosnick (Eds.), *Attitude strength: Antecedents and consequences* (pp. 215–245). Mahwah, NJ: Lawrence Erlbaum Associates Inc.

Grossman, R. P., & Till, B. D. (1998). The persistence of classically conditioned brand attitudes. *Journal of Advertising, 27,* 23–31.

Haddock, G. (2000). Subjective ease of retrieval and attitude-relevant judgments. In H. Bless & J. Forgas (Eds.), *The message within: The role of subjective states in social cognition and behavior* (pp. 125–142). Philadelphia, PA: Psychology Press.

Haddock, G., & Zanna, M. P. (1998). Assessing the impact of affective and cognitive information in predicting attitudes toward capital punishment. *Law and Human Behavior, 22,* 325–339.

Haire, M. (1950). Projective techniques in marketing research. *Journal of Marketing, 14,* 649–656.

Hammond, K. R. (1948). Measuring attitudes by error choice: An indirect method. *Journal of Abnormal and Social Psychology, 43,* 38–48.

Hass, R. G., & Grady, K. (1975). Temporal delay, type of forewarning and resistance to influence. *Journal of Experimental Social Psychology, 11,* 459–469.

Hastie, R. (1981). Schematic principles in human memory. In E. T. Higgins, C. P. Herman, & M. P. Zanna (Eds.), *Social cognition: The Ontario Symposium* (Vol. 1, pp. 39–88). Hillsdale, NJ: Lawrence Erlbaum Associates Inc.

Hastorf, A. H., & Cantril, H. (1954). They saw a game: A case study. *Journal of Abnormal and Social Psychology, 49,* 129–134.

Haugtvedt, C. P., & Petty, R. E. (1992). Personality and persuasion: Need for cognition moderates the persistence and resistance of attitude change. *Journal of Personality and Social Psychology, 63,* 308–319.

Haugtvedt, C. P., Petty, R. E., & Cacioppo, J. T. (1992). Need for cognition and advertising: Understanding the role of personality variables in consumer behavior moderates the persistence and resistance of attitude change. *Journal of Consumer Psychology, 1,* 239–260.

Haugtvedt, C. P., & Priester, J. R. (1997). Conceptual and methodological issues in advertising effectiveness: An attitude strength perspective. In W. D. Wells (Ed.), *Measuring advertising effectiveness: Advertising and consumer psychology* (pp. 79–93). Mahwah, NJ: Lawrence Erlbaum Associates Inc.

Haugtvedt, C. P., & Wegener, D. T. (1994). Message order effects in persuasion: An attitude strength perspective. *Journal of Consumer Research, 21,* 205–218.

Heider, F. (1946). Attitudes and cognitive organization. *Journal of Psychology, 21,* 107–112.

Heider, F. (1958). *The psychology of interpersonal relations.* New York: Wiley.

Herek, G. M. (1986). The instrumentality of attitudes: Toward a neofunctional theory. *Journal of Social Issues, 42,* 99–114.

Higgins, E. T. (1989). Knowledge accessibility and activation: Subjectivity and suffering from unconscious sources. In J. S. Uleman & J. A. Bargh (Eds.), *Unintended thought* (pp. 75–123). New York: Guilford.

Higgins, E. T., & King, G. A. (1981). Accessibility of social constructs: Information-processing consequences of individual and contextual variability. In N. Cantor & J. F. Kihlstrom (Eds.), *Personality, cognition, and social interaction* (pp. 69–121). Hillsdale, NJ: Lawrence Erlbaum Associates Inc.

Himmelfarb, S. (1993). The measurement of attitudes. In A. H. Eagly & S. Chaiken (Eds.), *The psychology of attitudes* (pp. 23–87). Fort Worth, TX: Harcourt Brace Jovanovich.

Houston, D. A., & Fazio, R. H. (1989). Biased processing as a function of attitude accessibility: Making objective judgments subjectively. *Social Cognition, 7,* 51–66.

Hovland, C. I., Janis, I. L., & Kelley, J. J. (1953). *Communication and persuasion.* New Haven, CT: Yale University Press.

Howard, D. J. (1997). Familiar phrases as peripheral persuasion cues. *Journal of Experimental Social Psychology, 33,* 231–243.

Howard, J., & Rothbart, M. (1980). Social categorization and memory for in-group and out-group behavior. *Journal of Personality and Social Psychology, 38,* 301–310.

Hymes, R. W. (1986). Political attitudes as social categories: A new look at selective memory. *Journal of Personality and Social Psychology, 51,* 233–241.

Insko, C. A. (1965). Verbal reinforcement of attitude. *Journal of Personality and Social Psychology, 2,* 621–623.

Insko, C. A., & Butzine, K. W. (1967). Rapport, awareness, and verbal reinforcement of attitude. *Journal of Personality and Social Psychology, 6,* 225–228.

Isen, A. M. (1987). Positive affect, cognitive processes, and social behavior. *Advances in Experimental Social Psychology, 20,* 203–253.

Isen, A. M., Shalker, T. E., Clark, M., & Karp, L. (1978). Affect, accessibility of material in memory, and behavior: A cognitive loop? *Journal of Personality and Social Psychology, 36,* 1–12.

Iyengar, S., & Kinder, D. R. (1987). *News that matters: Television and American opinion.* Chicago: University of Chicago Press.

Jaccard, J. J., & Davidson, A. R. (1972). Toward understanding of family planning behaviors: An initial investigation. *Journal of Applied Social Psychology, 2,* 228–235.

Jaccard, J., Weber, J., & Lundmark, J. (1975). A multitrait-multimethod analysis of four attitude assessment procedures. *Journal of Experimental Social Psychology, 11,* 149–154.

Jacoby, L. L., Kelley, C. M., Brown, J., & Jasechko, J. (1989). Becoming famous overnight: Limits on the ability to avoid unconscious influences of the past. *Journal of Personality and Social Psychology, 56,* 326–338.

Janis, I. L. (1959). Motivational factors in the resolution of decisional conflicts. In M. R. Jones (Ed.), *Nebraska Symposium on motivation* (Vol. 7, pp. 198–231). Lincoln, NE: University of Nebraska Press.

Janis, I. L., & King, B. T. (1954). The influence of role-playing on opinion change. *Journal of Abnormal and Social Psychology, 49,* 211–218.

Janis, I. L., & Mann, L. (1965). Effectiveness of emotional role-playing in modifying smoking habits and attitudes. *Journal of Experimental Research in Personality, 1,* 84–90.

Jarvis, W. B. G., & Petty, R. E. (1996). The need to evaluate. *Journal of Personality and Social Psychology, 70,* 172–194.

Johnson, B. T., & Eagly, A. H. (1989). Effects of involvement on persuasion: A meta-analysis. *Psychological Bulletin, 106,* 290–314.

Jonas, K., Diehl, M., & Brömer, P. (1997). Effects of attitudinal ambivalence on information processing and attitude-intention consistency. *Journal of Experimental Social Psychology, 33,* 190–210.

Jones, E. E., & Aneshansel, J. (1956). The learning and utilization of contravaluant material. *Journal of Abnormal and Social Psychology, 53,* 27–33.

Jones, E. E., & Sigall, H. (1971). The bogus pipeline: A new paradigm for measuring affect and attitude. *Psychological Bulletin, 76,* 349–364.

Joule, R.-V., & Beauvois, J.-L. (1998). Cognitive dissonance theory: A radical view. *European Review of Social Psychology, 8,* 1–32.

Judd, C. M., Kenny, D. A., & Krosnick, J. A. (1983). Judging the positions of political candidates: Models of assimilation and contrast. *Journal of Personality and Social Psychology, 44,* 952–963.

Judd, C. M., & Kulik, J. A. (1980). Schematic effects of social attitudes on information processing and recall. *Journal of Personality and Social Psychology, 38,* 569–578.

Kallick, S. M., Zebrowitz, L. A., Langlois, J. H., & Johnson, R. M. (1998). Does human facial attractiveness honestly advertise health? Longitudinal data on an evolutionary question. *Psychological Science, 9,* 8–13.

Kaplan, K. J. (1972). On the ambivalence–indifference problem in attitude theory and measurement: A suggested modification of the semantic differential technique. *Psychological Bulletin, 77,* 361–372.

Katona, G. (1975). *Psychological economics.* New York: Elsevier.

Katz, D. (1960). The functional approach to the study of attitudes. *Public Opinion Quarterly, 24,* 163–204.

Katz, D., & Stotland, E. (1959). A preliminary statement to a theory of attitude structure and change. In S. Koch (Ed.), *Psychology: A study of a science* (Vol. 3, pp. 423–475). New York: McGraw-Hill.

Kawakami, K., & Dovidio, J. F. (2001). The reliability of implicit stereotyping. *Personality and Social Psychology Bulletin, 27,* 212–225.

Keller, J., Bohner, G., & Erb, H.-P. (2000). Intuitive und heuristische Verarbeitung—verschiedene Prozesse? Präsentation einer deutschen Fassung des "Rational-Experiential Inventory" sowie neuer Selbstberichtskalen zur Heuristiknutzung. *Zeitschrift für Sozialpsychologie, 31,* 87–101.

Keller, L. M., Bouchard, T. J., Arvey, R. D., Segal, N. L., & Dawes, R. N. (1992). Work values: Genetic and environmental influences. *Journal of Applied Psychology, 77,* 79–88.

Kelley, H. H. (1967). Attribution theory in social psychology. In D. Levine (Ed.), *Nebraska Symposium on motivation* (Vol. 15, pp. 192–238). Lincoln, NE: University of Nebraska Press.

Kelley, H. H. (1972). Causal schemata and the attribution process. In E. E. Jones, D. E. Kanouse, H. H. Kelley, R. E. Nisbett, S. Valins, & B. Weiner (Eds.), *Attribution: Perceiving the causes of behavior* (pp. 151–174). Morristown, NJ: General Learning Press.

Kelly, C., & Breinlinger, S. (1995). Attitudes, intentions, and behavior: A study of women's participation in collective action. *Journal of Applied Social Psychology, 25,* 1430–1445.

Kenrick, D. T., Gutierres, S. E., & Goldberg, L. L. (1989). Influence of popular erotica on judgments of strangers and mates. *Journal of Experimental Social Psychology, 25,* 159–167.

Kim, K., & Shavitt, S. (1993). Toward a model of attitude reuse versus recomputation. In K. Finlay, A. A. Mitchell, & F. C. Cummins (Eds.), *Proceedings of the Society of Consumer Psychology* (pp. 105–110). Clemson, SC: CtC Press.

Kim, M., & Hunter, J. E. (1993). Attitude–behavior relations: A meta-analysis of attitudinal relevance and topic. *Journal of Communication, 43,* 101–142.

Kinder, D. R., & Sears, D. O. (1985). Public opinion and political action. In G. Lindzey & E. Aronson (Eds.), *Handbook of social psychology* (3rd ed., Vol. 2, pp. 659–741). New York: Random House.

King, B. T., & Janis, I. L. (1956). Comparison of the effectiveness of improvised versus non-improvised role-playing in producing opinion change. *Human Relations, 9,* 177–186.

Klinger, M. R., & Greenwald, A. G. (1994). Preferences need no inferences?: The cognitive basis of unconscious mere exposure effects. In P. M. Niedenthal & S. Kitayama (Eds.), *The heart's eye: Emotional influences in perception and attention* (pp. 67–85). San Diego, CA: Academic Press.

Knox, R. E., & Inkster, J. A. (1968). Postdecision dissonance at post time. *Journal of Personality and Social Psychology, 8,* 319–323.

Kokkinaki, F., & Lunt, P. (1997). The relationship between involvement, attitude accessibility and attitude–behaviour consistency. *British Journal of Social Psychology, 36,* 497–509.

Kothandapani, V. (1971). Validation of feeling, belief, and intention to act as three components of attitude and their contribution to prediction of contraceptive behavior. *Journal of Personality and Social Psychology, 19,* 321–333.

Kraus, S. (1995). Attitudes and the prediction of behavior: A meta-analysis of the empirical literature. *Personality and Social Psychology Bulletin, 21,* 58–75.

Krosnick, J. A., Betz, A. L., Jussim, L. J., & Lynn, A. R. (1992). Subliminal conditioning of attitudes. *Personality and Social Psychology Bulletin, 18,* 152–162.

Krosnick, J. A., Boninger, D. S., Chuang, Y. C., Berent, M. K., & Carnot, C. G. (1993). Attitude strength: One construct or many related constructs? *Journal of Personality and Social Psychology, 65,* 1132–1151.

Kruglanski, A. W., & Thompson, E. P. (1999). Persuasion by a single route: A view from the unimodel. *Psychological Inquiry, 10*(1), 83–109.

Kunda, Z. (1990). The case for motivated reasoning. *Psychological Bulletin, 108,* 480–498.

Laird, J. D. (1974). Self attribution of emotion: The effects of expressive behavior on the quality of emotional experience. *Journal of Personality and Social Psychology, 29,* 475–486.

LaPiere, R. (1934). Attitudes versus actions. *Social Forces, 13,* 230–237.

Latané, B., & Bourgeois, M. J. (2001). Successfully simulating dynamic social impact: Three levels of prediction. In J. P. Forgas & K. D. Williams (Eds.), *Social influence: Direct and indirect processes* (pp. 61–76). Philadelphia, PA: Psychology Press.

Lavine, H., & Snyder, M. (2000). Cognitive processes and the functional matching effect in persuasion: Studies of personality and poitical behavior. In G. R. Maio & J. M. Olson (Eds.), *Why we evaluate: Functions of attitudes* (pp. 97–131). Mahwah, NJ: Lawrence Erlbaum Associates Inc.

Lazarus, R. S. (1984). On the primacy of cognition. *American Psychologist, 39,* 124–129.

Lemon, N. (1973). *Attitudes and their measurement.* New York: Wiley.

Lepper, M. R., Greene, D., & Nisbett, R. E. (1973). Undermining children's intrinsic interest with extrinsic reward: A test of the "overjustification" hypothesis. *Journal of Personality and Social Psychology, 28,* 129–137.

Levine, J. M., & Murphy, G. (1943). The learning and forgetting of controversial material. *Journal of Abnormal and Social Psychology, 38,* 507–517.

Likert, R. (1932). A technique for the measurement of attitudes. *Archives of Psychology, 140,* 1–55.

Linder, D. E., Cooper, J., & Jones, E. E. (1967). Decision freedom as a determinant of the role of incentive magnitude in attitude change. *Journal of Personality and Social Psychology, 6,* 245–254.

Lipsitz, A., Kallmeyer, K., Ferguson, M., & Abas, A. (1989). Counting on blood donors: Increasing the impact of reminder calls. *Journal of Applied Social Psychology, 19,* 1057–1067.

Lord, C. G., & Lepper, M. R. (1999). Attitude representation theory. *Advances in Experimental Social Psychology, 31,* 265–343.

Lord, C. G., Ross, L., & Lepper, M. R. (1979). Biased assimilation and attitude polarization: The effects of prior theories on subsequently considered evidence. *Journal of Personality and Social Psychology, 37,* 2098–2109.

Losch, M. E., & Cacioppo, J. T. (1990). Cognitive dissonance may enhance sympathetic tonus, but attitudes are changed to reduce negative affect rather than arousal. *Journal of Experimental Social Psychology, 26,* 289–304.

Lott, A. J., & Lott, B. E. (1972). The power of liking: Consequences of interpersonal attitudes derived from a liberalized view of secondary reinforcement. *Advances in Experimental Social Psychology, 6,* 109–148.

Lumsdaine, A. A., & Janis, I. L. (1953). Resistance to "counterpropaganda" produced by one-sided and two-sided "propaganda" presentations. *Public Opinion Quarterly, 17,* 311–318.

Maass, A., Clark, R. D., & Haberkorn, G. (1982). The effects of differential ascribed category membership and norms on minority influence. *European Journal of Social Psychology, 12,* 89–104.

Maheswaran, D., & Chaiken, S. (1991). Promoting systematic processing in low motivation settings: The effect of incongruent information on processing and judgment. *Journal of Personality and Social Psychology, 61,* 13–25.

Maio, G. R., & Olson, J. M. (1998). Values as truisms: Evidence and implications. *Journal of Personality and Social Psychology, 74,* 294–311.

Maio, G. R., & Olson, J. M. (2000a). Emergent themes and potential approaches to attitude function: The function–structure model of attitudes. In G. R. Maio & J. M. Olson (Eds.), *Why we evaluate: Functions of attitudes* (pp. 417–442). Mahwah, NJ: Lawrence Erlbaum Associates Inc.

Maio, G. R., & Olson, J. M. (Eds.). (2000b). *Why we evaluate: Functions of attitudes.* Mahwah, NJ: Lawrence Erlbaum Associates Inc.

Mann, L., & Janis, I. L. (1968). A follow-up study on the long-term effects of emotional role-playing. *Journal of Personality and Social Psychology, 8,* 339–342.

Manstead, A. S. R., & Parker, D. (1995). Evaluating and extending the theory of planned behaviour. *European Review of Social Psychology, 6,* 69–95.

Martin, I., & Levey, A. B. (1994). The evaluative response: Primitive but necesssary. *Behaviour Research and Therapy, 32,* 301–305.

Martin, L. L. (1986). Set/reset: Use and disuse of concepts in impression formation. *Journal of Personality and Social Psychology, 51,* 493–504.

Martin, L. L., Abend, T., Sedikides, C., & Green, J. D. (1997). How would I feel if . . .? Mood as input to a role fulfillment evaluation process. *Journal of Personality and Social Psychology, 73,* 242–253.

Martin, L. L., Strack, F., & Stapel, D. A. (2001). How the mind moves: Knowledge accessibility and the fine-tuning of the cognitive system. In A. Tesser & N. Schwarz (Eds.), *Blackwell handbook of social psychology: Vol. 1. Intraindividual processes* (pp. 236–256). Oxford, UK: Blackwell.

Martin, L. L., Ward, D. W., Achee, J. W., & Wyer, R. S., Jr. (1993). Mood as input: People have to interpret the motivational implications of their moods. *Journal of Personality and Social Psychology, 64,* 317–326.

Martin, N. G., Eaves, L. J., Heath, A. R., Jardine, R., Feingold, L. M., & Eysenck, H. J. (1986). Transmission of social attitudes. *Proceedings of the National Academy of Science, 83,* 4364–4368.

Marwell, G., Aiken, M. T., & Demerath, N. J. (1987). The persistence of political attitudes among 1960s civil rights activists. *Public Opinion Quarterly, 51,* 359–375.

McGuire, W. J. (1960). A syllogistic analysis of cognitive relationships. In M. J. Rosenberg, C. I. Hovland, W. J. McGuire, R. P. Abelson, & J. W. Brehm (Eds.), *Attitude organization and change: An analysis of consistency among attitude components* (pp. 65–111). New Haven, CT: Yale University Press.

McGuire, W. J. (1964). Inducing resistance to persuasion: Some contemporary approaches. *Advances in Experimental Social Psychology, 1,* 191–229.

McGuire, W. J. (1969). The nature of attitudes and attitude change. In G. Lindzey & E. Aronson (Eds.), *The handbook of social psychology* (2nd ed., Vol. 3). Reading, MA: Addison-Wesley.

McGuire, W. J. (1981). The probabilogical model of cognitive structure and attitude change. In R. Petty, T. Ostrom, & T. Brock (Eds.), *Cognitive responses in persuasion.* Hillsdale, NJ: Lawrence Erlbaum Associates Inc.

McGuire, W. J. (1985). Attitudes and attitude change. In G. Lindzey & E. Aronson (Eds.), *Handbook of social psychology* (3rd ed., Vol. 2). New York: Random House.

McGuire, W. J., & Papageorgis, D. (1961). The relative efficacy of various types of prior belief-defense in producing immunity against persuasion. *Journal of Abnormal and Social Psychology, 62,* 327–337.

McGuire, W. J., & Papageorgis, D. (1962). Effectiveness of forewarning in developing resistance to persuasion. *Public Opinion Quarterly, 26,* 24–34.

Milgram, S., Mann, L., & Harter, S. (1965). The lost-letter technique: A tool of social research. *Public Opinion Quarterly, 29,* 437–438.

Millar, M. G., & Tesser, A. (1986). Effects of affective and cognitive focus on the attitude–behavior relation. *Journal of Personality and Social Psychology, 51,* 270–276.

Möntmann, V., & Irle, E. (1978). Bibliographie der wichtigen seit 1956 erschienenen Arbeiten zur Theorie der kognitiven Dissonanz [Bibliography of the important work appearing since 1956 on the theory of cognitive dissonance]. In L. Festinger (Ed.), *Theorie der kognitiven Dissonanz* [A theory of cognitive dissonance] (M. Irle & V. Möntmann, Trans.; pp. 366–413).

Bern, Switzerland: Huber. (Original work published 1957)

Moscovici, S., & Doise, W. (1994). *Conflict and consensus: A general theory of collective decisions*. London: Sage.

Moskowitz, G. B. (1996). The mediational effects of attributions and message processing in minority social influence. *British Journal of Social Psychology, 35,* 47–66.

Mugny, G., & Papastamou, S. (1980). When rigidity does not fail: Individualization and psychologization as resistances to the diffusion of minority innovations. *European Journal of Social Psychology, 10,* 43–62.

Newcomb, T. M. (1943). *Personality and social change: Attitude formation in a student community*. New York: Dryden.

Newcomb, T. M. (1961). *The acquaintance process*. New York: Holt, Rinehart, & Winston.

Newcomb, T. M. (1967). *Persistence and change: Bennington College and its students after twenty-five years*. New York: Wiley.

Newton, N., & Newton, M. (1950). Relationship of ability to breast feed and maternal attitudes towards breast feeding. *Pediatrics, 11,* 869–879.

Norman, R. (1975). Affective-cognitive consistency, attitudes, conformity, and behavior. *Journal of Personality and Social Psychology, 32,* 83–91.

Nuttin, J. M. (1985). Narcissism beyond Gestalt and awareness: The name letter effect. *European Journal of Social Psychology, 15,* 353–361.

Obrist, P. A. (1981). *Cardiovascular psychophysiology: A perspective*. New York: Plenum Press.

Orians, G., & Heerwagen, J. H. (1992). Evolved responses to landscapes. In J. H. Barkow, L. Cosmides, & J. Tooby (Eds.), *The adapted mind: Evolutionary psychology and the generation of culture* (pp. 555–580). New York: Oxford University Press.

Orne, M. T. (1962). On the social psychology of the psychological experiment: With particular reference to demand characteristics and their implications. *American Psychologist, 17,* 776–783.

Osgood, C. E., Suci, G. J., & Tannenbaum, P. H. (1957). *The measurement of meaning*. Urbana, IL: University of Illinois Press.

Ostrom, T. M. (1973). The bogus pipeline: A new ignis fatuus? *Psychological Bulletin, 79,* 252–259.

Ouellette, J. A., & Wood, W. (1998). Habit and intention in everyday life: The multiple processes by which past behavior predicts future behavior. *Psychological Bulletin, 124,* 54–74.

Papageorgis, D., & McGuire, W. J. (1961). The generality of immunity to persuasion produced by pre-exposure to weakened counterarguments. *Journal of Abnormal and Social Psychology, 62,* 475–481.

Paulhus, D. L. (1998). *Manual for the balanced inventory of desirable responding*. Toronto, Canada: Multi-Health Systems.

Pechmann, C. (1992). Predicting when two-sided ads will be more effective than one-sided ads: The role of correlational and correspondent inferences. *Journal of Marketing Research, 29,* 441–453.

Petty, R. E., & Brock, T. C. (1981). Thought disruption and persuasion: Assessing the validity of attitude change experiments. In R. E. Petty, T. M. Ostrom, & T. C. Brock (Eds.), *Cognitive responses in persuasion* (pp. 55–79). Hillsdale, NJ: Lawrence Erlbaum Associates Inc.

Petty, R. E., & Cacioppo, J. T. (1977). Forewarning, cognitive responding, and resistance to persuasion. *Journal of Personality and Social Psychology, 35,* 645–655.

Petty, R. E., & Cacioppo, J. T. (1979). Issue

involvement can increase or decrease persuasion by enhancing message-relevant cognitive responses. *Journal of Personality and Social Psychology, 37,* 1915–1926.

Petty, R. E., & Cacioppo, J. T. (1980). Effects of issue involvement on attitudes in an advertising context. In G. Gorn & M. Goldberg (Eds.), *Proceedings of the Division 23 program* (pp. 75–79). Montreal, Canada: Division 23 of the American Psychological Association.

Petty, R. E., & Cacioppo, J. T. (1981). *Attitudes and persuasion: Classic and contemporary approaches.* Dubuque, IA: Brown.

Petty, R. E., & Cacioppo, J. T. (1986a). *Communication and persuasion: Central and peripheral routes to attitude change.* New York: Springer.

Petty, R. E., & Cacioppo, J. T. (1986b). The elaboration likelihood model of persuasion. *Advances in Experimental Social Psychology, 19,* 124–203.

Petty, R. E., Cacioppo, J. T., & Goldman, R. (1981). Personal involvement as a determinant of argument-based persuasion. *Journal of Personality and Social Psychology, 41,* 847–855.

Petty, R. E., Cacioppo, J. T., & Schumann, D. (1983). Central and peripheral routes to advertising effectiveness: The moderating role of involvement. *Journal of Consumer Research, 10,* 134–148.

Petty, R. E., Haugtvedt, C. P., & Smith, S. M. (1995). Elaboration as a determinant of attitude strength: Creating attitudes that are persistent, resistant, and predictive of behavior. In R. E. Petty & J. A. Krosnick (Eds.), *Attitude strength: Antecedents and consequences* (pp. 93–130). Mahwah, NJ: Lawrence Erlbaum Associates Inc.

Petty, R. E., & Krosnick, J. A. (Eds.). (1995). *Attitude strength: Antecedents and consequences.* Mahwah, NJ: Lawrence Erlbaum Associates Inc.

Petty, R. E., Ostrom, T. M., & Brock, T. C.

(Eds.). (1981). *Cognitive responses in persuasion.* Hillsdale, NJ: Lawrence Erlbaum Associates Inc.

Petty, R. E., Priester, J. R., & Wegener, D. T. (1994). Cognitive processes in attitude change. In R. S. Wyer, Jr., & T. K. Srull (Eds.), *Handbook of social cognition: Vol. 2. Applications* (2nd ed., pp. 69–142). Hillsdale, NJ: Lawrence Erlbaum Associates Inc.

Petty, R. E., & Wegener, D. T. (1998a). Attitude change: Multiple roles for persuasion variables. In D. Gilbert, S. T. Fiske, & G. Lindzey (Eds.), *Handbook of social psychology* (4th ed., pp. 323–390). New York: McGraw-Hill.

Petty, R. E., & Wegener, D. T. (1998b). Matching versus mismatching attitude functions: Implications for scrutiny of persuasive messages. *Personality and Social Psychology Bulletin, 24,* 227–240.

Petty, R. E., & Wegener, D. T. (1999). The elaboration likelihood model: Current status and controversies. In S. Chaiken & Y. Trope (Eds.), *Dual process theories in social psychology* (pp. 41–72). New York: Guilford.

Petty, R. E., Wegener, D. T., & Fabrigar, L. R. (1997). Attitudes and attitude change. *Annual Review of Psychology, 48,* 609–647.

Petty, R. E., Wells, G. L., & Brock, T. C. (1976). Distraction can enhance or reduce yielding to propaganda: Thought disruption versus effort justification. *Journal of Personality and Social Psychology, 34,* 874–884.

Pilkington, N. W., & Lydon, J. E. (1997). The relative effect of attitude similarity and attitude dissimilarity on interpersonal attraction: The moderating roles of prejudice and group membership. *Personality and Social Psychology Bulletin, 23,* 107–122.

Plessner, H., & Banse, R. (Eds.). (2001). Attitude measurement using the Implicit Association Task (IAT).

Zeitschrift für Experimentelle Psychologie,
48 (Whole no. 2), 79–175.

Pomazal, R. J., & Jaccard, J. J. (1976). An informational approach to altruistic behavior. *Journal of Personality and Social Psychology, 33,* 317–326.

Pomerantz, E., Chaiken, S., & Tordesillas, R. S. (1995). Attitude strength and resistance processes. *Journal of Personality and Social Psychology, 69,* 408–419.

Powell, M. C., & Fazio, R. H. (1984). Attitude accessibility as a function of repeated attitudinal expression. *Personality and Social Psychology Bulletin, 10,* 139–148.

Pratkanis, A. R. (1988). The attitude heuristic and selective fact identification. *British Journal of Social Psychology, 27,* 257–263.

Pratkanis, A. R. (1989). The cognitive representation of attitudes. In A. R. Pratkanis, S. J. Breckler, & A. G. Greenwald (Eds.), *Attitude structure and function* (pp. 71–98). Hillsdale, NJ: Lawrence Erlbaum Associates Inc.

Prentice, D. A., & Carlsmith, K. M. (2000). Opinions and personality: On the psychological functions of attitudes and other valued possessions. In G. R. Maio & J. M. Olson (Eds.), *Why we evaluate: Functions of attitudes* (pp. 223–248). Mahwah, NJ: Lawrence Erlbaum Associates Inc.

Prislin, R. (1996). Attitude stability and attitude strength: One is enough to make it stable. *European Journal of Social Psychology, 26,* 447–477.

Raghubir, P., & Menon, G. (1998). AIDS and me, never the twain shall meet: The effects of information accessibility on judgments of risk and advertising effectiveness. *Journal of Consumer Research, 25,* 52–63.

Razran, G. H. S. (1940). Conditioned response changes in rating and appraising sociopolitical slogans. *Psychological Bulletin, 37,* 481.

Reber, R., Winkielman, P., & Schwarz, N. (1998). Effects of perceptual fluency on affective judgments. *Psychological Science, 9,* 45–48.

Reeder, G. D., & Pryor, J. B. (2000). Attitudes toward persons with HIV/ AIDS: Linking a functional approach with underlying process. In G. R. Maio, & J. Olson (Eds.), *Why we evaluate: Functions of attitudes* (pp. 295–323). Mahwah, NJ: Lawrence Erlbaum Associates Inc.

Regan, D. T., & Fazio, R. H. (1977). On the consistency between attitudes and behavior: Look to the method of attitude formation. *Journal of Experimental Social Psychology, 13,* 28–45.

Regan, D. T., & Kilduff, M. (1988). Optimism about elections: Dissonance reduction at the ballot box. *Political Psychology, 9,* 101–107.

Regan, D. T., Straus, E., & Fazio, R. H. (1974). Liking and the attribution process. *Journal of Experimental Social Psychology, 10,* 385–397.

Roberts, C. A., & Johannson, C. B. (1974). The inheritance of cognitive interest styles among twins. *Journal of Vocational Behavior, 4,* 237–243.

Roberts, J. V. (1985). The attitude–memory relationship after 40 years: A meta-analysis of the literature. *Basic and Applied Social Psychology, 6,* 221–241.

Roese, N. J., & Jamieson, D. W. (1993). Twenty years of bogus pipeline research: A critical review and meta-analysis. *Psychological Bulletin, 114,* 363–375.

Roese, N. J., & Olson, J. M. (1994). Attitude importance as a function of repeated attitude expression. *Journal of Experimental Social Psychology, 30,* 39–51.

Rokeach, M. (1973). *The nature of human values.* New York: Free Press.

Rosenbaum, M. E. (1986). The repulsion hypothesis: On the nondevelopment of relationships. *Journal of Personality and Social Psychology, 51,* 1156–1166.

Rosenberg, M. J. (1960). An analysis of affective-cognitive consistency. In M. J. Rosenberg, C. I. Hovland, W. J. McGuire, R. P. Abelson, & J. W. Brehm (Eds.), *Attitude organization and change* (pp. 15–64). New Haven, CT: Yale University Press.

Rosenberg, M. J. (1968). Hedonism, inauthenticity, and other goads toward expansion of a consistency theory. In R. P. Abelson, E. Aronson, W. J. McGuire, T. M. Newcomb, M. J. Rosenberg, & P. H. Tannenbaum (Eds.), *Theories of cognitive consistency: A sourcebook* (pp. 73–111). Chicago: Rand-McNally.

Rosenthal, R., & Rosnow, R. L. (1991). *Essentials of behavioral research* (2nd ed.). New York: McGraw-Hill.

Roskos-Ewoldsen, D. R., & Fazio, R. H. (1992). On the orienting value of attitudes: Attitude accessibility as a determinant of an object's attraction of visual attention. *Journal of Personality and Social Psychology, 63,* 198–211.

Ross, L., Greene, D., & House, P. (1977). The "false consensus effect": An egocentric bias in social perception and attribution processes. *Journal of Experimental Social Psychology, 13,* 279–301.

Ross, M., McFarland, C., & Fletcher, G. J. O. (1981). The effect of attitude on the recall of personal history. *Journal of Personality and Social Psychology, 40,* 627–634.

Ryan, R. M., & Deci, E. L. (2000). Self-determination theory and the facilitation of intrinsic motivation, social development, and well-being. *American Psychologist, 55,* 68–78.

Sadler, O., & Tesser, A. (1973). Some effects of salience and time upon interpersonal hostility and attraction during social isolation. *Sociometry, 36,* 99–112.

Saegert, S. C., Swap, W. C., & Zajonc, R. B. (1973). Exposure, context, and interpersonal attraction. *Journal of Personality and Social Psychology, 25,* 234–242.

Sanbonmatsu, D. M., & Fazio, R. H. (1990). The role of attitudes in memory-based decision making. *Journal of Personality and Social Psychology, 59,* 614–622.

Sayre, J. (1939). A comparison of three indices of attitude toward radio advertising. *Journal of Applied Psychology, 23,* 23–33.

Scarr, S. (1981). The transmission of authoritarian attitudes in families: Genetic resemblance in social political attitudes? In S. Scarr (Ed.), *Race, social class and individual differences* (pp. 399–427). Hillsdale, NJ: Lawrence Erlbaum Associates Inc.

Scarr, S., & Weinberg, R. A. (1978). Attitudes, interest and IQ. *Human Nature, 1,* 29–36.

Schaller, M. (1992). In-group favoritism and statistical reasoning in social inference: Implications for formation and maintenance of group stereotypes. *Journal of Personality and Social Psychology, 63,* 61–74.

Schlenker, B. R. (1982). Translating actions into attitudes: An identity–analytic approach. *Advances in Experimental Social Psychology, 15,* 59–101.

Schuette, R. A., & Fazio, R. H. (1995). Attitude accessibility and motivation as determinants of biased processing: A test of the MODE model. *Personality and Social Psychology Bulletin, 21,* 704–710.

Schuman, H., & Converse, J. M. (1971). The effects of black and white interviewers on black responses in 1968. *Public Opinion Quarterly, 35,* 44–68.

Schuman, H., & Presser, S. (1981). *Questions and answers in attitude surveys: Experiments on question form, wording, and context.* San Diego, CA: Academic Press.

Schwartz, G. E., Ahern, G. L., & Brown,

S. L. (1979). Lateralized facial muscle response to positive and negative emotional stimuli. *Psychophysiology, 16,* 561–571.

Schwartz, S. H. (1992). Universals in the content and structure of values: Theoretical advances and empirical tests in 20 countries. *Advances in Experimental Social Psychology, 25,* 1–65.

Schwarz, N. (1990). Feelings as information: Informational and motivational functions of affective states. In E. T. Higgins & R. Sorrentino (Eds.), *Handbook of motivation and cognition: Foundations of social behavior* (Vol. 2, pp. 527–561). New York: Guilford.

Schwarz, N., & Bless, H. (1992). Constructing reality and its alternatives: An inclusion/exclusion model of assimilation and contrast effects in social judgment. In L. L. Martin & A. Tesser (Eds.), *The construction of social judgment* (pp. 217–245). Hillsdale, NJ: Lawrence Erlbaum Associates Inc.

Schwarz, N., Bless, H., & Bohner, G. (1991). Mood and persuasion: Affective states influence the processing of persuasive communications. *Advances in Experimental Social Psychology, 24,* 161–199.

Schwarz, N., Bless, H., Strack, F., Klumpp, G., Rittenauer-Schatka, H., & Simons, A. (1991). Ease of retrieval as information: Another look at the availability heuristic. *Journal of Personality and Social Psychology, 61,* 195–202.

Schwarz, N., & Bohner, G. (2001). The construction of attitudes. In A. Tesser & N. Schwarz (Eds.), *Blackwell handbook of social psychology: Vol. 1. Intraindividual processes* (pp. 436–457). Oxford, UK: Blackwell.

Schwarz, N., & Clore, G. L. (1983). Mood, misattribution and judgments of well-being: Informative and directive functions of affective states. *Journal of*

Personality and Social Psychology, 45, 513–523.

Schwarz, N., & Clore, G. L. (1988). How do I feel about it? The informative function of affective states. In K. Fiedler & J. Forgas (Eds.), *Affect, cognition, and social behavior* (pp. 44–62). Toronto, Canada: Hogrefe International.

Schwarz, N., & Hippler, H.-J. (1995). The numeric values of rating scales: A comparison of their impact in mail surveys and telephone interviews. *International Journal of Public Opinion Research, 7,* 72–74.

Schwarz, N., & Strack, F. (1981). Manipulating salience: Causal assessment in natural settings. *Personality and Social Psychology Bulletin, 6,* 554–558.

Schwarz, N., Strack, F., Kommer, D., & Wagner, D. (1987). Soccer, rooms, and the quality of your life: Mood effects on judgments of satisfaction with life in general and with specific domains. *European Journal of Social Psychology, 17,* 69–79.

Schwarz, N., & Sudman, S. (Eds.). (1992). *Context effects in social and psychological research.* New York: Springer.

Schwarzwald, J., Bizman, A., & Raz, M. (1983). The foot-in-the-door paradigm: Effects of second request size on donation probability and donor generosity. *Personality and Social Psychology Bulletin, 9,* 69–79.

Sears, D. O., & Funk, C. L. (1990). The limited effect of economic self-interest on the political attitudes of the mass public. *Journal of Behavioral Economics, 19,* 247–271.

Shavitt, S. (1989). Operationalizing functional theories of attitude. In A. R. Pratkanis, S. J. Breckler, & A. G. Greenwald (Eds.), *Attitude structure and function* (pp. 311–337). Hillsdale, NJ: Lawrence Erlbaum Associates Inc.

Shavitt, S. (1990). The role of attitude objects in attitude functions. *Journal of*

Experimental Social Psychology, 26, 124–148.

Shavitt, S., & Brock, T. C. (1986). Self-relevant responses in commercial persuasion: Field and experimental tests. In J. Olson & K. Sentis (Eds.), *Advertising and consumer psychology* (pp. 149–171). New York: Praeger.

Shavitt, S., & Fazio, R. H. (1991). Effects of attribute salience on the consistency between attitudes and behavior predictions. *Personality and Social Psychology Bulletin, 17,* 507–516.

Shavitt, S., Swan, S., Lowrey, T. M., & Wänke, M. (1994). The interaction of endorser attractiveness and involvement in persuasion depends on the goal that guides message processing. *Journal of Consumer Psychology, 3,* 137–162.

Shavitt, S., & Wänke, M. (2001). Consumer behavior. In A. Tesser & N. Schwarz (Eds.), *Blackwell handbook of social psychology: Vol. 1. Intraindividual processes* (pp. 569–590). Oxford, UK: Blackwell.

Sheppard, B. H., Hartwick, J., & Warshaw, P. R. (1988). The theory of reasoned action: A meta-analysis of past research with recommendations for modifications and future research. *Journal of Consumer Research, 15,* 325–343.

Sherif, M., & Hovland, C. I. (1961). *Social judgment: Assimilation and contrast effects in communication and attitude change.* New Haven, CT: Yale University Press.

Sia, T. L., Lord, C. G., Blessum, K. A., Ratcliff, C. D., & Lepper, M. R. (1997). Is a rose always a rose? The role of social category exemplar change in attitude stability and attitude–behavior consistency. *Journal of Personality and Social Psychology, 72,* 501–514.

Sia, T. L., Lord, C. G., Blessum, K. A., Thomas, J. C., & Lepper, M. R. (1999). Activation of exemplars in the process of assessing social category attitudes.

Journal of Personality and Social Psychology, 76, 517–532.

Siemer, M., & Reisenzein, R. (1998). Effects of mood on evaluative judgements: Influence of reduced processing capacity and mood salience. *Cognition and Emotion, 12,* 783–805.

Sinclair, R. C., Mark, M. M., & Clore, G. L. (1994). Mood-related persuasion depends on (mis)attributions. *Social Cognition, 12,* 309–326.

Singh, D. (1993). Adaptive significance of female physical attractiveness: Role of waist-to-hip-ratio. *Journal of Personality and Social Psychology, 65,* 293–307.

Sivacek, J., & Crano, W. D. (1982). Vested interest as a moderator of attitude–behavior consistency. *Journal of Personality and Social Psychology, 43,* 210–221.

Skinner, B. F. (1957). *Verbal behavior.* New York: Appleton-Century-Crofts.

Smetana, J. G., & Adler, N. E. (1980). Fishbein's valence × expectancy model: An examination of some assumptions. *Personality and Social Psychology Bulletin, 6,* 89–96.

Smith, B. L., Lasswell, H. D., & Casey, R. D. (1946). *Propaganda, communication, and public opinion.* Princeton, NJ: Princeton University Press.

Smith, E. R. (1996). What do connectionism and social psychology offer each other? *Journal of Personality and Social Psychology, 70,* 893–912.

Smith, E. R., & DeCoster, J. (2000). Dual-process models in social and cognitive psychology: Conceptual integration and links to underlying memory systems. *Personality and Social Psychology Review, 4,* 108–131.

Smith, E. R., Fazio, R. H., & Cejka, M. A. (1996). Accessible attitudes influence categorization of multiple categorizable objects. *Journal of Personality and Social Psychology, 71,* 888–898.

Smith, E. R., & Mackie, D. M. (1995). *Social psychology.* New York: Worth.

Smith, E. R., & Zárate, M. A. (1992). Exemplar-based model of social judgment. *Psychological Review, 99,* 3–21.

Smith, G. H. (1947). Beliefs in statements labelled fact and rumor. *Journal of Abnormal and Social Psychology, 42,* 80–90.

Smith, M. B., Bruner, J. S., & White, R. W. (1956). *Opinions and personality.* New York: Wiley.

Snyder, M. (1974). Self-monitoring of expressive behavior. *Journal of Personality and Social Psychology, 30,* 526–537.

Snyder, M., & DeBono, K. G. (1985). Appeals to images and claims about quality: Understanding the psychology of advertising. *Journal of Personality and Social Psychology, 49,* 586–597.

Snyder, M., & DeBono, K. G. (1987). A functional approach to attitudes and persuasion. In M. P. Zanna, J. M. Olson, & C. P. Herman (Eds.), *Social influence: The Ontario Symposium* (Vol. 5, pp. 107–125). Hillsdale, NJ: Lawrence Erlbaum Associates Inc.

Snyder, M., & DeBono, K. G. (1989). Understanding functions of attitudes: Lessons from personality and social behavior. In A. R. Pratkanis, S. J. Breckler, & A. G. Greenwald (Eds.), *Attitude structure and function* (pp. 339–359). Hillsdale, NJ: Lawrence Erlbaum Associates Inc.

Snyder, M., & Kendzierski, D. (1982). Acting on one's attitudes: Procedures for linking attitude and behavior. *Journal of Experimental Social Psychology, 18,* 165–183.

Snyder, M., & Swann, W. B. (1976). When actions reflect attitudes: The politics of impression management. *Journal of Personality and Social Psychology, 34,* 1034–1042.

Sparks, P. (1999, July). *Attitudinal and moral evaluations.* Paper presented at the 12th general meeting of the European Association of Experimental Social Psychology, Oxford, UK.

Srull, T. K. (1984). Methodological techniques for the study of person memory and social cognition. In R. S. Wyer & T. K. Srull (Eds.), *Handbook of social cognition* (Vol. 2, pp. 1–72). Hillsdale, NJ: Lawrence Erlbaum Associates Inc.

Staats, A. W. (1983). Paradigmatic behaviorism: Unified theory for social-personality psychology. *Advances in Experimental Social Psychology, 16,* 125–179.

Staats, A. W., & Staats, C. K. (1958). Attitudes established by classical conditioning. *Journal of Abnormal and Social Psychology, 57,* 37–40.

Staats, A. W., Staats, C. K., & Crawford, H. L. (1962). First-order classical conditioning of meaning and the parallel conditioning of a GSR. *Journal of General Psychology, 67,* 159–167.

Steele, C. M. (1988). The psychology of self-affirmation: Sustaining the integrity of the self. *Advances in Experimental Social Psychology, 21,* 261–302.

Steele, C. M., & Liu, T. J. (1983). Dissonance processes as self-affirmation. *Journal of Personality and Social Psychology, 45,* 5–19.

Stern, S. E., & Faber, J. E. (1997). The lost e-mail method: Milgram's lost-letter technique in the age of advertising. *Behavior Research Methods, Instruments, and Computers, 29,* 260–263.

Stevens, S. S. (1946). On the theory of scales of measurement. *Science, 103,* 677–680.

Strack, F. (1992). The different routes to social judgments: Experiential versus informational strategies. In L. L. Martin & A. Tesser (Eds.), *The construction of social judgments* (pp. 249–275). Hillsdale, NJ: Lawrence Erlbaum Associates Inc.

Strack, F., & Bless, H. (1994). Memory for nonoccurrences: Metacognitive and presuppositional strategies. *Journal of Memory and Language, 33*, 203–217.

Strack, F., Martin, L. L., & Schwarz, N. (1988). Priming and communication: Social deteminants of information use in judgments of life satisfaction. *European Journal of Social Psychology, 18*, 429–442.

Strack, F., Martin, L. L., & Stepper, S. (1988). Inhibiting and facilitating conditions of the human smile: A nonobtrusive test of the facial feedback hypothesis. *Journal of Personality and Social Psychology, 54*, 768–777.

Strack, F., Schwarz, N., Chassein, B., Kern, D., & Wagner, D. (1990). Salience of comparison standards and the activation of social norms: Consequences for judgements of happiness and their communication. *British Journal of Social Psychology, 29*, 303–314.

Strack, F., Schwarz, N., & Wänke, M. (1991). Semantic and pragmatic aspects of context effects in social and psychological research. *Social Cognition, 9*, 111–125.

Stroebe, W., & Diehl, M. (1981). Conformity and counterattitudinal behavior: The effect of social support on attitude change. *Journal of Personality and Social Psychology, 41*, 876–889.

Stroebe, W., & Diehl, M. (1988). When social support fails: Supporter characteristics in compliance-induced attitude change. *Personality and Social Psychology Bulletin, 14*, 136–144.

Stroebe, W., & Jonas, K. (1996). Principles of attitude formation and strategies of change. In M. Hewstone, W. Stroebe, & G. M. Stephenson (Eds.), *Introduction to social psychology* (2nd ed., pp. 240–275). Oxford, UK: Blackwell.

Stults, D. M., Messé, L. A., & Kerr, N. L. (1984). Belief-discrepant behavior and the bogus pipeline: Impression management or arousal attribution. *Journal of Experimental Social Psychology, 20*, 47–54.

Sudman, S., Bradburn, M. N., & Schwarz, N. (1996). *Thinking about answers: The application of cognitive processes to survey methodology.* San Francisco: Jossey-Bass.

Sutton, S. (1998). Predicting and explaining intentions and behavior: How well are we doing? *Journal of Applied Social Psychology, 28*, 1317–1338.

Tajfel, H. (1981). *Human groups and social categories: Studies in social psychology.* Cambridge, UK: Cambridge University Press.

Tassinary, L. G., & Hansen, K. A. (1998). A critical test of the waist-to-hip-ratio hypothesis of female physical attractiveness. *Psychological Science, 9*, 150–155.

Taylor, S. E. (1981). The interface of cognitive and social psychology. In J. H. Harvey (Ed.), *Cognition, social behavior, and the environment.* Hillsdale, NJ: Lawrence Erlbaum Associates Inc.

Teahan, J. E. (1975). A longitudinal study of attitude shifts among black and white police officers. *Journal of Social Issues, 31*(1), 47–56.

Tedeschi, J. T. (1981). *Impression management.* New York: Academic Press.

Tedeschi, J. T., Schlenker, B. R., & Bonoma, T. V. (1971). Cognitive dissonance: Private ratiocination or public spectacle? *American Psychologist, 26*, 685–695.

Tesser, A. (1978). Self-generated attitude change. *Advances in Experimental Social Psychology, 11*, 289–338.

Tesser, A. (1993). The importance of heritability in psychological research: The case of attitudes. *Psychological Review, 100*, 129–142.

Tesser, A., & Martin, L. L. (1996). The psychology of evaluation. In E. T. Higgins & A. W. Kruglanski (Eds.), *Social psychology: Handbook of basic principles* (pp. 400–432). New York: Guilford.

Tesser, A., Martin, L., & Mendolia, M. (1995). The impact of thought on attitude extremity and attitude–behavior consistency. In R. E. Petty & J. A. Krosnick (Eds.), *Attitude strength: Antecedents and consequences* (pp. 73–92). Mahwah, NJ: Lawrence Erlbaum Associates Inc.

Tesser, A., & Shaffer, D. R. (1990). Attitudes and attitude change. In M. R. Rosenzweig & L. W. Porter (Eds.), *Annual review of psychology* (Vol. 41, pp. 479–523). Palo Alto, CA: Annual Reviews.

Tetlock, P. E., & Manstead, A. S. R. (1985). Impression management versus intrapsychic explanations in social psychology: A useful dichotomy? *Psychological Review, 92,* 59–77.

Thistlethwaite, D. L. (1950). Attitude and structure as factors in the distortion of reasoning. *Journal of Abnormal and Social Psychology, 45,* 442–458.

Thompson, M. M., Zanna, M. P., & Griffin, D. W. (1995). Let's not be indifferent about (attitudinal) ambivalence. In R. E. Petty & J. A. Krosnick (Eds.), *Attitude strength: Antecedents and consequences* (pp. 361–386). Mahwah, NJ: Lawrence Erlbaum Associates Inc.

Thurstone, L. L. (1928). Attitudes can be measured. *American Journal of Sociology, 33,* 529–554.

Thurstone, L. L., & Chave, E. J. (1929). *The measurement of attitude.* Chicago: University of Chicago Press.

Tordella, M. A., & Neutens, J. J. (1979). An instrument to appraise attitudes of college students toward euthanasia. *Journal of School Health, 49,* 351–352.

Tougas, F., Brown, R., Beaton, A. M., & Joly, S. (1995). Neosexism: Plus ça change, plus c'est pareil. *Personality and Social Psychology Bulletin, 21,* 842–849.

Tourangeau, R., & Rasinski, K. A. (1988). Cognitive processes underlying context

effects in attitude measurement. *Psychological Bulletin, 103,* 299–314.

Tourangeau, R., Rasinski, K. A., Bradburn, N. M., & D'Andrade, R. (1989). Belief accessibility and context effects in attitude measurement. *Journal of Experimental Social Psychology, 25,* 401–421.

Triandis, H. C. (1980). Values, attitudes, and interpersonal behavior. In H. E. Howe, Jr., & M. M. Page (Eds.), *Nebraska Symposium on motivation 1979.* Lincon, NE: University of Nebraska Press.

Trivers, R. L. (1972). Parental investment and sexual selection. In B. Campbell (Ed.), *Sexual selection and the descent of man* (pp. 136–179). Chicago: Aldine.

Upshaw, H. S. (1969). The personal reference scale: An approach to social judgment. *Advances in Experimental Social Psychology, 4,* 315–371.

Vallone, R. P., Ross, L., & Lepper, M. R. (1985). The hostile media phenomenon: Biased perception and perceptions of media bias in coverage of the Beirut massacre. *Journal of Personality and Social Psychology, 49,* 577–585.

Waller, N. G., Kojetin, B. A., Bouchard, T. J., Lykken, D. T., & Tellegen, A. (1990). Genetic and environmental influences on religious interests, attitudes and values: A study of twins reared apart and together. *Psychological Science, 1,* 138–142.

Wänke, M. (1997). Making context effects work for you: Suggestions for improving data quality from a construal perspective. *International Journal of Public Opinion Research, 9,* 266–276.

Wänke, M., Bless, H., & Biller, B. (1996). Subjective experience versus content of information in the construction of attitude judgments. *Personality and Social Psychology Bulletin, 22,* 1105–1113.

Wänke, M., Bohner, G., & Jurkowitsch, A. (1997). There are many reasons to drive a BMW: Does imagined ease of argument generation influence attitudes? *Journal of Consumer Research, 24,* 170–177.

Wänke, M., & Schwarz, N. (1997). Reducing question order effects: The role of buffer items. In L. Lyberg, P. Biemer, M. Collins, E. DeLeeuw, C. Dippo & N. Schwarz (Eds.), *Survey measurement and process quality* (pp. 115–140). Chichester, UK: Wiley.

Webb, E. J., Campbell, D. T., Schwartz, R. D., Sechrest, L., & Grove, J. B. (1981). *Nonreactive measures in the social sciences* (2nd ed.). Boston, MA: Houghton Mifflin.

Wegener, D. T., Downing, J., Krosnick, J. A., & Petty, R. E. (1995). Measures and manipulations of strength-related properties of attitudes: Current practice and future directions. In R. E. Petty & J. A. Krosnick (Eds.), *Attitude strength: Antecedents and consequences* (pp. 455–487). Mahwah, NJ: Lawrence Erlbaum Associates Inc.

Wegener, D. T., & Petty, R. E. (1994). Mood-management across affective states: The hedonic contingency hypothesis. *Journal of Personality and Social Psychology, 66,* 1034–1048.

Wegener, D. T., & Petty, R. E. (1997). The flexible correction model: The role of naive theories of bias in bias correction. *Advances in Experimental Social Psychology, 29,* 141–208.

Wegener, D. T., Petty, R. E., & Smith, S. M. (1995). Positive mood can increase or decrease message scrutiny: The hedonic contingency view of mood and message processing. *Journal of Personality and Social Psychology, 69,* 5–15.

Weick, K. E. (1985). Systematic observational methods. In G. Lindzey & E. Aronson (Eds.), *The handbook of social psychology* (3rd edition, Vol. 1, pp. 567–634). New York: Random House.

Weigel, R. H., & Newman, L. S. (1976). Increasing attitude–behavior correspondence by broadening the scope of the behavioral measure. *Journal of Personality and Social Psychology, 33,* 793–802.

Wells, G. L., & Petty, R. E. (1980). The effects of overt head movements on persuasion: Compatibility and incompatibility of responses. *Basic and Applied Social Psychology, 1,* 219–230.

Wicker, A. W. (1969). Attitude versus action: The relationship of verbal and overt behavioral responses to attitude objects. *Journal of Social Issues, 25*(4), 41–78.

Wicklund, R. A., & Brehm, J. W. (1976). *Perspectives on cognitive dissonance.* Hillsdale, NJ: Lawrence Erlbaum Associates Inc.

Wilson, D. T., Mathews, H. L., & Harvey, J. W. (1975). An empirical test of the Fishbein intention model. *Journal of Consumer Research, 1,* 39–48.

Wilson, T. D., & Dunn, D. S. (1986). Effects of introspection on attitude–behavior consistency: Analyzing reasons versus focusing on feelings. *Journal of Experimental Social Psychology, 22,* 249–263.

Wilson, T. D., Dunn, D. S., Kraft, D., & Lisle, D. J. (1989). Introspection, attitude change, and attitude–behavior consistency: The disruptive effects of explaining why we feel the way we do. *Advances in Experimental Social Psychology, 22,* 287–343.

Wilson, T. D., & Hodges, S. D. (1992). Attitudes as temporary constructions. In L. L. Martin & A. Tesser (Eds.), *The construction of social judgments* (pp. 37–65). Hillsdale, NJ: Lawrence Erlbaum Associates Inc.

Wilson, T. D., Hodges, S. D., & LaFleur, S. J. (1995). Effects of introspecting about reasons: Inferring attitudes from accessible thoughts. *Journal of Personality and Social Psychology, 69,* 16–28.

Wilson, T. D., Lindsey, S., & Schooler,

T. Y. (2000). A model of dual attitudes. *Psychological Review, 107,* 101–126.

Wilson, T. D., Lisle, D. J., & Kraft, D. (1990). Effects of self-reflection on attitudes and consumer decisions. *Advances in Consumer Research, 17,* 79–85.

Wilson, T. D., Lisle, D. J., Schooler, J. W., Hodges, S. D., Klaaren, K. K., & LaFleur, S. J. (1993). Introspecting about reasons can reduce post-choice satisfaction. *Personality and Social Psychology Bulletin, 19,* 331–339.

Wilson, T. D., & Schooler, J. W. (1991). Thinking too much: Introspection can reduce the quality of preferences and decisions. *Journal of Personality and Social Psychology, 60,* 181–192.

Winston, S. (1932). Birth control and the sex-ratio at birth. *American Journal of Sociology, 38,* 225–231.

Wood, W. (1982). Retrieval of attitude-relevant information from memory: Effects on susceptibility to persuasion and on intrinsic motivation. *Journal of Personality and Social Psychology, 42,* 798–810.

Wood, W., & Eagly, A. H. (1981). Stages in the analysis of persuasive messages: The role of causal attributions and message comprehension. *Journal of Personality and Social Psychology, 40,* 246–259.

Worchel, S., & Arnold, S. E. (1973). The effects of censorship and attractiveness of the censor on attitude change. *Journal of Experimental Social Psychology, 9,* 365–377.

Worchel, S., Arnold, S. E., & Baker, M. (1975). The effects of censorship on attitude change: The influence of censor and communication characteristics. *Journal of Applied Social Psychology, 5,* 227–239.

Worth, L. T., & Mackie, D. M. (1987). Cognitive mediation of positive affect in persuasion. *Social Cognition, 5,* 76–94.

Wyer, R. S., Jr. (1970). Quantitative prediction of belief and opinion change: A further test of a subjective probability model. *Journal of Personality and Social Psychology, 166,* 559–570.

Wyer, R. S., Jr., & Hartwick, J. (1980). The role of information retrieval and conditional inference processes in belief formation and change. *Advances in Experimental Social Psychology, 13,* 241–284.

Wyer, R. S., Jr., & Srull, T. K. (1989). *Memory and cognition in its social context.* Hillsdale, NJ: Lawrence Erlbaum Associates Inc.

Yu, D. W., & Shepard, G. H. (1998). Is beauty in the eye of the beholder? *Nature, 396,* 321–322.

Zajonc, R. B. (1968). Attitudinal effects of mere exposure. *Journal of Personality and Social Psychology Monograph, 9* (Suppl. 2, Pt. 2), 1–27.

Zajonc, R. B. (1980). Feeling and thinking: Preferences need no inferences. *American Psychologist, 35,* 151–175.

Zajonc, R. B. (1984). On the primacy of affect. *American Psychologist, 39,* 117–123.

Zajonc, R. B. (2000). Feeling and thinking: Closing the debate over the independence of affect. In J. P. Forgas (Ed.), *Feeling and thinking: The role of affect in social cognition* (pp. 31–58). New York: Cambridge University Press.

Zajonc, R. B., Murphy, S. T., & Inglehart, M. (1989). Feeling and facial efference: Implications of the vascular theory of emotion. *Psychological Review, 96,* 395–416.

Zanna, M. P., & Cooper, J. (1974). Dissonance and the pill: An attribution approach to studying the arousal properties of dissonance. *Journal of Personality and Social Psychology, 29,* 703–709.

Zanna, M. P., & Fazio, R. H. (1982). The attitude–behavior relation: Moving toward a third generation of research.

In M. P. Zanna, E. T. Higgins, & C. P. Herman (Eds.), *Consistency in social behavior: The Ontario Symposium* (Vol. 2, pp. 283–301). Hillsdale, NJ: Lawrence Erlbaum Associates Inc.

Zanna, M. P., Olson, J. M., & Fazio, R. H. (1980). Attitude–behavior consistency: An individual difference perspective.

Journal of Personality and Social Psychology, 38, 432–440.

Zimbardo, P. G., Weisenberg, M., Firestone, I., & Levy, B. (1965). Communicator effectiveness in producing public conformity and private attitude change. *Journal of Personality, 33,* 233–255.

Author index

Subject index